AF644416

Globalization, State and Governance

GLOBALIZATION,
State and Governance

Edited by

Shaji Varkey

Head, Department of Political Science,
University of Kerala, Thiruvananthapuram

New Century Publications
New Delhi, India

NEW CENTURY PUBLICATIONS
4800/24, Bharat Ram Road,
Ansari Road, Daryaganj,
New Delhi - 110 002 (India)

Tel.: 011-2324 7798, 4358 7398, 6539 6605
Fax: 011-4101 7798
E-mail: indiatax@vsnl.com • info@newcenturypublications.com
www.newcenturypublications.com

Editorial office:
LG–7, Aakarshan Bhawan,
4754-57/23, Ansari Road, Daryaganj,
New Delhi - 110 002

Tel.: 011-4356 0919

Copyright © 2014 by the editor

All rights reserved. No part of this book may be reproduced, stored in a retrieval system, or transmitted in any form or by any means, mechanical, photocopying, recording, or otherwise without the prior written permission of the publisher.

First Published: **2014**

ISBN: **978-81-7708-382-8**

Published by New Century Publications and printed at Salasar Imaging Systems, New Delhi.

Designs: Patch Creative Unit, New Delhi.

PRINTED IN INDIA

(A Festschrift Volume in Honour of Dr. G. Gopa Kumar)

About Dr. G. Gopa Kumar

Born on February 12, 1951, Dr. G. Gopa Kumar obtained his M.A. and Ph.D. degrees in political science from the Department of Political Science, University of Kerala. Dr. Kumar became Lecturer in Political Science at the age of 24 in Government College, Chittur, Palghat in Kerala State.

Between 1982 and 2011, he served the Kerala University as Lecturer, Reader, Professor and finally the Dean of Social Sciences. He also served as the Director of the V.K. Krishna Menon Study Centre for International Relations in Kerala University. Between 2009 and 2011, he was appointed as the Director General of the Institute of Parliamentary Affairs, Government of Kerala and edited its *Journal of Parliamentary Studies*.

Dr. Kumar was awarded Indo-French Cultural Exchange Fellowship in 1990 to study the French party politics and coalition game. Earlier, he was UGC Research Scientist during 1988-1989 working on Comparative Politics. In 1996, the US International Agency, Washington DC selected him as the only candidate from India to study on *American Federalism* in various universities of USA.

In 1998, he was a Fulbright Visiting Lecturer to teach *Comparative Public Policy* in the Department of Politics and Policy, Claremont Graduate University, California. In 2000, he was awarded the Shastri Indo-Canadian Fellowship at the University of Calgary, Canada to work on *Canadian Multiculturalism*. In 2001, he was invited by the same University to teach a semester course on *Comparative Politics* and *Political Economy of Development.*

In 2009, he was selected as a Senior Fellow by the Australia-India Council to work on *Australian Multiculturalism and its Linkages with Federalism* at Monash University, Melbourne. Besides this, he has visited and lectured at Australian National

University, Canberra University, University of New South Wales, Sydney, University of South Australia, Adelaide, Royal Melbourne Institute for Technology, Melbourne. In 2010, the University of New South Wales awarded him Visiting Research Fellowship to work on *Environmental Issues and Development*. He has published 12 books and over 135 research papers.

Dr. Kumar is married to Mrs. Jayasree Gopa Kumar who is Principal of a school in Thiruvananthapuram. They have two children, G. Govind Kumar and Gayathri Kumar. Govind is Assistant Manager in Idea Cellular Company located in Kochi and lives with his wife Sruthi Govind, a software engineer. Gayathri is a software engineer in Infosys and lives with her husband Deepak in the United States.

About the Book

Globalization is understood, theorised and defined in diverse ways. For the mainstream theorists of the west, globalization marked the triumph of capitalism and a market economy. For the critiques of this argument, globalization facilitated a worldwide expansion of capital by breaking the legal-political barriers put up by the nation states. For some it ensued the universalisation of consumerism through transnational ruling elites. For *network society* theorists, the engine of globalization is the ever-expanding information and communication revolution.

Governance being essentially ambiguous connotes different things to different people. The governance paradigm, that appeared in the early 1990s is not exclusively a market-based one but a mélange of experimentations like new public management, regulatory governance, network governance, participatory governance, good governance, multi-level governance and global governance.

The relationship between state and governance is very complex in modern times. As a political institution—with monopoly over the legitimate use of physical force within a given territory—the power of state was unique and unchallenged for long. The state in the neo-liberal times has been *hollowed out* on account of its shrinking leverage.

The present volume contains 16 well-researched scholarly essays which provide deep insights into the emerging political order in the world.

Editor's Profile

Dr. Shaji Varkey (b. 1962) is currently Head of the Department of Political Science, University of Kerala, Thiruvananthapuram. He did his M.A. and Ph.D. from University of Kerala. He was the Director of V.K. Krishna Menon Centre for International Relations, University of Kerala during 2009-2012. His major publications are in the field of international relations, development and environment.

He was a visiting scholar at Claremont Graduate University, USA in 2007. He has several international collaboratory projects to his credit. Presently, he is working on a project on Spaces of Political Protests in Kerala, sponsored by Indian Council of Social Science Research (ICSSR), New Delhi.

Contents

Contributors

Neera Chandhoke	Professor, Department of Political Science, University of Delhi, Delhi.
A.K. Pasha	Director, Gulf Studies Programme, Centre for West Asian Studies, School of International Studies, Jawaharlal Nehru University (JNU), New Delhi.
Ashutosh Kumar	Professor, Department of Political Science, Punjab University, Chandigarh.
S.N. Sangita	Professor, Institute for Social and Economic Change (ISEC), Bangalore.
Biju B.L.	Assistant Professor, Department of Political Science, Central University, Hyderabad.
B. Ramesh Babu	Visiting Professor, Institute of Public Enterprise (IPE), Hyderabad.
V. Anil Kumar	Assistant Professor, Institute for Social and Economic Change (ISEC), Bangalore.
D. Jeevan Kumar	Professor of Political Science, Bangalore University, Bangalore.
K.M. Sajad Ibrahim	Director, UGC-Nehru Studies Centre, University of Kerala, Thiruvananthapuram.
M.J. Vinod	Professor, Department of Political Science, Bangalore University, Bangalore.
Mohanan B. Pillai	Professor and Director, UNESCO Madanjeet Singh Institute of South Asia Regional Co-operation, Pondicherry University, Puducherry.

P.M. Joshy	Lecturer, School of International Relations and Politics, Mahatma Gandhi University, Kottayam.
Josukutty C.A.	Assistant Professor, Department of Political Science, University of Kerala, Thiruvananthapuram.
G.D.R.U.U. Abeyrathne	Senior Lecturer in Political Science, Department of Economics, University of Ruhuna, Matara, Sri Lanka.
S.Y. Surendra Kumar	Assistant Professor, Department of Political Science, Bangalore University, Bangalore.
Ashalekshmi B.S.	Assistant Professor, Centre for Research in Social Sciences and Education (CERSSE), Jain University, Bangalore.
Devi Parvathy	Assistant Professor, St. Johns College, Anchal.
Veena R.	Assistant Professor, Department of Political Science, Madras Christian College, Tambaram, Chennai.

Introduction

By Shaji Varkey

The contemporary epoch of globalization has razed many of the existing structures, processes and ideologies and replaced it with a universal, neo-liberal framework to which everything else was sought to be reduced. The unfolding of events with great speed, on great scales to great extents and with great impact has reconfigured the social life in unpredictable and diverse ways. Seemingly fixed notions like state, sovereignty, territoriality, citizenship etc. have collapsed giving rise to a multiple and fluid regimes. In place of the traditional state structure with a top-down and hierarchically-ordered bureaucracy, a multi-layered and de-centred political/ institutional project facilitated and enabled through a technological revolution, and legitimized through a neo-liberal ideological framework has come into being. What is most important in the understanding about globalization and governance is the recognition that both tend to converge to produce a governmentality conforming largely to the logic of capital.

Globalisation is understood, theorised and defined in diverse ways. For the mainstream theorists of the west, globalization marked the triumph of capitalism and a market economy. For the critiques of this argument, globalization facilitated a world-wide expansion of capital by breaking the legal-political barriers put up by the nation states. For some it ensued the universalisation of consumerism through transnational ruling elites. For "network society" theorists, the engine of globalization is the ever-expanding information and communication revolution.

Globalisation connects people through space and time, in real and virtual manner. National sovereignty has become a myth of the past and no more considered as sacrosanct in international affairs. State borders have rendered increasingly porous through which pass communications, merchandise, microbes, migrants, money, organisations, pollutants and weapons. These trans-planetary exchanges have reached unprecedented scales, ranges, frequencies, speeds, intensities and impacts. A plethora of institutions from the local to the national and global have been created to govern these diverse forces and actors.

Governance being essentially ambiguous connotes different things to different people. It is a buzzword, a fad, a framing devise, a bridging concept, un umbrella concept, a descriptive concept, a slippery concept, an empty signifier, a weasel word, a fetish, a field, an approach, a theory and a perspective. The governance paradigm, that appeared in the early 1990s is not exclusively a market-based one but a mélange of experimentations like new public management, regulatory governance, net work governance, participatory governance, good governance, multi-level governance and global governance. The addition of adjectives to governance however, has the advantage of making it infinitely flexible and adaptable to the neo-liberal structure that witnessed a concurrent growth during the same period.

Emergence of multiple locus of power in the society, weather in the private or in the public domain creates novel structures and relations of governance.

The relationship between state and governance is very complex in modern times. As political institution with monopoly over the legitimate use of physical force within a given territory, the power of state was unique and unchallenged for long. The neo-liberal state negates this notion and therefore spawned a variety of actors that accept the logic of capitalism. The state is not only an abstract entity but constituted by a 'relational rationality' with embedded structures of power spread across and beyond the territorial borders. The state in the neo-liberal times has been "hollowed out" on account of its shrinking leverage. The state power has been dispersed and reconstituted across new sites of action augmented through new strategies and technologies. The changing boundary of state and civil society has resulted in the collapse of the top-down, bureaucratized and highly politicized structure and witnessed the emergence of a horizontal network of associations. Governance literature is rife with structure-agency issues.

The state-centric governance relies heavily on structural explanations, with state institutions responsible for governing and their characteristics being crucial for defining outcomes. In "governance without government", however, the importance of agency-of-people as individuals and collectivities is emphasized whereas in the former, citizen participation is only done at the receiving end. The governmental rationality suggests that it has superior wisdom in all matters and that the structures are capable of performing the tasks assigned to it in an impeccable manner. In rational choice approaches, agents are perceived as decision makers with rational capacity to make strategic choices.

The governance structure that the early-modern state established was based on three core priorities: to provide external security, maintaining internal order and thirdly, raising revenue. The order, security and revenue imperative underwent change during the age of capitalist accumulation. Capitalism as a mode of production succeeded in generating income and wealth that enabled the creation of an expansive state structure with functional differentiation. Capitalism, however, is prone to periodic bouts of boom and bust and a total collapse would have the impact of undermining the whole structure. Welfarism in fact was a political vent that saved the system from overheating and the eventual breakdown. As state remained the fulcrum in a welfare structure, the untrammelled accumulation spree of capitalism was constrained.

Areas of operation were earmarked and the private sector was denied entry to areas that has strategic significance for the nation and the population. The *dirigiste* system that was put in place not only excluded the private capital from certain sectors but also regulated the inflow of global capital by strengthening the domestic rules. By invoking domestic sovereignty, states selectively stemmed the surge of global capital. However, with the onset of neo-liberal globalization, state welfarism has entered a phase of diminishing growth, stagnation and 'immovable and irresistible' compulsion towards retrenchment.

The whole idea of good governance gained currency in the post-Washington consensus phase (after 1995), when new forms of institution-building and governmental interventions began to appear in the global south. Several authors in the early 1990s argued that economic development is facilitated in countries where institutional resilience is available. This institutionalist argument has particular salience in third world countries, where the existing structures are archaic, corrupt, opaque and impenetrable to the global circulation of capital. Gilley goes a step further by arguing that general governance (which includes rule of law, control of corruption and government effectiveness) has a large, even overarching importance in global citizen evaluations of states.

The discourse of good governance gained significance towards the closing decades of 20th century when governance, state and market are considered to be complimentary institutions. Though the notion of good governance appears to be founded on certain normative foundation, the fact is that good governance literature does not take up such issues in its philosophical depth. On the contrary, the supposed normativism yields to crass utilitarianism.

Governance has four meanings: a structure, a process, a mechanism and a strategy. As structure, governance involves formal and informal institutions; as a process it implies the regulation and direction of the policy-making process; as a mechanism it connotes institutional procedures of decision making and as a strategy it means actors involvement in shaping and changing institutions.

Governance as a complex phenomenon involves multiple agents such as governments, private and corporate actors, non-governmental, inter-governmental and global institutions. The new governance revolution has *adapted* the information and communication technology (ICT) promising to deliver all citizens improved services, reliable information and greater knowledge in order to facilitate access to the governing process and encourage deeper citizen participation.

ICT brings about three major tasks: improving government processes: that is e-administration; secondly connecting citizens: e-citizens and e-services and thirdly; building interactions with and within civil society: e-society. E-administration involves cutting process costs, managing process performance, making strategic connections in government and creating empowerment. E-citizens are not political entities alone but stakeholders and consumers in a competitive world. Connecting to citizen implies talking to citizen, listening to citizen and improving public services. Building an e-society involves intensive networking and interaction between and among individuals, groups, communities, institutions and state. The social embeddedness of digital technology is what is most important in a digital society. In most third world societies, the yawning digital divide limits the democratisation process. Digital divide is symptomatic of an economic divide as well.

The present volume on *Globalization, State and Governance* is a collective effort of scholars and colleagues. I take this opportunity to place on record my deep sense of gratitude to all the contributors to this work for their though-provoking research papers which will surely ignite debate and discussion on the emerging political order in the world.

Thiruvananthapuram **Shaji Varkey**

1

Globalisation and the State in India

Neera Chandhoke

Globalisation must be one of the most extensively observed, intellectually stalked, comprehensively analysed, and perhaps over-researched processes in the recent history of the world. For this very reason, perhaps, we find little consensus either on the nature, or on the effects of globalisation in the relevant literature. Consider for instance, some of the questions that continue to bedevil scholars of globalisation.

1. Is globalisation a new historical process, or has a set of processes which had been initiated in the sixteenth century—that of flows of financial capital, trade, and commerce from, mainly Europe, to countries of the South, acquired new forms and dimensions?
2. Does the integration of the countries of the South, into the international system of markets, trade, financial flows, and labour processes via globalisation bring benefits to all countries, to just a few, or to none?
3. Has globalisation increased poverty, global and national inequalities and caused harm, or has the process reduced, if not redeemed these persistent ills of the human condition?
4. How does the globalisation of issues that were formerly considered to fall within the provenance of national governments, such as the environment, climate change, human rights, and governance, impinge upon state sovereignty?
5. What has happened to the state in countries of the South? For most of the twentieth century the state has been

conceived of not only as an institution of power, but also as an institution that is expected to look after the welfare of, as well as be responsive to the demands of its citizens? Has the state in times of globalisation been hollowed out, reinvented, or transformed into a facilitator and a regulator of multiple transactions, which range from trade, to telecommunications, to power generation? Or does the state, compelled as the institution is by factors that are undeniably political, continue as much as the same?

Even though much of the debate on globalisation remains shot through with highly polemical hues, increasingly scholars realise that globalisation is much more a plural and much more a contradictory process than originally conceived of. [1] Take the issue of international policy on globalisation. In direct contrast to neo-liberal orthodoxy that underpinned the onset of globalisation, by the 1990s it came to be widely acknowledged that the state plays a key role in: (a) negotiating globalisation, and (b) providing social goods to citizens, particularly to those citizens who are unable to participate in market transactions.

The role of the state in managing globalisation was highlighted by the 1999 UNDP Report on Human Development. The report held that without regulation the market can generate far reaching imbalances. "When the market goes too far in dominating social and political outcomes, the opportunities and rewards of globalisation are spread unequally and inequitably, concentrating power and wealth among a select group of persons, nations, and corporations while marginalising the others. When the market gets out of hand, instabilities show up in "boom and bust" economies, as in the financial crisis in East Asia and its world wide repercussions cutting global output by an estimated US$ 2 trillion in 1998-2000. When the profit motive of market players gets out of hand, they challenge people's ethics and sacrifice respect for justice and human rights' (UNDP, 1999: 2). The market, was the fairly stark message of the report, needs to be regulated, and market transactions have to be administered, simply because uncontrolled markets propel serious distortions in society.

The other core task of the state, i.e., providing to the citizens well being, was fore grounded by the World Bank Report of 1997. The special report on the state held that efficient development is well nigh impossible without the state playing a direct role in the process, and that there can be neither economic nor social development without a good government. The report concluded rather sharply that a 'State that ignores the needs of large sections of the population in setting and implementing policy is not a capable state' (World Bank 1997: 110).

These two reports marked an important shift in international policy, which in the 1980s, took the form of what came to be known as the Washington consensus. In pursuance of the objectives of this consensus, ten policy recommendations were imposed on particularly debt-ridden Third World countries, by international financial and lending institutions. Among these recommendations were the following: trade liberalisation, clearing all hurdles to foreign direct investment, privatisation, deregulation, strengthening property rights, and tax reforms.

If we translate these economic imperatives into political terms, we find that the consensus dictated the following: (a) the state, particularly in Third World countries, should withdraw from the social sector; (b) the market should be freed from all constraints; and (c) people should organise their own social and economic reproduction instead of depending on the state. The state in other words was expected to roll back both from regulating economic transactions, and from providing social goods to its citizens at affordable prices. If state regulation of the market was considered to be a hurdle to the efficient functioning of the market; state provisioning of social goods, such as subsidized or free health care and education, it was held, interfered with the logic of the market, i.e., the pursuit of profit. People were consequently thrown onto the not so tender mercies of the market.

The mid-1990s were, however, to witness a sharp swing in the mood of international trade and financial institutions. Resultantly, these institutions were to move away from an emphasis on a free and untrammelled market, to the idea that both the market and the generic processes of globalisation had to be governed. The shift had largely to do with the economic and financial crisis of the nineteen nineties. Doctrines of free trade and unregulated markets had run into trouble ever since 1994, when Mexico was hit by financial devastation. The second financial crisis, which began when the government of Thailand devalued the Baht, and which then spread to the rest of East Asia, Japan, Brazil, and Russia in 1997 and 1998, impoverished millions, and generated rage and discontent. We saw an inkling of this dissatisfaction when Korean workers rose to defy the IMF. Many scholars saw these economic and financial crises as a consequence of unfettered globalisation; as a result of the working of the free and unregulated market (Higgot 2000: 131-153).

It was clear that the neo-liberal agenda had failed to deliver the much-promised benefits of greater growth, stabilisation of financial markets, and a beneficial political order. Income disparities had increased, and the number of the poor had grown drastically even as people were deprived of livelihoods and security. A global economic order had been forged through globalisation without any prospect of justice, or democracy, or distribution. And this posed problems for the defenders of globalisation. For if a system is widely perceived as unjust, it will necessarily engender resistance.

Therefore, whereas in the 1980s and the early 1990s free market liberalism had been left to private corporations, this strategy had to be rethought since it had proved counter-productive. In fact, as early as in 1995 the journalist Paul Krugman had suggested that the Mexican crisis marked the beginning of the deflation of the Washington consensus (Krugman 1995: 28-44). The very idea that globalisation had rendered capitalism efficient came to be questioned, because what was witnessed was the globalisation of a crisis. Consequently, managers of international financial and economic institutions were to realise, somewhat late, what Marx had argued in the late nineteenth century: that there is nothing natural or self-regulating about markets and that markets are inherently self-destructive. If markets were to endure they had to be controlled or, in the new parlance of international financial institutions, 'governed'.

By the closing decades of the twentieth century, it became clear that if globalisation brought opportunities in its wake; the process has adversely affected that section of society which is unable to make the transition from one system of production (industrial), to another system based on rapid and efficient communication and flows of information (post-industrial). Above all neo-liberal prescriptions which resulted in the lifting of subsidies, and the withdrawal of the state from providing employment, health care, education, and shelter, had intensified deprivation and misery. All of this bode ill for any argument that globalisation would herald an era of rapid growth and well being.

This realisation led to a radical shift in the rhetoric of globalisation: the replacement of the language of the market by that of governance, accountability, transparency, democracy, and the indispensability of the state. The World Bank, under the influence of the economist Joseph Stiglitz, known for his critique of the unfettered market, moved from a narrow economistic focus on development to what came to be known as the comprehensive development framework. Even as policies of structural adjustment were replaced by notions of partnership between the Bank and borrowing governments, the language of the Bank shifted from macroeconomic theory that focused on economic growth to the recognition of the centrality of governance. The Bank had no choice. For global civil society actors in various demonstrations insisted that 'Fifty Years is Enough', a slogan that overshadowed the golden jubilee of the Bank.

Yet Two Questions

Despite a plethora of literature on the subject of globalisation and the shifts therein, two questions remain unsettled. One why has the process [of globalisation] borne different consequences for different countries? It is clear by now that globalisation has not impacted all countries in the South in quite the same manner. If China and India seem to have benefited from globalisation; others, particularly countries belonging to the Sub-Saharan African region, appear to have lost out completely. [2] Further even within countries such as India that have benefited from globalisation in terms of higher economic growth and economic transformations, *some regions have profited from globalisation and others lag far behind. Evidently, some countries, and some regions within countries, have been able to take advantages of the opportunities offered by globalisation. These countries and regions have also been able to negotiate the constraints that are embedded in the process with some skill. Others have simply not been able to do so.*

The interesting question then becomes—what are the reasons for the uneven response to globalisation across the South? Are the experiences of Southern countries, which have successfully negotiated globalisation generalisable in as much as other countries can learn from them? Perhaps not, because as the record of the developing world in the last twenty five years shows us, the ability of a state to profit from, or be constrained by globalisation, is dependent on a number of historically specific factors: processes of capital formation, industrial and agricultural development, accumulation of professional skills, development of infrastructure, technological advances, labour laws, and, regulatory regimes, all of which impart to the state flexibility, as well as the capacity to respond to new challenges. The ability of a state to negotiate the processes of globalisation appears to be *country specific*. This ability also depends on the position of the said country in the global system of markets, capital transactions, trade flows, and communications.

The second question is the following: how does globalisation impact the capacity of the state to deliver social goods to its citizens? [I assume that the task of providing social goods to people is a constituent part of the democratic agenda, or that political democracy and social/economic democracy are not distant or even first cousins, *they are constitutive of democracy itself*]. Is there a direct and unmediated relationship between: (a) processes intrinsic to globalisation such as the lifting of government controls on economic transactions, trade, and commerce, leading to the integration of the state into the global market, and (b) rendering of obligations by the state?

In countries which have been subjected to stringent regulations by international financial institutions through structural adjustment programmes the state has been compelled to roll back from social provisioning. The state has also had to do away with subsidies to vulnerable sectors of the economy and society, withdraw from the regulation of economic activities, truncate the public sector, cut down on recruitment to public jobs, loosen protective labour laws, and in general pull out from the social sector in the pursuit of one main objective; correcting the fiscal deficit by freeing capital from non-productive expenditure.

However, if in institutionalised democracies such as India, the withdrawal of the state from social welfare has not followed globalisation as a matter of course, this is because of one basic reason; institutionalised democracy that enables mobilisation in civil society on the one hand, and allows citizens to pronounce their verdict on the government during elections on the other. It can be added that the globalisation of political norms relating to poverty, human rights, and human development has deeply impacted policy making. In India, the effects of globalisation have been, to put it mildly, contradictory.

If greater integration into the world market has resulted in the liberalisation of the economy as well as economic reforms to offset the fiscal deficit, issues of social welfare and of state responsibility for providing for the poorer sections of society have also been raised onto the political agenda with renewed force. Kundu points out that 'within the discordant discourse on globalisation, we can discern elements of a new politics and the emergence of a sense of social responsibility in the country'. Social development, he goes on to argue, figured importantly in the policy debate during the early 1990s, when neo-liberal orthodoxy was at its peak (Kundu 2006: xv).

This is not to suggest that all this has been carried through effectively, or that India is in the throes of a social revolution in the midst of an economic transformation. It is merely to suggest that the effects of globalisation on the capacity of the state to negotiate the imperatives of globalisation on the one hand, and discharge its obligations to the citizens on the other, is dependent on a number of mediating factors, which are partly historical, and mainly political. *The objective of this essay is to investigate these mediating factors in India* through a study of the way in which the state has addressed the provisions of social goods.

Globalisation and Transformation of the Economy

Since Independence, India had pursued a classic policy of import substitution industrialisation, with the state playing a dominant role in the economy. It is generally felt that the grip of the state over the economy led to a burgeoning license raj, to corruption, and to inefficiency is well known.

By the 1970s, Government reports began to acknowledge the problems that had arisen out of low levels of productivity, lack of development finance, and absence of export promotion strategies. After P.M. Indira Gandhi came back to power in 1980-83, a major shift in development policy was initiated by the government. Kohli notes that instead of the statist and the nationalist model of development of the Nehru era, which had been accentuated in a populist direction by P.M. Indira Gandhi in the 1970s, P.M Gandhi 'shifted India's political economy around 1980 in the direction of a state and business alliance for economic growth' (Kohli 2006: 1251-1259, 1255).

The Prime Minister, who had begun to stress economic growth instead of redistribution in sharp contrast to the political rhetoric of the 1970s, adopted an anti-labour stance, sought an alliance with big business, put brakes on the growth of the public sector industries, and demoted the importance of economic planning. A New Industrial Policy that prioritized maximising production was adopted, the government lifted restrictions on the expansion of big business into new areas, encouraged the private sector to invest in areas formerly closed to it such as production of power, diluted the Monopolies and Restrictive Trade Practices Act, removed licensing restrictions, provided some tax relief to business, and altered the legal framework within which business functioned. The government also provided incentives to the private sector, in order to encourage it to finance new investments by raising resources directly from the public. Since political considerations ruled out a cutback in public expenditure, the government sought to raise revenues through indirect taxes (Kohli 2006: 1251-1259, 1255).

These policies were furthered by P.M. Rajiv Gandhi's regime from 1984-89. P.M. Rajiv Gandhi attempted to promote economic liberalisation, but substantial promotion of competitiveness and exports could not be realised in the 1980s for largely political reasons. Though the budgets of 1984 and 1985 had tried to institutionalise economic reforms, these reforms were rolled back due to internal pressure from the Congress party (Kohli 2006: 1361).

By the end of the 1980s, India began to confront great economic difficulties. The fiscal deficit had increased to over 8 percent of the GDP. By the turn of the decade of the nineteen nineties, inflation had reached 14 percent, and external debt had increased from US$ 18 billion in 1980, to nearly US$ 72 billion. With the Iraqi invasion of Kuwait in 1990, remittances from Indian workers in the Gulf collapsed because labour fled the conflict torn region, exports to Kuwait and Iraq fell, and India faced a considerably higher oil bill as the price of oil skyrocketed. The adverse credit rating of the Moody's in October 1990, pointed to a rise in the debt service ratio and the debt export ratio, to the budget deficit, and to India's dependence on short-term commercial borrowings. India was on the verge of a liquidity crisis in June 1991, with not enough foreign exchange to cover a fortnight of imports (Kohli 2006: 1361). 1991 also brought the collapse of the Soviet Union, which used to be a major trade and strategic partner of India, with attendant consequences (Corbridge and Harriss 2000: 151).

In June 1991, the severe financial crisis, which might have forced the country to default on its international obligations, acted as a powerful incentive for the government to intensify economic reforms that had been undertaken in the 1980s. Arguably, the liberalisation of the economy, which had been institutionalised in the decade of the 1980s, had encouraged some business groups to be more competitive. These groups were now ready to compete with international capital. Corbridge and Harriss point out that there is need for caution for accepting the view that the economic reforms were a response to the economic and especially the fiscal crisis of the 1980s. The view, 'discounts the successes of the 1980s, and it ignores the role played by some of India's business leaders in arguing for reforms that served their private or corporate interests'.

In sum, a combination of strong factors provided strong incentives to lift controls that had earmarked state intervention in the economy since independence. The central government under P.M. Narasimha Rao, enacted several measures to extend existing reforms and initiate new ones, even though the anti-liberalization lobby voiced protest. The Bombay Club of industrialists began to articulate concern about competition from multinationals, and the trade unions struck work against the exit policy that would displace jobs. Despite great opposition P.M. Narasimha Rao and Finance Minister Dr. Manmohan Singh dramatically transformed the domestic and the international context of India's economic strategy. The objective of policy makers was dual: (a) to bail the country out of the balance of payments deficit, and (b) to promote competitiveness and export orientation in the economy to cushion the country against further shocks. Post-1991, the process of dismantling controls over the economy accelerated at a fast pace.

These objectives resulted in an extraordinary shake up of the system. In 1991, the Indian government introduced a New Economic Policy with the objective of liberalising the Indian economy, and thus enabling its firmer integration into the world market through some of the following measures. The aim of these measures was to create an environment that would allow national and international business the freedom to enter and exit. Consequently, crucial public sectors enterprises have been privatised, public equity in many enterprises has been diluted, and service areas formerly reserved for the public sector have been opened to the private sector such as health, insurance, banking, infrastructure, roads, air transport, and retail. In the sphere of external trade, financial relations, and foreign investment, the government heralded a decisive shift. By India's own past standards' writes Kohli, 'the changes [in external economic relations] were quite dramatic' (Atul Kohli 2006: 1361).

These measures have borne some spectacular results. In 2008, Bardhan noted that from 1993 onwards the economy, powered by the services sector, has been growing at a rate of 6 percent per annum, and since the last four years at an astonishing 9 percent per annum. This compares very well with the rest of the world, except China. From 1977 to 1990, India's foreign reserves remained at US$ 5 billion and occasionally dropped to a precarious level of US$ 6 billion. From 1990, reserves began to rise and are now well over US$ 600 billion. [3] Thus, a process which had been initiated in the early years of the decade of the1980s by P.M. Indira Gandhi came to fruition in the 1990s.

It is clear by now that high rates of economic growth have not been accompanied by a substantial reduction of poverty and deprivation. According to Bardhan, the outstanding average figures for GDP and growth are being achieved largely by a small segment of the well of population; the middle income groups growing well but less rapidly, and a bottom segment of around 20 percent. The record however varies between states. This raises one basic question for, and of globalisation. Why have some states within the Indian Union and regions within states, done better than others to ameliorate the ill being of substantial sections of the population?

But before we take this up, one basic point needs to be registered. One, although the Indian state has been committed to social welfare since independence, and this commitment is coded in Chapter IV of the Constitution of India, the historical record of the Indian state has been rather poor in this regard. Public investments in basic social sectors have been low, and the implementation of the many programmes for social welfare has been both inefficient and inadequate, as well as marked by corruption and mismanagement. It would be irresponsible to put the blame for this grim record onto processes of globalisation alone, and thereby emancipate the state from non-performance in these sectors.

A Case Study of Selected States

Globalisation, it is generally observed, has led to regional inequalities in India. We might add that states within the Indian Union have shown different results as far as social welfare is concerned. In this section we study how different states have managed to balance the two sets of imperatives laid out above: globalisation and the need to deliver on social welfare. The states have been ranked according to the globalisation and liberalisation index created by the survey carried out for the project by Indicus. The globalisation index looks at the State wise per capita exports (value) 2002-03, State-wise per capita FDI Approved value between 2000 and 2005, and State-wise per capita migration (emigration clearances granted between 1993 and 2001).

We carried out intensive case studies of Tamil Nadu, Kerala, Gujarat, Karnataka, which can be considered high globalisers (ranking 1-5), Punjab and Andhra Pradesh are middle globalisers, and Bihar can be considered to be a low globaliser (Table 1.1).

Table 1.1: Globalisation Index

State	Ranking
Maharashtra	1
Tamil Nadu	2
Kerala	3
Gujarat	4
Karnataka	5
Punjab	6
Andhra Pradesh	7
West Bengal	8
Rajasthan	9
Odisha	10
Uttar Pradesh	11
Madhya Pradesh	12
Assam	13

When it came to liberalisation, the index was constructed on the following variables: privatization or selling of government owned business, de-regulation or levels of removal of legal and quasi-legal regulations. The variables according to Debroy and Bhandari are: size of government expenditures: taxes and enterprises; legal structure and security of property rights, and regulation of credit, labour and business.

The results of our study are paradoxical (Table 1.2).

Table 1.2: Liberalisation Index

State	Ranking
Tamil Nadu	1
Gujarat	2
Kerala	3
Andhra Pradesh	4
Madhya Pradesh	5
Uttar Pradesh	6
Karnataka	7
Maharashtra	8
West Bengal	9
Rajasthan	10
Odisha	11
Punjab	12
Assam	13

Some state governments have managed to maintain their commitment to social welfare *even though* they are highly globalised, such as Tamil Nadu. And some state governments are not committed to social welfare *even though* they are not globalised, such as Bihar. It appears that the link between globalisation and the capacity of the state to deliver social goods to its citizens is highly *contingent* upon a variety of factors.

1. Measures that are generally associated with the regulatory regime that accompanies globalisation: downsizing of the state; liberalisation of trade, lifting of controls on private investment, withdrawal of the state from the public sector and services, tax reforms, stringency in labour laws, opening up of the market to FDI's, reduction of subsidies, and withdrawal of the state from the social sector, were adopted, because most states confronted a fiscal deficit. If in Kerala the fiscal deficit can be traced to heavy involvement in the field of social development without concomitant economic growth, in Punjab this deficit was due to investment in the security apparatus to counter militancy. This involved a shift away from the social sector. In Andhra Pradesh and Tamil

Nadu the fiscal deficit was due to the adoption of populist measures which catered to electoral constituencies. In Gujarat and Karnataka, the origins of the fiscal deficit can be traced to high salaries, and an overburdened state sector. And in Bihar, the fiscal deficit can be attributed to general administrative and fiscal inefficiency.

2. The measures that were adopted by state governments to counter the deficit and to create conditions favourable to investment generated different sets of political responses. In Tamil Nadu the sacking of government employees, particularly school teachers, and the conversion of the public distribution system into a targeted one, gave rise to discontent and led to electoral defeats for the government in 2004. The successor government reversed these measures. But in the state commitment to social policy, and the dominant role played by an entrepreneurial class in industrial development, has resulted in a balancing of social development and economic development, despite problems in the quality of services. In Andhra Pradesh, the populist measures by the NTR government, which substituted for social policy, were reversed by the Chandra Babu Naidu regime. The regime concentrated on transforming the economy through taking advantage of the opportunities offered by globalisation. This was paralleled by the rhetoric of empowerment and democracy. However, neglect of the rural sector has led to agrarian distress and farmer's suicides. The defeat of the Chandra Babu regime and the installation of a new government did not result, as in the case of Tamil Nadu, in the restoration of commitment to social policy. In Karnataka, the government managed to transform the economy but at the cost of the rural sector. In Kerala a major cutback in the social sector was ruled out by an ideologically charged political party, and by politically charged social movements. Punjab which has been heavily dependent on the state for economic growth and for social development is one state that has not been able to cope with the withdrawal of the state

from both sectors, and decline in funds by the central government. Punjab's status in the country has deteriorated in economic terms, and there is little involvement of either the state or private players in the social sector. This is in complete contrast to Gujarat where private entrepreneurship has played a large role in industry Gujarat has been able to respond to the opportunities offered by globalisation, as well as meet certain social goals. The fiscal deficit in Bihar is the product of developments internal to the state; such as administrative mismanagement.

3. Notably, states with high social development indicators might or might not be highly globalised or states with highest incomes. Kerala is a reluctant globaliser but performs best on literacy and infant mortality indicators. But Tamil Nadu achieves both goals, that of globalising the economy as well as securing high social indicators. The explanation for this has to be non-economic. One possible explanation is political mobilisation in civil society. The other is the quality of governance.
4. In Kerala, the achievements in health and education is dependent more on the quality of these services, and the efficiency with which they are used, rather than in higher allocations of resources (Dev and Mooij 2005: 86-107, 97).
5. This is remarkable considering that when the state of Kerala was constituted the Malabar region lagged behind Travancore and Cochin in terms of social development. By the 1980s, the Malabar region had caught up with other regions, mainly due to well directed state action. Public participation and state leadership has also played a crucial role in this respect. The anti-caste movement, missionary activities, and left movements have aided in raising human development and social security for the poor. Women have played an especially important role in these movements.
6. If Tamil Nadu represents one example of the state possessing the capacity to achieve both economic growth via globalisation, as well as social development, this is due to a

number of historical factors. The nature of the anti caste movement ensured that the claims of the backward classes did not stay confined to reservations in public jobs. Therefore, members of these classes were able to achieve a competitive edge in the professions. Tamil Nadu has the added advantage of being a well administered state, and has an efficient bureaucracy. A dynamic entrepreneurial class, which has been given a great deal of space in the state, has facilitated industrial development. This has been facilitated by the considerable attention given to infrastructure. The state is most highly industrialised in the country, and ranks after Maharashtra, accounting for 11 percent of the country's industrial output. And considerable progress in higher education means that the state leads the country, in particularly technical education. For these reasons, the state attracts FDI, and is the third most important destination in India for FDI. At the same time, Tamil Nadu as the state, has led the country in nutrition schemes and in protective social security measures. The Chief Minister's Nutrition Meal Programme and the Tamil Nadu Integrated Nutrition Project, has increased the nutrition levels of school going children.

7. At the other end of the pole, Bihar has not been able to achieve either economic growth or social development for a variety of historical reasons: administrative inefficiency, the shift in political priorities from development to caste empowerment, apathy rather than concentrated public action, and the subordination of the administrative class to the political class for reasons of politics. Consequently whereas Bihar has not been able to attract FDI's, it has also not performed at all in the field of social policy. Extreme forms of social inequality have created an environment marked by subordination to the political class. The result is the increasing migration from the state to the rest of the country.

In sum, a number of historical and political factors mediate the relationship between globalisation and the state's capacity to meet the needs of its citizens particularly the poorer sections of society.

Mediations

This essay set out to examine whether globalisation has significantly impacted the capacity of the Indian State to deliver social goods to the citizens, particularly to the poorer sections who are unable to participate in market transactions. The broad findings of the project indicate that an entire range of factors mediate the relationship between globalisation, and the capacity of the state to deliver social welfare to its people. What are these factors?

1. In comparison to the rest of the developing world, particularly Sub-Saharan Africa, India has been able to negotiate globalisation from a relatively stronger plane. The reason why it has been able to do so is due to relatively high rates of savings, availability of a pool of professional talent, infrastructure, and the ability to shift from classic import substitution model of development, to one that is based on the service sector particularly information technology, and manufacturing. Arguably, the state led model of planned development that was institutionalised in India in the 1950s has strengthened the capacity of the state.
2. The experience of globalisation has been uneven between states. Two factors need to be noted in connection with inter-state disparities. Firstly, states with the highest social development indicators such as Kerala; are not necessarily states which have the highest incomes. Secondly, some states which have globalised such as Tamil Nadu, have performed much better on the social welfare front than states that have not globalised such as Bihar.

   Since we find little correlation between economic growth and social welfare policies, and between social welfare policies and globalisation, the explanation for this phenomenon must be non-economic; it must necessarily lie in the realm of the political. Three conceivable explanations are the following:
3. Electoral Democracy: Electoral democracy carries its own political reverberations in three senses.

- It enables mobilisation on issues that are of significance for daily lives of people.
- Politicians desiring election or re-election have no choice except to respond. They are more likely to respond when civil society is politically mobilised, when voter turnouts are high, and when governments have been dismissed on policies. This is particularly the case in the 2004 General Elections, and the elections in Tamil Nadu.
- A competitive party systems are a strong incentive for politicians to deliver, politicians will be more likely to implement the preferences of the voters if they face strong competition. It is instructive to note in this connection that Kerala has consistently high voter turn outs, a competitive party system, and a history of political mobilisation.

4. Nature of the State: States that have a good record of delivering on social welfare such as Kerala and Tamil Nadu have had:

- Governments that are committed to social welfare,
- Political parties that have strong ideological orientations,
- Efficient and committed bureaucracies.

5. Civil society mobilisation:

- The Government of India has responded to civil society campaigns and accepted that citizens have a right to employment, to information, and to education. The role of the Supreme Court has been particularly important in this context because the Court has mediated between these campaigns and the Government.
- Networks in global civil society have fore-grounded various issues from eradication of poverty as a human right, to social protection.
- Human development reports of the UNDP by ranking governments on the basis of performance in human developments, have served to 'name and shame' these governments.

The Indian state has responded to combined interventions, which lie in the realm of the political by initiating several programmes of which the NREGA is the flagship programme of the UPA government. These programmes are significant, but they cannot serve to substitute for institutionalised and targeted interventions in the sphere of social welfare. If the context in which these programmes; that of indifference, corruption, mismanagement, and inefficiency, is not streamlined, and government officials and local self-government functionaries not impressed upon that these programmes are central to the projects of the government, and that they form an integral part of development planning, then many of these programmes will fall by the way side.

Therefore, there is urgent need to institutionalise the stress on employment generation, education, health, and nutrition, to restructure the administrative environment that seems to be marked by apathy on the one hand, and intent to subvert on the other in the directions of transparency and accountability, and to promote participation of the citizens in the administration of these programmes. Otherwise, the gains of current movements in national and global civil society will result in policies and programmes that continue to reproduce the gap between rhetoric and the reality of much of the poverty in India.

Conclusion

A review of developments in India, post-1991, will show us that not all major transformations in Indian society have been produced and reproduced through globalisation alone. These transformations are the product of complex transactions between different sets of factors, some of which are structural and some which are contingent. The question of whether the state does or does not deliver on social goods in times of globalisation cannot be answered in terms of a simple yes or no. The factors which intervene between the intention of a country to globalise, and its performance in the field of social welfare, are contingent upon the history, the economics, but particularly of the politics of the country. It is difficult and perhaps irresponsible to try to trace a direct and an unmediated relationship between globalisation and social policies. Even though globalisation can be considered a catalyst in the restructuring of Indian society, the relationship between the processes of globalisation and the state is mediated by a number of factors.

For these reasons, it is difficult to either acclaim globalisation with some enthusiasm as the one answer to the ills of the contemporary world, or to reject it as the defining ill of this world. Any discussion of globalisation, particularly one that is embedded in a political discourse cannot but be nuanced and brimming over with 'ifs' and 'buts'. In sum, it is difficult to adopt a simple and one dimensional position on globalisation as a political process, just as it is difficult to adopt such a position on any political process, whether the process in question is the objective of politics in a dissent mode, or the form of dissent politics.

End Notes

1. For instance Hardt and Negri interpret globalization as constituting a historically novel form of global domination, i.e. a dynamic, decentred, and diffused global system under the rule of Empire. Jagdish Bhagwati defends globalization in his, book, *In Defence of Globalisation*, and Joseph Stigliz argues in his work *Globalisation and its Discontents* that globalization needs to be controlled.
2. Mittelman identifies three broad characteristics of globalisation literature as firstly a tendency towards economism or a focus on material factors to the exclusion of political and cultural aspects, secondly, state centricity, and thirdly an overemphasis on detailed descriptions without grasp of linkages to evolving global structures, p. 3.
3. Pranab Bardhan estimates that the growth period began in 1975 when the economy grew at the rate of 9 percent, and barring one year, it has never looked back. The reasons for economic growth Bardhan traces to the rise in savings and investment rates largely propelled by the nationalization and the extension of the banking system in the late 1960s, acceleration of the savings rate in the 1990s, economic reforms of the 1990s, the surge in outsourcing activities, and what he calls a cultural revolution.

References

Bardhan, Pranab (2008), 'India's Dilemmas: The Political Economy of Policymaking in a Globalised World', *Economic and Political Weekly*, 2nd February, pp. 53-62.

Bhagwati, Jagdish (2004), In Defence of Globalisation, Oxford University Press, New York.

Corbridge, Stuart and John Harriss (2000), Reinventing India: Liberalisation, Hindu Nationalism and Popular Democracy, Oxford University Press, New Delhi, p. 151.

Dev, S. Mahendra and Jos Mooij (2005), 'Patterns in Social Sector Expenditure: Pre- and Post-Reform Periods' in Kirit S. Parikh and R. Radhakrishnan (ed.) India Development Report 2004-2005, Oxford University Press, New Delhi.

Hardt, Michael and Antonio Negri (2000), Empire, Harvard University Press, Cambridge, Mass.

Higgot, Richard (2000), 'Contested Globalisation: The Changing Context and Normative Challenges', *Review of International Studies*, 26.

Kohli, Atul (2006), 'Politics of Economic Growth in India: 1980-2005', Part I, *Economic and Political Weekly*, April 1.

Krugman, Paul (1995), 'Dutch Tulips and Emerging Markets', *Foreign Affairs*, 74: 4.

Kundu, Amitabh (2006), 'Introduction: A Framework for Analysing Economic and Social Backwardness' in Kundu (ed.) India Social Development: A Report, Council for Social Development, Oxford University Press, New Delhi.

Mittelman, J.H (2000), The Globalisation Syndrome: Transformation and Resistance, Princeton University Press, New Jersey, p. 241.

Stigliz, Joseph (2003), Globalisation and its Discontents, W.W Norton, New York.

UNDP (1999), Human Development Report 1999, New Delhi, Oxford University Press.

World Bank (1997), World Development Report: The State in a Changing World, Oxford University Press, Oxford.

2

India and Gulf Co-operation Council (GCC) States

A.K. Pasha

Introduction

Throughout recorded history India has had close maritime trade and other relations with the Magan, Dilmun and other civilizations which flourished in present day GCC States. Indian and Arab merchants settled in each other's ports and other territories. After the rise of Islam, contacts increased between the two as also commerce. The European imperial powers starting with Portuguese with a crusader mentality had introduced new rules like showing of flags, drawing of boundaries, forts to safeguard their interests as also their cultural and religious values. The British came to control India by early 19th century and soon the British with Indian soldiers and resources came to dominate the present day GCC states even though some parts were under Ottoman control. For the British the Gulf was a key communication link between India and London. Despite European attempts to cut ties, both India and the Gulf Arabs managed to retain some contacts.

The British had over whelming influence over all Gulf States and the rulers obviously came to establish close political, military and economic ties with London. The US established its military presence in Bahrain [naval] and Saudi Arabia as also close political ties. Both UK and USA encouraged the GCC States to have close ties with Pakistan mainly on the basis of its Islamic identity. Pakistan as an ally of US used this opportunity to raise Kashmir and other domestic Indian issues.

After the Iranian revolution in 1979, there was a sense that

GCC states may see major upheavals and so India was cautious in developing other than purely normal trade and political ties. Since the end of the Cold War, all Indian governments have been tirelessly working to establish close ties with the USA in all fields including military. Pakistan, Kashmir, emergence of China and mounting domestic security challenges should be kept in mind in this developing relationship.

The GCC States under the combined threat from Iran and Iraq came to establish all round close ties with the USA including stationing of US troops in their territories. After its invasion and occupation of Iraq in 2003 there is Pax-Americana in the Gulf notwithstanding protests from Iran. In the background of this ground reality in the Gulf [global as well] and emergence of US as the sole super power since 1991 is the overall framework under which India's growing ties with GCC States are assessed. High-level political, military visits from both sides indicate new warmth and dynamism, including willingness to enhance defence and security ties which were unthinkable until recently.

The GCC states preoccupation with terrorism and stability both internal and Gulf security and support to India on Kashmir issue is seen by India as welcomes changes. Pakistan is no longer seen as a stumbling bloc in closer GCC-India bilateral ties. India's growing proximity with GCC States has put India's ties with Iran under strain as also due to US-Iran conflictual ties. There is no denying of the fact that as Indo-US ties get closer this is bound to have a positive impact on India-GCC ties. It is in this framework that this article explores the multifaceted GCC-India relations. The subject of this essay is divided into four parts.

The first part deals briefly with the historical developments as a background to the contemporary issues. The second part deals in detail India's bilateral relations with each of the six GCC States. The third part examines issues like democracy, security and other challenges. The final section briefly attempts to study the challenges India faces in the Gulf region and attempts an assessment of the new opportunities available in a region undergoing rapid transformation.

India and Saudi Arabia

Soon after Independence, Pakistan tried hard to mobilize Arab and Islamic states to its side on the Kashmir and other issues. In this, Pakistan's relations with Saudi Arabia were to prove most rewarding. But soon India established close ties with Egypt's President Gamal Abdel Nasser. Many Arab states resented Pakistan's attempt to raise the Kashmir issue in Islamic meetings. Pakistan's membership in western sponsored military pacts was also denounced. Saudis attacked Pakistan's decision to join the Baghdad Pact which subsequently became CENTO after Iraq withdrew from the military alliance in the wake of the Iraqi revolution in July 1958.

In fact, Riyadh was astonished to find that the "Islamic state of Pakistan should accede to those who have joined hands with the Zionists Jews" and spoke of the Pact as a "stab in the heart of the Arab and Muslim states" and urged it "to return to the right path", by withdrawing from the widely unpopular western military pact. Pakistan, which had launched a campaign against India on the issue of treatment of Indian Muslims, also got a setback when Riyadh publicly sided with India on the issue. King Saud Bin Abdul Aziz of Saudi Arabia paid tribute to the Government of India for its policy of equality and equity towards the forty million Muslims in India. Giving impressions of his 17-day long tour of India [from 26th November] in a now famous public statement, the Saudi King on 10 December 1955 told the Indo-Arab Society in Bombay, "I desire to say to my Muslim brethren all over the world with satisfaction that the fate of the Indian Muslims is in safe hands.

In my capacity as the guardian of Muslim holy places, I desire to express my gratitude to the great Indian leader, Mr. Nehru, and all those lieutenants of his, through whom he executes this policy of equality and equity". When India's

Prime Minister Jawaharlal Nehru returned the visit in September 1956, he was given a rousing welcome with slogans of "Welcome Prophet of Peace" which obviously angered Pakistan. Soon after India's independence, Prime Minister Jawaharlal Nehru had to tackle amongst other things, Pakistan's relentless propaganda against India over Kashmir and other issues.

By the end of 1952, Pakistan's attempt to forge a Pan-Islamic alliance was in shambles and had to be subsequently abandoned. Among all its allies in the West Asian region, Pakistan's relations with Saudi Arabia were to prove most rewarding. King Abdul Aziz Ibn Saud after consolidating his territorial gains and having obtained financial security in terms of oil revenues, he charted to follow a more autonomous foreign policy. When King Saud visited Pakistan in 1953, he extended Riyadh's political support to Pakistan on the Kashmir issue.

India's recognition of Israel on 17th September 1950 came as a surprise to many in the Arab/Islamic world in view of India's persistent opposition to the partition of Palestine. Pakistan tried to paint India in the darkest colours in the eyes of the Arabs on this issue. But New Delhi's unequivocal support to the Palestine cause and subsequently her diplomatic and moral support to Arab national liberation movements in Algeria, Morocco, Tunisia, South Yemen and elsewhere brought it closer even to many conservative Arab states in the area.

India's support to the Egyptian stand during the 1956 Suez crisis and opposition to western attempts to pressurize Arab countries which followed non-aligned policies further improved India's credibility among the Arabs. Pakistan on the other hand by siding with the British alienated itself in the region. Egypt went to the extent of declaring that Kashmir was an integral part of India and that "Suez was as dear to Egypt as Kashmir was to India".

In a u-turn in Saudi Foreign Policy, King Ibn Saud after

his visit to the US (after the Suez crisis) became close to the US and endorsed the 'Eisenhower Doctrine'. The US wanted Arab support in the cold war which it failed to get through the Baghdad Pact. No wonder Egypt's Nasser denounced the US Doctrine as imperialist attempt to dominate the WANA region. The secession of Syria from the UAR in 1961, Egypt's military intervention in North Yemen after the 1962 revolution, US decision to supply offensive weapons to Israel under President Johnson, emergence of Faisal as Saudi King and his emphasis on Pan-Islamism rather than Pan-Arabism which Nasser advocated, all this brought about radical changes in the region with implications on India's policy towards the region which had come to be identified as Cairo-centric.

In the US-Israeli scheme to contain Nasser and Arab nationalist forces, Saudi Arabia and Pakistan, together with Turkey and Iran (CENTO partners) became prominent players in the game. Moreover, Pakistan's rabid hostility towards Arab nationalism and communism was well appreciated by the House of Saud. Thus, a Saudi-Pakistan alliance virtually came to be established in mid-1960 with Riyadh terming India as an aggressor in the 1965 Indo-Pak war and warned New Delhi not to take undue advantage of its close ties with the Arab/Islamic states. Saudi Arabia at the Arab Heads of States meeting in September 1965 joined with Jordan in demanding a collective Arab disapproval of the Indian stand on the War.

No Indian Prime Minister or high dignitary had been to Saudi Arabia since Jawaharlal Nehru visited the Kingdom in 1956, until Mrs. Indira Gandhi paid an official visit to Riyadh in April 1982. The only exception was the visit by Fakhruddin Ali Ahmed, President of India, who attended King Faisal's funeral in March 1975. This was the first time an Indian President personally represented India at the funeral of another Head of State, since the practice had been to depute the Vice President or senior Cabinet minister. It indicated the importance India attached to relations with the Kingdom of Saudi Arabia. During the period 1956 to 1982, India's relations with Saudi Arabia had never been unfriendly but at the same time they were not close either. A variety of factors worked at, such as close Indo-Egyptian ties, Treaty relationship between India and USSR, close Indo-Iraqi ties, Indian support to the Iranian revolution and policies [initially], and on top of it the Indo-Pak 1965 and 1971 Wars.

However, what materially affected Indo-Saudi ties was the close Saudi-Pakistan relationship. Despite the lack of political understanding, Indo-Saudi economic ties flourished. It is in this backdrop one should see Mrs. Gandhi's visit to Saudi Arabia in April 1982 which ended the 26 years long "communication gap" between India and the Saudi Kingdom. Her visit paved the way for better relations and "heralded a new era" in Indo-Saudi ties. She praised the Kingdom's "constructive role" in the global arena and its contribution in solving many international problems. She supported the Fahd Peace Plan on the Arab-Israeli issue saying "we have welcomed it. It is in line with our basic principles to which we must adhere to resolve the crisis in West Asia". She also described the Fahd Plan as "new hope, conforming to India's stand". Mrs. Indira Gandhi also sought Riyadh's cooperation to strengthen peace and stability in the South Asian region.

While political relations have been far from bonhomie as a result of Cold War alignments and Saudi-Pakistani affinity, Indo-Saudi economic cooperation took a more realistic form and flourished. Mrs. Gandhi's visit to the kingdom paved the way for a new chapter in economic cooperation. The most tangible gain was the setting up of an Indo-Saudi joint commission to promote economic and technical collaboration. The assumption that a combination of Indian technology, skilled manpower and Saudi money could work to strengthen South-South Cooperation yielded tremendous economic gains during the last 25 years, forcing a rethink on the political front, which could see a new dawn with the visit of King Abdullah in January 2006, the first by a Saudi head of state to India in 50 years. The Joint Commission was established under an economic and technical cooperation agreement signed in April 1981. The Commission has been meeting regularly since 1983 in Riyadh, and in New Delhi (Burke 1974: 134; Ahsan 1988: 11-12,109).

Prime Minister Manmohan Singh visited Saudi Arabia [three-day visit from February 27 to March 1, 2010 at the invitation of King Abdullah. This was the first visit by an Indian prime minister in 28 years, which was widely covered by the Saudi press with the *Arab News* headlining the front page with 'Indian PM on historic visit'. Stating that the visit was long overdue, the daily, in its editorial, said that both countries have much in common. 'Each has been undergoing far-reaching changes and each has set out to assert a high profile role on the world stage, for instance as members of the G20', it wrote. Stating that high hopes rested on the renewal of what has been a historic relationship, the editorial went on to say: 'Saudi Arabia's trading importance to India extends beyond the fact that we supply a quarter of India's oil needs. Our non-oil exports have grown strongly in recent years. As India's spectacular economic growth continues, Saudi capital can help finance new ventures.

Commenting on growing Indo-Israel military relation Singh said Arab concern about growing Indo-Israeli defence cooperation is "misplaced." Our relationship with no single country is at the expense of our relations with any other country", he said. As to India's support for Palestine, it was "an article of faith for us", he added, "our solidarity with the people of Palestine predates our independence", Singh said. "India supports a peaceful solution that would result in a sovereign, independent, viable and united state of Palestine living within secure and recognized borders, with East Jerusalem as its capital, side by side at peace with Israel", he added. [1]

Prime Minister Man Mohan Singh at the end of his 3-day visit to Saudi Arabia disclosed that he asked Saudi Arabia to persuade Pakistan to act against Pakistan-based Islamist militant groups. Only time will tell whether Riyadh can or will use its clout over Pakistan as far as Indian security concerns are concerned. [2]

India and Saudi Arabia have also agreed to increase strategic cooperation although mutual convergence is yet to be seen. In this connection, both in 2006, signed an initial agreement to tackle terrorism and trans-national crime. Whereas India expects Riyadh to use its influence over Pakistan to contain export of terrorism to India especially Kashmir and also facilitate meaningful cooperation, peace, security and stability in South Asia as Islamabad is seen by India as a spoiler. Saudi Arabia's driving motive to seek strategic cooperation with India is partly to improve the geopolitical environment in Pakistan and Afghanistan. Also Riyadh is under pressure from neighbouring Iran among other things due to Tehran's quest for nuclear technology [weapons in Saudi perception] and domestically from Al-Qaeda and other religious groups calling for the overthrow of the Saudi monarchy. India and Saudi Arabia also share a common desire for political stability and security in the Gulf region.

India and the UAE

A large number of India's public and private companies have taken active part in the industrialization of the UAE. They are either contracts or joint ventures. Some of them are the refinery in the Ruwais area in Abu Dhabi by Engineering Projects [India] Limited [EPI], a tube blending plant and a turnkey project by the Balmer Lawrie group, consultancy works for the Abu Dhabi National Oil Co. by ONGC, the laying of a multi purpose pipeline by Engineers India Limited [EIL] and, civil construction work for .the Airport at Abu Dhabi by Engineering Construction Corporation [ECC]. Dubai now allows ownership of real estate to foreigners. Reputed Indian companies like the Tatas, Kamanis, Dastur and others have taken part in the industrial development of UAE. In the Jebel Ali free trade zone about 160 Indian companies—the largest number from any one country have taken part, of which 56 are joint ventures.

The Sadiyat free trade zone is attracting many Indian companies. Software is the new field in bilateral trade with firms like Satyam and Infosys active in business. The UAE has about 20 joint ventures—mostly in private sector, in India especially in Gujarat and Maharashtra. The offshore and onshore oil drilling platforms plant in Maharashtra is the most significant. A very large and growing number of Indian companies are established in all the UAE Emirates especially in the Free Trade Zones.

This includes both private and public sector companies who make huge profits which are mostly sent back to India. UAE held its first exhibition in Mumbai at the end of 2003 where contracts worth US$ 140 million were signed. Dubai and Sharjah Chambers of Commerce and Industry in March 2004 signed a MoU with India for investments in Indian infrastructure worth US$ 20 billion. Many IT firms are heading to UAE and IT exports to UAE in 2004 were US$ 149 million, an increase from US$ 100 million in 2003. Dubai Ports International [DPI] won a contract for US$ 450 million to manage, operate and develop the Rajiv Gandhi Container Terminal in Kochi [Kerala] on a BOT basis for 38 years. This will get 33.3 percent revenue to Kochi Port Trust annually. This is DPI's second contract after 30 year agreement for the Vishakhapatanam port. [3]

The stand adopted by the UAE on Kashmir at all meetings until 1991 had been remarkably restrained. But since the Babri Masjid event and Bombay bomb blasts, the UAE shifted from its earlier position. At the OIC foreign ministers at Karachi in 1994 the UAE called for guaranteeing the "national rights and the Islamic identity of Kashmiri people". The UAE minister of state for foreign affairs in his speech expressed concern over the situation in Kashmir and called for settlement of the problem. He said: "The situation in Kashmir is still tense and could flare up unless tension is defused, before it is too late".

He further added: "We appeal to all parties concerned to work for resolving this problem through wisdom and objectivity and we hope to see a peaceful solution that is acceptable to all parties within the framework of international resolutions and bilateral agreements that will guarantee the national rights and the Islamic identity of people there [Kashmir]".

A change that too a significant one, had taken place in UAE's position towards India and this was obvious since the demolition of the Babri Masjid when it took series of steps to express its displeasure, including its disagreement to immediately receive India's Minister of State for External Affairs R.L. Bhatia, its attempts to cold shoulder goodwill Indian naval visit and its lack of enthusiasm to specify dates for a visit by Prime Minister Narashima Rao. Some have linked the UAE's attitude with the extradition related issues. R.L Bhatia finally visited the UAE on 25th May 1993 where he rejected any mediation bid by a country to resolve the Kashmir issue.

He said, "people can advice on friendly basis, but we cannot accept any mediation". He also said that the Kashmir issue is a bilateral matter and we do not want any outside interference. But the UAE gave every possible support to India in connection with the Bombay bomb blasts. It condemned all sorts of terrorism and violence which resulted in the killing of innocent people. It agreed to work with India to curb terrorism and step up cooperation in security measures. The former Indian Ambassador to UAE Ranjit Sethi said: "There has been no adverse impact on our relations in any manner. We have been given much assistance by the UAE authorities, at every level". Moreover, he added that the UAE is ready to help in every possible way in matters vital to the security of India. The refuge given by UAE to Indian nationals whom the, "government of India wants them for crimes committed" in India has become an issue in bilateral relations.

In this connection, L.K. Advani, India's Home Minister

visited UAE from 13th July 2001 for issues related to extradition treaty. He called on the President of UAE and discussed with him regional and international issues of mutual interest. Some in the government bureaucracy and mass media of India continue to portray UAE as a country, especially Dubai as a haven for Indian terrorists. The UAE also gets negative publicity in India. This image needs to be corrected as this might lead to unpleasant problems in future. In order to further improve ties Mr. Natwar Singh visited UAE in 2004 and signed an agreement to boost economic cooperation through reviving the joint commission. Since then, a number of high level visits from both sides have taken place putting the bilateral ties on a firm footing (Alani 2007: 8-9).

India and Kuwait

The Gulf crisis over Kuwait when Iraq marched into the oil rich Emirate on 2nd August 1990 posed India a major challenge. Due to India's close political and economic ties with Iraq, an impression was created in the initial stages of the crisis that New Delhi tended to support Baghdad. This led to misunderstanding between Kuwait [and also with other GCC states] with India. To be correct, India strongly disapproved the Iraqi invasion of Kuwait and called it illegal and should be vacated but stopped short of condemning the invasion. Since India did not openly take sides, Kuwait and other GCC states assumed India's sympathies lay with Iraq. The Kuwait crisis affected India in many ways. New Delhi mainly due to domestic turmoil displayed no apparent enthusiasm to resolve the crisis.

The minority government of V.P. Singh appeared to be primarily concerned with the evacuation of more than one lakh Indian citizens from Kuwait and 25,000 in Iraq. Public pressure mounted along with the decision of MP's from Kerala to sit on a day long fast at the Parliament House on 16th August 1990 to protest against the "inaction of the government regarding the plight of Indians" in both the Gulf states. This forced the government to accord the safe evacuation of Indians top priority. It partly explains India's decision not to condemn the Iraqi action as it could have jeopardized the repatriation of Indians from the Gulf. India was also faced with the loss of crude oil supplies from both Kuwait and Iraq, which compelled New Delhi to look for alternative supplies.

During 1990, Kuwait had agreed to sell India about 1.5 million tones of oil and Iraq 6.25 million tones, which included about 4.5 million tones that Iraq was transferring to India on behalf of the USSR against rupee payment. Before the crisis began India had received only half the oil from the total of about 7.75 million tones and it was difficult for India to immediately procure the rest. Moreover, increase in oil prices in the spot market from about US$ 16-17 per barrel in July 1990 to US$ 35 per barrel upset India's budget [economy]. According to one conservative estimate, India lost nearly US$ 3 billion [US] in foreign exchange alone.

This included US$ 2.36 billion for extra import of oil, US$ 200 million to evacuate Indians from the Gulf States and US$ 200 million as loss of exports to these two states and also about US$ 200 million as loss of remittances sent by Indian workers from both the countries. All of these economic compulsions pushed India to seek IMF loan where US support was crucial. The Indian government partly shared the fear of the West in particular the US, that Saddam Hussein would control fifty percent of the world's oil reserves, if he were not pushed out of Kuwait. No wonder India allowed [initially] the-refuelling of US military planes and went along with the sole superpower at the UN. According to K.P. Fabian, who was Joint Secretary, Gulf, Ministry of External Affairs [MEA], "we did not join the US-led coalition as we were engaged in finding a non-military resolution.

The US resented this. Its friends outside India told us that we were getting isolated. Since our principled position conveyed the impression of a pro-Iraq tilt, the decision was taken at the highest level under pressure to agree to US request for refuelling facilities". In reality, India isolated due to acute domestic crisis, and also the regional and global factors, had no worthwhile role to play in most of the UN resolutions which were passed before it became a non-permanent member of the UNSC. Under the leadership of Yugoslavia, NAM went along with the West and UN Resolutions and unfortunately India's role was marginal. Many have attacked India's approach to the Iraq-Kuwait crisis as "malleable", "deliberate ambiguity", "wait and see", "opportunism", so on.

Undoubtedly, getting back Indian workers and their welfare and safety in other Gulf States was uppermost in the minds of the policy makers, besides securing oil supplies, but New Delhi was equally concerned over the escalation of the crisis and its probable spill over effects. On the other hand, India was committed to adhere to the UN resolutions on Iraq, but at the same time, took care not to openly condemn Iraq's aggression. This was in line with India's policy to seek friendly ties with all states in the West Asian region. India by neither condoning nor condemning the Iraqi takeover of Kuwait justified its position by saying that "condemnation is not part of the Indian nature".

India, of course by simply "regretting" the invasion did not win the gratitude of either party. It was in fact misunderstood by both the parties and by others as well. Room for India to manoeuvre in the Gulf crisis was rather limited, given the resolve of the West and the GCC to contain Iraq. India on its own could not take any peace initiatives to resolve the crisis, because as mentioned earlier the Indian government was beset with serious domestic problems. But as a leading member of NAM, it did take some feeble initiatives, but these came too late, partly because of deep differences within the movement, especially Yugoslavia's one-sided stance (Koch, 2008: 4-7 and Pasha 1998: 66-74).

It must be mentioned that India expressed serious reservations about 'the right to interference' in the internal affairs of a member nation [Iraq] on humanitarian grounds, especially in the case of Kurds and Shias in Iraq. This was on UN Resolution 688 of 5th April 1991. Moreover, India is a member of the 35-nation United Nations Iraq-Kuwaiti Observer Mission [UNIKOM] to patrol the Demilitarized zone [DMZ] along the Iraq-Kuwait border. India is also associated in the monitoring commissions and teams meant to supervise Iraqi payment of compensation and elimination of weapons of mass destruction.

Due to the ambiguous stand taken by India on Iraq's aggression towards Kuwait, this strained India's ties with the Kuwaiti's who began asking embarrassing questions: Why did India take Iraq's side during the Gulf war? Why did the Indian government refuse an audience to Kuwait's ambassador in New Delhi? Why was India the only country in the world to move its embassy from Kuwait to Basra during the war? Did Kuwait cease to exist as a nation in 1990? These were very difficult questions for Indian officials to answer. Kuwait's Foreign Minister expressed the hope that India would rebuild the Babri Masjid and hand over it to the Indian Muslims.

He said: "we hope that the Prime Minister Narashima Rao who had earlier promised to rebuild the structure will stick to his resolve". In an interesting development, the Kuwaiti government blocked a decision by a community run supermarket to dismiss Hindu employees from India in protest at the Babri Masjid demolition. The Kuwaiti Minister of Social Affairs and Labour Mr. Jassem Mohammed al Qun ordered the Al Sabaahiya al Ahmadi Cooperative Society supermarket to rescind its 15th December 1992 decision. In a related development in a letter to the editor of Kuwait's Arab Times, writers requested GCC states not to recruit Indian Hindu workers and send back those who were already in the country.

It was also reported that many in Kuwait were very keen to organize demonstrations and close shops in protest against India, but apparently this could not materialize in view of the Kuwaiti government's tough opposition to such activities. India's External Affairs Minister Madhavsinh Solanki visited

Kuwait in mid-February 1992 the first ministerial visit to Kuwait since the 1990-91 Iraq-Kuwait war. The visit was primarily aimed at building bridges with Kuwait after India's ambivalent attitude during its occupation by Iraq.

As seen earlier, relations between the two had deteriorated and Kuwaiti leaders publicly expressed anguish and surprise at India's stand during the Kuwaiti crisis. After the talks with the Kuwaiti leaders, Solanki said, Kuwait wanted India and Pakistan to resolve the Kashmir issue through peaceful negotiations in accordance with international norms. L.L. Mehrotra, Secretary in the MEA who accompanied the Minister claimed that the visit was a "diplomatic triumph". Apparently both were impressed by Kuwait's support to the Shimla agreement and India was also satisfied with Kuwait's explanation about its criticism of India at the OIC meeting (Pasha 2004: 56-57).

In protest against the demolition of the Babri Masjid, a proposal was tabled by two Kuwaiti independent MP's, Khalid al Adwah [an Islamist] and Mohammed Sharar, in the Kuwaiti National Assembly in January 1994 for boycott of Indian Hindu workers and a ban on their entry and recruitment into Kuwait. The Kuwaiti government on 15th August 1994 rejected the proposal saying such a move would worsen Kuwait's relations with "friendly India" and stressed that the proposal violated political and religious norms.

The state minister for cabinet affairs Abdul Aziz al Dakheel said Kuwait was not solely responsible for Muslim affairs around the world. "Defence of Muslims should be made in a collective way through Islamic organizations concerned especially the OIC", he said. Dhakeel also said "only a small group of Hindus were terrorizing Muslims in India and this should not be generalized. By taking a decision to ban Hindus such relations will worsen and India may take a decision to ban Kuwaitis from visiting India", he added. Dhakeel stressed that Muslim countries like Pakistan, Bangladesh and Indonesia had not even thought of taking such a measure.

He felt the proposal was likely to give the impression that Islam was a racial religion and thus harm the cause of Muslims rather than serving them. He felt that the adoption of the proposal would spoil Kuwait's image and its human rights record. Moreover, Kuwait is still subject to criticism on several issues, including that of human rights, Dhakeel said. Acceptance of the MP's demand would also have encouraged the Islamic fundamentalists groups in Kuwait, the Minister pointed out.

The Kuwaiti government's firm position in rejecting the call by the two MP's to punish the whole Indian Hindu community for the mistake of a fraction of the community is commendable and demonstrates the progressive character of the Al Sabah regime in Kuwait. Moreover, any acceptance of the MP's demand would have weakened Kuwait's struggle against Iraq as several groups in India would have publicly called for an end to the UN sanctions against Iraq from which India had been suffering in terms of lost export opportunities, stop in remittances, the need to find alternative sources to offset loss of oil supplies from Iraq. Kuwait-India total trade turnover during 1999-2000 was US$ 2.07 billion.

India and Oman

It is only since 1970 that Oman has been following an independent foreign policy under Sultan Qaboos. During the 1971 Bangladesh crisis, Oman was the only Arab [Muslim] country that did not completely side with Pakistan. In recent times high level visits have taken place between the two states. P.M. Narashima Rao visited Oman in June 1993. The turning point when P.M. Rajiv Gandhi visited Oman in November 1985. Since then all Indian P.M.'s have visited Oman along with all foreign and many other ministers underlining the importance both attach to their friendship. India's President S.D. Sharma visited Oman in October 1996. In a rare visit abroad Oman's Sultan Qaboos visited India in April 1997. The high level political visits from both sides have not only given impetus to ties but have impacted in all sectors.

Both have a special vision for bilateral relationships and such visits are used to find new ways in which the two countries could concretize this vision into a broad and mutually beneficial cooperative framework. Shared objectives and experiences and mutual desire to strengthen ties have assumed importance in recent times. But the fundamental basis for growing Oman-India relations is the realization that both can work closely together to ensure a stable and prosperous Gulf Region and South Asia which are increasingly getting inter-linked in a number of ways.

Due to Oman's strategic location at the Straits of Hormouz and its proximity to the Bab-el-Mandeb both are willing to cooperate in relation to Gulf security and maritime security near the Somalia coast. Oman-India military relations are also growing including air and naval exercises. Due to India's growing energy imports from the Gulf region and mounting turmoil over there due to wars, revolutions, foreign interventions/presence, cooperation with Oman assumes strategic dimensions for India. In this connection, there are over 38 bilateral agreements signed between India and Oman covering most aspects of their ever expanding bilateral relations.

Oman has decided to participate in two oil refineries in India. Oman-India Fertilizer Company (Omifco) is US$ 1 billion project and is producing 1.65 million tones of granulated urea and 0.25 mn tones of surplus ammonia per year. There is modest military-security cooperation between the two states. Indo-Oman trade improved from US$ 96 million in 1990 to US$ 134 million in 1996. India's exports to Oman increased from US$ 56 million to US$ 114 million in 1996. India's imports from Oman declined from US$ 40 million in 1990 to US$ 20 million in 1996. Among all the six GCC states, Oman is the only state in the GCC with which India has balance of trade surplus.

A delegation from National Defence College visited Oman

from 20-25 May 2001. The delegation called on the Ministers of Defence and Foreign Affairs and interacted with the Omani defence officials and visited defence institutes in Oman. Also, an Indian military delegation led by Vice Admiral M.J. Singh visited Oman from 27-31, October 2001 to observe the Oman-British Joint exercises at the invitation of Oman and had extensive interaction with their Omani and British counterparts. George Fernandez, Indian Defence Minister visited Muscat in September 2002 and both are exploring the possibility of joint ventures related to the defence production.

In 2005, both India and Oman celebrated 50 years of diplomatic relations and a number of programs in both the countries were held. E. Ahamed, Minister of State for External Affairs, Natwar Singh, MEA and Minister of State for Overseas Indian Affairs Jagdish Tytler visited Oman in 2004. Both signed an extradition treaty. Both agreed to intensify cooperation in the IT, tourism, education and HRD, health care and small and medium industries sectors. . Oman is also keen to upgrade its technical and vocational skills and this offers a good [lucrative] opportunity for Indian investors and companies for investments. An estimated 150 Indian companies [the number is growing] are operating in Oman covering almost all Omani economic sectors and also making huge profits.

Many new joint ventures are in the pipeline. Indo-Oman Joint Commission Meetings have been regularly held in Muscat and New Delhi which have reviewed the entire gamut of bilateral economic relations and means of enhancing bilateral trade between the two countries. Also the Joint Business Council Meetings have been held at Oman Chamber of Commerce organized by OCCI and Federation of Indian Chambers of Commerce and Industries (FICCI). The two way total non-oil trade between Oman and India which was less than US$ 200 mn in 2000, has gone up during 2009-10 to US$ 4.5 billion which needs to be increased further to reflect the growing India-Oman business relations.

The pride of place in India-Oman economic relations is occupied by the US$ 969 million Oman India Fertilizer Company at Sur. India imports its entire production of urea and ammonia which is crucial for increasing its food production to feed its growing population and for its food security. The acquisition of the Shadeed Iron and Steel plant in the port city of Sohar for US$ 464 million; raising of its stake to 26 percent from 4 percent in the US$ 1 billion refinery at Bina in Madhya Pradesh by Oman Oil Company are a few shining examples of burgeoning economic and bilateral co-operation. There has been an increase in investments in each other's countries during the last 2-3 years.

India emphasized the priority it attached for cooperation with Oman in Petroleum, Gas and fertilizer sectors while Oman underscored the need for greater cooperation in capacity building and information technology. Omani side has agreed in-principle to invest in India for revival of few closed plants of Fertilizer Corporation of India (FCI) and Hindustan Fertilizer Corporation Ltd. (HFCL) and the expansion in RCF (Public Sector Unit of Government of India) through investment by Oman Oil Company. Oman and India have agreed to in principle to form a senior level Working Group representing Government of India, RCF, KRIBHCO from Indian side and Oman Oil Company from Omani side for initiating early due diligence.

Future Ahead

India after having consolidated its multifaceted ties with the ASEAN countries through a balanced and pragmatic approach is gradually focusing on deepening and widening the multifaceted relations with the GCC states. There are serious attempts being made at the highest levels to identify new areas where there is potential for growth and also sombre and pragmatic assessment to see the old and new and emerging challenges in a new perspective so as to visualize a future trajectory in order to devise new and innovative policies. The key factor driving its policy is India's quest for energy security. Due to uncertainty over IPI pipeline due to US opposition, Qatar is emerging as reliable supplier of LNG to India. Despite global search for oil/gas resources, the focus remains on the Gulf region to ensure adequate supplies to sustain its high economic growth.

The Gulf region had been an important foreign exchange earning zone from the standpoint of growing trade, workers remittances, and investment opportunities and tourism but now there are new policy initiatives to realize the huge potential in these areas which remained unexplored. One can notice numerous meaningful steps being taken both by India and the GCC states to strengthen bilateral ties in all of these areas. But instability in the region poses a greater threat than ever before, as India's reliance on Gulf oil is growing. It is well known that all the GCC states have security agreements with the USA and with their consent the presence of US troops and a huge naval fleet in the Gulf region. [4] Issues related to security [including maritime] and stability issue in the Gulf region is bringing India-GCC States-USA closer.

A modest beginning has been made for cooperation in the field of security with the GCC states, which has a rich potential field ahead. There is absolutely no doubt of the growing three-way convergence and all round close cooperation will be the new feature in the near and medium term. Gulf region being extended neighbourhood of the Indian sub-continent makes India pursue pragmatic policies in the near and medium term horizon taking into consideration the sensitivities of the USA, GCC states and India's own growing interests in the region. The economic-commercial content in India-GCC relationship is growing and has more potential to expand for mutual benefit. Indian leaders have been urging investors in the GCC to invest their surplus liquidity in infrastructure sector in India.

If India needs to maintain a growth rate of 7-8 percent over the next 10 years—for financing of Indian infrastructure in the next five years alone it needs an estimated over US$ 500 billion. The new development for which support is being mobilized is that, India would be working in tandem with the USA in the GCC region, to further promote its core interests. Major highlights in GCC-India Relations have been the steps both have taken towards initiating negotiations for a free trade pact. India considers the GCC region as its "natural economic hinterland". The presence of over five million Indian workers in the GCC states serves as a bridge contributing to wealth and prosperity for both India and the GCC States. [5]. They are an important link as also their growing remittances which act as a cushion to the increasing oil prices/bill.

As the job profile of Indian workers is changing and switching over to white collar jobs, salaries are increasing and with it the need for new financial institutional cooperation. India's public and private financial institutions are seeking greater cooperation with financial institutions in GCC states so as to cater to the growing financial needs of both the peoples. More and more recruiting agencies are coming into the picture, as getting skilled people to GCC states become lucrative.

There is also in India growing concern about the religions extremist groups in the GCC states targeting Indian workers due to developments in Iraq and elsewhere in the region as also due to India's close proximity to the USA and Israel and now strain in Indo-Iranian ties. From India's perspective Qatar has emerged as a reliable supplier of LNG, Bahrain for financial cooperation, UAE for trade, educational and cultural contacts, Oman for naval, security cooperation, Kuwait for oil and petroleum products, trade and investments; and Saudi Arabia for (Hajj) pilgrimage, oil, trade and Indian workers. All the GCC states have retained their diverse ties with India amid special areas (Pasha 2006: 116-122).

This is not to overlook the new challenges emerging from the Gulf Region. It would be fair to mention that most GCC regimes are on the defensive due to mounting internal security challenges and India implicitly has been supporting conservative Arab regimes lately. For New Delhi to fight terrorism in Kashmir and other parts of India and in the larger context of peace and stability in South Asia, it needs cooperation from GCC States especially Saudi Arabia and UAE. It remains to be seen how the GCC States use their influence over Pakistan to stop its mischievous attempts to undermine Indian interests. At the same time, India is also working closely with the few secular and democratic forces in the region as also the dominant world powers which have vast stakes in the region to maintain security and stability so very essential to protect its vital interests and also to prevent the spread of violence and terrorism from this volatile region [especially from Palestine, Iraq, Afghanistan Pakistan], to India in future.

Hence there is urgent need to enhance India's interaction with the GCC countries to seek greater role in cooperation with the states vital to our interests especially to enhance our maritime and energy security. [6] At the same time, India should not hesitate from actively encouraging the process of political change and modernization because once the Arab regimes become democratic and responsive to popular demands, not only their legitimacy would be enhanced but more significantly their dependence on outside states especially the US would come down and this may lead to reduction in outside military and political intervention. Not only this will take care of the growing anti-Americanism as reflected in the numerous religious groups articulating this resentment but we can avoid Iran [1979]-like situations which impacted India for decades and others as well. The big question is: Are the GCC monarchies willing to share real power with their own people/elites and have vibrant democratic structures thereby reduce their dependence on US? The other big question is: will the US allow them to become truly democratic and independent from US influence.

End Notes

1. Z.A. Bhutto called Pak-Saudi ties as "indestructible solidarity",

King Khalid called for a settlement of the Kashmir problem in accordance with relevant UN resolutions. The Saudi King was on a visit to Pakistan in October 1976. See also: Anwar H. Syed 1977, and Rashid Jamal 1986.

2. See: Sheikh (2003). In May 2004, the Lancet report found that about 100,000 additional Iraqi deaths had taken place since the US invasion in March 2003. A team from Johns Hopkins University identified more than 12,000 family members and tracked those who had died since the invasion–an estimated 650,000 additional Iraqi civilian casualties. Most of these deaths have been of men aged 15-44.
3. In Pasha (2008), cited that during 2007-08, India paid almost $50 billion for the import of oil and related products.
4. But J.N. Dixit (2003), says "at the UN India took a vacillating and ambiguous stand till the unanimity of international opinion persuaded us to go along with the UNSC Resolution. Indian policies fell short of moral principles and political adroitness in dealing with this crucial development", Dixit, n. 3, p. 366. See also: Singh 2007, Mudiam 1996; Singh 1979; and Pasha 2000. J.N. Dixit says: "There was even an extraordinary unrealistic assessment from our mission in Baghdad that Saddam Hussein should be treated with kid gloves because he was not likely to be defeated by the combined forces of the international community under the UN umbrella led by the US", see also The Hindu, 14-04-2008. Pasha (1993), Pasha (ed.) 1999.
5. The Lancet report found that about 1,00,000 additional Iraqi deaths had taken place sine the US invasion in March 2003.A team from Johns Hopkins University identified more than 12,000 family members and tracked those who had died since the invasion- an estimated 6,50,000 additional Iraqi civilian casualties. Most of these deaths have been of men aged 15- 44; A.K. Pasha, "The US Invasion of Iraq and the Muslim World", in V.D. Chopra (ed.), 2004.
6. A.K. Pasha (2008), During 2007-08 India paid almost $50 billion for oil and products imports.

References

Ahsan, Abdullah (1988), The Organization of Islamic Conference: An Introduction to the Islamic Political Institution, The International Institute of Islamic Thought, Herndon, Virginia, pp. 11-12 and p. 109.

Alani, Mustafa (2007), 'The Curse of Oil and the Disintegration of Iraq,' *Gulf Monitor,* Vol. 4, June.

Alani, Mustafa, Dhafer Al Ani and Mahmood Sariolghalam (2004), 'Developments in Iraq and Iran', in Gulf Research Centre Year Book, Dubai.

Al-Naqeeb, Khaldoun Hasan (1990), Society and State in the Gulf and Arab Peninsula: A Different Perspective, Routledge, London.

Al-Qallab, Musa Hamad (2007), 'Analyzing the Military Posture of US and Iranian troops in the Gulf Region', *Gulf Monitor,* Vol. 1, No. 4, June.

Baba, Noor Ahmed (1992), 'Nasser's Pan-Arab Radicalism and the Saudi Drive for Islamic Solidarity: A Response for Security', *India Quarterly,* Vol. XLVIII, Nos. 1-2, January-June.

Burgat, Francois (2003), Face to Face with Political Islam, IB Tauris, London.

Burke, S.M. (1974), Mainsprings of Indian and Pakistani Foreign Policies, Minneapolis, University of Minnesota Press.

Chomsky, Noam (1994), World Orders: Old and New, American University, Cairo; Chopra, V.D. (ed.) (2004), Genesis and Fallout of US-UK Military Action in Iraq, Delhi, Kalpaz.

Dixit, J.N. (2003), India's Foreign Policy, 1947-2003, Picus Books, New Delhi.

Ehteshami, Anoushiravan (2005), 'The Year of Crisis in Iran', in Gulf Research Centre, Year Book, 2005-06, Dubai.

Fabian, K.P. (2003), The Commonsense on the War on Iraq, Somaiya Publications, New Delhi.

Gupta, Bhabhani Sen (ed.) (1987), The Persian Gulf and South Asia: Prospects and Problems of Inter-Regional Cooperation, South Asian Publishers, New Delhi.

Jamal, Rashid (1986), 'Pakistan as the Central Command', *Middle East Report*, July-August.

Kapur, Harish (2009), Foreign Policies of India's Prime Ministers, Lancer, New Delhi.

Koch, Christian (2008), 'Iran, the National Intelligence Estimate and the Gulf Security', *Gulf Monitor*, Vol. 2, No. 1, January.

Kozicki, Richard J., 'India and the Arab World after Indira Gandhi: Continuity in Foreign Policy', Arab-American Affairs, Fall, 1985, No. 14, pp. 1-17.

Mishra, Rajesh Kumar (2007), 'Nuclear Proliferation Challenges and India's Response', *Strategic Analysis,* Vol. 31, No. 5, September, pp. 791-814.

Mudiam, P.R., India and the Middle East, British Academic Press, London, p. 56.

Murphy Jr., Johan F. (2002), Sword of Islam: Muslim Extremism from the Arab Conquests to the Attack on America, Prometheus Books, New York.

Pasha, A.K. (2008), 'India's Cultural Diplomacy in West Asia and North Africa', in Anwar Alam (ed.), India and West Asia in an Era of Globalization, New Century Publications, New Delhi.

—(2007), 'India and West Asia: Past and Future', in N.S. Sisodia and Ashok K. Behuria, (eds.), West Asia in Turmoil: Implications for Global Security, New Delhi: Academic Foundation.

—(2007), 'India and the Persian Gulf: An Overview', World Focus, Vol. 28, No. 2, February.

—(2007), 'India's Cultural Diplomacy in West Asia', in M.H. Ilias and P.J. Vincent (eds.), India-West Asia Relations: Understanding Cultural Interplays, New Century Publications, New Delhi.

—(2006), 'India-Saudi Ties Ready for a New Dawn', *GCC-India Research Bulletin,* Issue No.1, January.

—(2006), 'India's Policy Towards the Arab World in 21st Century' in V.D. Chopra, (ed.), India's Foreign Policy in 21st Century, Kalpaz, New Delhi.

—(2006), 'Pax Americana in the Gulf Region: Implications for India's Quest for Energy Security', in S.N. Malakar (ed.) India's Energy Security and the Gulf, Academic Excellence, Delhi.

—(2005), 'India and the Gulf States: Challenges and Opportunities' in Rajen Harshe and K.M. Seethi (ed.), Engaging with the World: Critical Reflections on India's Foreign Policy, Orient Longman, New Delhi.

—(2004 a), 'India and West Asia', *World Focus*, Vol. 25, October-December.

—(2004 b), 'Why is the Islamic World Important for India?', *Hard News*, Vol. 1, Issue, 7, June.

—(2004 c), 'The Iraq Crisis: An Overview', *World Focus*, Vol. 25, No.1, January.

—(2004 d),'The US Invasion of Iraq; and the Muslim World', in VD Chopra, (ed.), Genesis and Fallout of US-UK Military

Action in Iraq, Kalpazpp, Delhi.
—(2003), 'India and the GCC States: Challenges and Opportunities', *World Focus*, Vol. 24, No. 202, February.
—(2002), 'Arab Response to Peace Process', *World Focus*, 23:3, March.
—(2000), Arab-Israeli Peace Process: An Indian Perspective, Manas, New Delhi.
—(1999 a), Aspects of Political Participation in the Gulf States, Kalinga Publishers, New Delhi.
—(1999 b), India and West Asia: Continuity and Change, Gyan Sagar Publications, Delhi.
— (1999 c), Kuwait: Strategies of Survival, Har Anand, New Delhi.
—(1999 d), Contemporary Gulf: State, Society, Economy and Foreign Policy, Détente Publications, New Delhi.
—(1998), "India, Iran and the GCC States: Common Political and Strategic Concerns", *Encounter*, March-April.
—(1995), India and Kuwait: Strategic, Economic and Political Developments, Gyan Sagar Publications, Delhi.
—(1994), 'Demography, Political Reforms and Opposition in GCC States', in G. Pant, (ed.), The West Asian Political economy: Demography, Democracy and economic Reforms, Manak, New Delhi.
—(1993), 'India and Israel: Growing Cooperation', *World Focus*, Vol. 14, No. 8, August.
—(1991), 'Effects of the Gulf war on Political formations in West Asia', Détente, ix: 6, March-June.
—(1990), 'Nehru and Crisis in West Asia', Détente, Vol. 9, No. 1, May-June, pp. 4-9.
Pasha, S.A.M. (2006), Islam in Pakistan's Foreign Policy, Global Media Publications, New Delhi.
Pearson, Michael N. (1996), Pilgrimage to Mecca: The Indian Experience, 1500-1800, Princeton, Markur Wiener.
Petras, James (2008), 'Zionists and the US Joint Intelligence Report', *Economic and Political Weekly*, Vol. XLIII, No.1, January 5, 2008.
Sabini, John (1981), Armies in the Sand: The Struggle for Mecca and Medina, London: Thames and Hudson.
Salam, Mohammed Abdel (2007), 'Civilian Nuclear Program in Arab Countries', *Security and Terrorism Research Bulletin*, Gulf Research Centre, Issue, No. 7, December.

Sheikh, Naveed S. (2003), The New Politics of Islam: Pan-Islamic Foreign Policy in a World of States, Routledge Curzon, London.
Sikri, Rajiv (2009), Challenge and Strategy: Rethinking India's Foreign Policy, Sage Publications, New Delhi.
Singh, K.R. (2007), 'Energy Insecurity and Military Misadventures in the Persian Gulf Region', International Studies [JNU], Vol. 44, No.4, October-December.
—(1979), 'India and WANA', in Bimal Prasad (ed.), India's Foreign Policy: Studies in Continuity and Change, Vikas, New Delhi, pp. 247-259.
Syed, Anwar H. (1977), 'Pakistan in 1976: Business as Usual', Asian Survey, Vol. 17, No. 2, February.
Tertrais, Bruno (2007), The Iranian Nuclear Crisis: Prospects and Scenarios, in Gulf Research Centre, Year Book, 2006-07, Dubai.
Uri M., Kupferschmidt (1978), 'The General Muslim Congress of 1931 in Jerusalem', Asian and African Studies (Haifa), Vol. 12, No. 1, March.
Verindar Grover (1993) (ed.), International Relations and Foreign Policy of India, Vol. 4, West Asia and India's Foreign Policy, Deep and Deep Publications, New Delhi.

3

Quest for a Land of Their 'Own' in Kashmir: The Autonomy Argument

Ashutosh Kumar

Even after more than two decades of the ethnic conflict, Kashmir continues to receive the attention of the whole world as the world in general and India in particular grapples with the escalation of violence in the sub-continent that is clearly linked to the non-fulfilment of the demand for what people of Kashmir call *azadi* based on the right to self-determination. The demand for *azadi* persists as the recent mass protest that swept the Kashmir valley in the wake of the alleged sexual assault on two Kashmiri women or the proposed shifting of the Central University from Kashmir valley to Jammu region or 'diversion' of forestland to the Shri Amarnath Shrine Board for the Amarnath Yatra showed clearly. The present essay presents an analysis of the conflict situation in Kashmir while contemplating the possible pathways to conflict resolution and restoration of peace in the valley.

For the purpose the essay is divided into four parts. The first part addresses to the dominant concerns of the both nation states of India and Pakistan who are directly involved in the conflict. It also refers to the growing concerns of the western liberal democracies led by US. In the second part the possible 'solutions' to the Kashmir 'problem' being suggested by the Kashmir specialists are taken up for with focus on their feasibility aspects. The third part brings in the people of Kashmir and their aspirations into the discourse. The essay suggests that any possible long-term solution to the seemingly intractable Kashmir issue would involve an understanding of the bases on which the ethno-religious identity of the Kashmiri people has been constructed. For the purpose of analysing the bases, one also needs to recount the tragic consequences of the failed 'Kashmir policy' of India. In the fourth part, the essay hypothesises that the autonomy option appears to be the only viable solution given the uniqueness of the Kashmiri identity, as the other options as discussed earlier are neither credible nor feasible.

Kashmir: Dominant Concerns

Let us first address what may be termed as the 'dominant' concerns of the western liberal world led by US over the decades? Kashmir right since its accession to India has received attention of both UK and US primarily due to its geo-political location. Kashmir as a region shares common frontiers with India, Pakistan, Afghanistan, and China and also the oil and natural gas rich Central Asian Republics. As such, it is perceived as a gateway to South, Southwest and Central Asia thus holding the key to the strategic balance in the region- a fact recognized even by the early Kashmir leadership (Abdullah, 1977: 1).

The ongoing 'global war on terror' has brought other western liberal democracies also into the picture. Second, Kashmir has been a witness to three developments that arouse the US concerns namely ever increasing flow of arms and drugs from the frontiers, growth of cross-border as well as home grown terrorism as well as the rise of pan-Islamic fundamentalism (Navlakha, 2000: 47).

Third, US has a stake in keeping South Asia region as a conflict free zone as it engages Pakistan as its strategic ally in its fight against the Taliban forces in Afghanistan. [1] Four wars and simmering war like situation between India and Pakistan over the last six decades notwithstanding the intermittent thaw that has once again been broken post-Mumbai carnage, has been a major source of concern for the whole world that view the south Asia as one of the 'most dangerous flashpoint on earth' (Mehta, 2003: 201).

The fact that the conflict over Kashmir has outlasted the

conflicts in Indo-China, Middle East and even the Cold War and also that both the feuding states hold nuclear power underlines the critical need felt to resolve the Kashmir issue (Ramesh, 1999: 35-37). The American frantic diplomatic intervention in bringing a thaw in India-Pakistan relationship after the Pakistani terrorist attacks on Mumbai in November 2008 and the move to appoint a special envoy for South Asia by Obama administration showed the increasing concern of US. Fourth, denial of the right of Kashmiri people to self-determination by India and frequent incidents of the violation of the human rights both by the state agents including the state sponsored 'counter insurgent groups' as well as the Islamist groups has focused the attention of the global civil society to strife torn Kashmir and its helpless masses.

The violation of human rights, the loss of human lives both by the sate security agents and the militants during the last two decades has been colossal. Just consider the grim details. Till the date the death toll has been around 70,000 civilians, at least 60,000 people have been arrested and tortured, 8-10,000 people have been missing and there have been 33 recorded massacres. Before the mayhem started in the valley, as many as 1,25,000 Kashmiri Pandits were forced to migrate from the valley, becoming refugees in their own state (Navlakha, 2008: 47). As for the governmental responsibility in these deaths, an independent study conducted in 2000 showed that 80 percent of the deaths that happened till then were due to cross fire, killings by security forces, or in custody, and of renegades' (Navlakha, 2000: 27). The major concern of the human rights groups has been to prevent custodial deaths, even if in the short-term this means accepting greater use of detention. The fact that the Indian government in the past has not allowed the human rights groups like Asia Watch and Amnesty International to visit Kashmir on their fact-finding missions raises further western liberal concern.

Kashmir has remained an obsession with Pakistan. One can broadly refer to four factors to explain as to why Kashmir runs 'in the blood of Pakistan' as a former President of Pakistan succinctly put it. First, Kashmir has always been treated by a significant section of both the classes and masses in Pakistan as the 'unfinished agenda' of the partition as in accordance with the two-nation theory a Muslim majority Kashmir 'should' have been part of Pakistan. Pakistan considers Kashmir as a disputed territory as it does not accept the validity of the instrument of accession. [2]

It also insists on carrying out of the UN resolution regarding holding the plebiscite so that the people of Kashmir could exercise their right to self-determination as to whether they want to opt for India and Pakistan. Second, Pakistan continues to remain what Alavi in early seventies described as an 'overdeveloped' post-colonial state still ruled by an oligarchy of military, bureaucracy and politicians that has thrived on a 'political economy of defence' (Alavi, 1972: p. 52). It remains true even after the recent episode of the restoration of civilian rule. In a Pakistan torn by ethnic strife and civil war between the Islamist forces and the Pakistani Army, Kashmir has become the very basis of the process of legitimisation of the idea of a militarised and increasingly authoritarian Pakistan.

Third, the growing Islamisation of Pakistan since the Zia regime has created a significant constituency of the Islamist forces not only among the masses but also more importantly in the ruling stratum forces including the military elite. For these forces, 'Muslim' Kashmir under a 'Hindu' India remains an anathema as they look for the creation of *Darul-e-Islam*. Fourth, even among the moderates in Pakistan the painful memory of partition and then more recently the creation of Bangladesh continue to rankle for which they hold India responsible citing it as the testimony to the Indian hostility to the very existence of Pakistan.

As for Indian State, Kashmir as the sole Muslim majority constituent state in the union represents the 'shining example' or 'litmus test' of its secular credential. In the nationalist discourse, Kashmir stands at the 'core' as its retention is considered critical for the preservation of absolute, indivisible sovereignty and political integrity of the nation-state. Second is the cost factor in retaining Kashmir for India that causes the concern. The loss of human lives and resources over the period has simply been tremendous. Only the annual economic costs to combat militancy and retaining Siachin runs into more than ₹ 10,000 crore (Navlakha, 2001: 8). It goes without saying that this public money could have had better utilization for the developmental purposes.

Third, at a time when the economy guides the politics, it is clear that a peaceful solution to Kashmir problem would have promoted the regional cooperation mooted under the auspices of SAARC (South Asian Free Trade Area and SAARC Chambers of Commerce and Industry, located in Karachi). The success achieved by ASEAN has been instructive in this regard as its member countries have been able to resolve their bilateral issues (Harshe, 1998: 37). An economically resurgent India is much to gain from the heightened economic activities in the region. Fourth, in the present globalizing world that shows immense respect for human rights, Indian democracy has embarrassingly being seen in the poor light on account of her poor human rights record in the valley. Ironically India has been among the first signatories to the human rights bills, which recognizes the right of all peoples of the world to self-determination (Puri, 2001: 263).

There is no doubt that India gets a poor world opinion for it bungled Kashmir issue. It has come under criticism for displaying a self-righteous rhetoric, cleverness and reluctance to compromise. At the domestic level, the Kashmir's post-accession past demonstrates to some that 'the Indian government…listens only when people take up arms, valorises armed groups and has contempt for non-violent movements' (Navlakha, 2001: 8).

As the media coverage of the people's movements on the shrine board issue showed, there has been a marked reluctance to report fairly about the tragic happenings in the valley. The inadequate response of the civil society is sought to be justified on the ground that what Kashmiri people have been asking for in the name of the right to self-determination is primarily a masked communal demand being raised by the Kashmiri Muslims and that too only those who are fundamentalists (Balagopal, 1996: 29). It is further argued that in the existing situation of strife and turmoil dominated by the militants, how does one gauge 'what the people really think'? In recent times, holding of the peaceful elections in the valley and large scale participation of the people in them has been put forward as the proof of peoples' desire to join the political mainstream. The fact of the matter is that there remains a groundswell of support for autonomy/azadi among the people that is why the movement has sustained itself. Then, both the state agents as well as the militants have been responsible for creating a culture of fear and silence in the valley.

Kashmir thus poses a serious question mark about the success of democracy in India. As a critical challenge to the democratic credential of India, the ongoing movement has tended to 'sap the energy of the people, divert resources, encourage chauvinists, undermine democratic rights, and threaten regional stability and economic cooperation, all of which is detrimental to the country and region's interests (Bose, 1992: 115).

Looking for Possible 'Options'

What can be the possible pathways to enduring peace in the valley? One needs to understand that the demand for *azadi/* autonomy cannot be analysed merely in the context of the militancy (Puri, 2003: 16-21). Even the Indian army commanders posted in the valley have long been admitting that Kashmir 'problem' is not a law and order problem but is political in nature that needs a permanent political solution.

As one understands that granting independent status to Kashmir or handing over the territory of Kashmir to Pakistan are simply out of question, the question arises as to which are the other options left? The options being suggested by the 'Kashmir experts' fall into one of the two broad categories either as plebiscitary or partitionsist in nature. The plebiscitary option would be to settle the sovereignty question by taking into consideration the will of the people expressed through the democratic method of free and impartial plebiscite held under the auspices of the UN as per the Security Council resolution. Indian state has consistently rejected the plebiscite option as irrelevant, obsolete and unnecessary as in her opinion the people of Jammu and Kashmir have exercised their democratic rights repeatedly in the elections periodically held in the state. It also refers to the fact that the duly constituted constituent assembly of the state had accepted the accession of Kashmir to India.

The partitionsist option, mooted during Shimla talks in 1971 between the two states, is to convert the existing line of control into an international border and the maintenance of peace on the border with the active role of the United Nations Military Observer Group, formed in the wake of the 1949 Karachi agreement (Kumar, 2001: 16).

As the growing Talibanizaton and militarization of civil society in Pakistan rules out this option even when India seems willing to consider it, another option that is contemplated is to integrate non-Muslim dominated Jammu and Ladakh into India and having a shared sovereignty over a united valley with soft border. The idea of softening the border has been pushed forward as a humanitarian initiative that would enable the divided families and villages to reaffirm their age-old ties as well as facilitate trade on old routes (Chowdhary, 2000: 3). This is an option, which in the recent years has been partially worked out but then it at most fulfil one of the urge of the Kashmiris on the both sides of the border but does not meet their demands.

Another variant of the partitionsist option being argued is to trifurcate the state on the basis of religion as demanded by as diverse quarters such as Rashtriya Swayam Sewak Sangh (RSS),

KSG and the People's Initiative for peace and Unity over the years (Mattoo, 2000: 87). The idea was originally mooted by Sir Owen Dixon's 1950 proposal of 'regional plebiscites'. These groups have been asking for the creation of a separate Muslim state of Kashmir incorporating the Muslim dominated areas of Jammu regions like Doda, Poonch and Rajouri. The Hindu-dominated districts of Jammu and Buddhist-dominated district of Leh are proposed as autonomous political units (Balagopal, 2003: 24).

Such a formulation only foregrounds religious identity and shows a disregard for the immense ethnic and linguistic variety of the state. Political trifurcation of the state can be rejected on the following grounds: 'first, trifurcation will destroy the composite identity of the state, which has existed as one unit since 1846, and send a dangerous message to the whole nation. If Hindus, Muslims and Buddhists cannot live in one state, can they do so in a larger entity? Second, it will most probably lead to a transfer of Muslims from various parts of the city but also Doda, Rajouri and Poonch, assuming that the entire province is made into a separate state. Finally, it will lead to such deep communal polarization that bloody communal riots will inevitably follow'. [3]

Leaving aside the above options, can there be any '*outright*' solution being advocated by the popular jingoist media after every terrorist attacks on India? The strategic analysts rule out the possibility in the absence of a decisive military superiority over Pakistan as well as the nuclear power status of Pakistan (Mehta, 2003: 201).

As for the role of the third party mediation, it has long been ruled out by Indian state after the mediation of Britain and US failed in 1962-63 following the China-India war. Opposition to Obama administration's reported move to appoint a special envoy for Kashmir was the most recent illustration of India's reluctance. As for the track two and three diplomacy, advocating people to people contact or back channel discussion, it has mostly of the interest for the media and the retired civil servants.

Bringing in the Kashmiri People

The above makes it clear that the Kashmir 'problem' remains intractable due to the entrenched positions as well as the antagonisms that mark the ruling class politics in both India and Pakistan. The invisibility of the people of the valley in the whole territorialized discourse on solving the issue is palpable as the national interests of the two 'nation-states' overshadow them. Both states have been taking the maximalist positions to serve what they consider their national interests without realising that nationalism sometimes may become the enemy of the national interest.

The present essay would argue that there is a critical need to develop a civic political culture that can enable the civil society in the two states to transcend the 'sediments of history' that are weighing them down. Only then would it be recognized that the Kashmir 'problem' is first and foremost a problem between the people of both Indian and Pakistan parts of Kashmir asking for autonomy/*azadi* and the two nation states that refuse to listen to them with sincerity and not as much between the two states.

To reiterate, the essay argues that in the absence of a rational analysis of the historical bases of the Kashmiri people's political alienation and political responses, their demand for democratic space and their urge to maintain their political distinctiveness remains suspect.

In what follows is an exploration of the nature and bases of assertion of collective political consciousness that underlies the distinct Kashmiri ethno-regional identity.

Making of the Kashmiri Identity

In philosophical terms, the ethno-cultural identity of Kashmiri masses can be interpreted to have both cognitive as well as abstract basis. [4] In cognitive terms, this distinct identity gets reflected in all those societal and cultural factors that underlay the construction of a distinctive identity of Kashmiri nation (qaum)- the language, the customs, and the traditions. In abstract terms, *Kashmiriat* has been historically reflected in the common philosophical underpinnings governing the vital aspects of Kashmiri life. This philosophical and cultural substance of the Kashmiri identity underlies the humanist and eclectic basis of society on the one hand and the liberal and non- dogmatic attitude of the people towards religion, on the other (Chowdhary and A. Kumar, 2000: 201). *Kashmiriyat* has reflected the seminal values of the three great religious traditions, namely, the Buddhism, Shivism, and Islam that influenced the social and cultural life of the people of Kashmir at different periods. As a result, a synthetic liberal character is easily discernable in the philosophical orientation of the people of Kashmir (Sufi, G.M.D., 1949).

It follows that Islamic consciousness, which has been an integral part of Kashmir's nationalist and democratic movement, in its '*Sufi*' form, has been the 'preserver, consolidator and perpetuator of Kashmiri identity' (Bazaz, 1954: 83). Prioritising the 'Islamic' identity of the people in the valley by the Islamist forces has not succeeded in undermining the secular, pluralist, tolerant and accommodative nature of *Kashmiriat* (Puri, 1995: 60).

In politico-religious terms right since the early twentieth century, the people of Kashmir have imagined themselves as a distinct political community demanding for separate territorial homeland. The geographical insularity of the valley has provided them with 'historical existence of individuality' (Stein, 1979). That is the reason why the valley people find it difficult to respond to any other wider political identity/political centre that have its nucleus outside.

The process of formation and assertion of the collective political consciousness among the people of Kashmir has been determined by a number of factors, the most important of which has been the peoples' perception of history. Kashmir has been, for a long period, under the alien control. It has been ruled by the Mughals, Afghans, Sikhs and Dogras successively

(Puri, 2008: 20). Long period of outside control has left in the minds of people a memory of continued subjugation of the community and its economic oppression.

In the popular political discourse that evolved way back in the 1930s, the Dogra monarchical rule, against which the quit Kashmir movement was organized came to be depicted as the archetype of continuous outside control and domination. The Treaty of Amritsar (1846) by which Kashmir was transferred by the British authorities to the Dogra rules on the payment of a paltry sum of seventy-five lakh rupees has always rankled in the popular memory as the symbol of the degradation and slavery of the community as a whole (Abdullah, 1993). Hence, the lingering hope for *azadi* that is reflected in evoking the terms likes *mulk* (country) and *quam* (nation) (Chowdhary and A. Kumar, 2000: 3).

As per the early assertion of the Kashmiri identity on religious basis it was essentially a consequence of the pitiable socio-economic situation in which the community was placed at that time under the Hindu Dogra rule (Zusthi, 1986: 25). The landless Muslim peasants and artisans were 'taxed to the limit of the endurance and subject to an administrative that ... (was) corrupt from top to bottom, were vote less, unorganised and helpless in their ignorance' (Mohammad, 1947:2). There was also a bias against the Muslims in terms of employment in the bureaucracy and army which heightened the sense of exclusion of an entire community by a Hindu ruler.

The substantive political and economic form of the mass politics, however, enabled the people in rising above their Muslim consciousness in the subsequent years (Dhar, 1951: 143). In organizational terms, this was reflected in the conversion of the Muslim Conference, the party that led the Kashmiri uprising, into the National Conference (NC) in 1939 enabling it to succeed in transcending the narrow religious limitations. In terms of ideology the NC prioritised the radical land reforms as well as the emancipation of the people including the women from the oppressive feudal elite.

The secular character of the NC was obvious as Sheikh Abdullah averred: 'my fight is for the emancipation of my country. Let us all rise above petty communal bickering and work jointly for the welfare of the masses'. Thus, the politics that evolved as a result of the changing process of mobilization resulted in the assertion of ethnic identity that had an overarching Kashmiri rather than an Islamic character. The political issues that emerged were the issues of political dignity, independent political space and the self-rule as Kashmir came out of the feudal monarchical shackle to be part of Indian Union.

What Went Wrong: Narrating the Political Tale?

A number of inter-related developments in the post-1950 period, however, contributed to the accumulation of discontent and gradually allowed the return of the communal consciousness, now in its virulent form. These included the increasing intervention of the centre in the politics of the state; the process of constitutional integration of the state with India; the failure of the structures of articulation of democratic responses; and failure of ideology and the decline of the socially purposive politics.

While analysing the impact of the above, it is imperative to emphasize that the bases of Kashmir's negotiated relationship with India were both ideological and emotional in nature.

On ideological grounds, the political leadership had a reason for preferring India to Pakistan because of the former's commitment to the radical land reforms. Such reforms may not have been as easily accomplished in a feudal Pakistan. The secular democratic values that underpinned the nationalist movement in India also assured the Kashmiri leadership. On emotional plane there persisted a personal relationship between the Kashmiri and Indian leadership. The fact that the leaders like Gandhi and Nehru were sensitive to the Kashmiri urge for self-governance and independent political space was a satisfying matter to the Kashmiris (Raza, 1996: 30).

Unfortunately, the above relationship witnessed an early

setback as the *Praja Parishad* led movement in Jammu, supported by Rashtriya Swayem Sewak Sangh (RSS), and raised the question mark over the constitutional autonomy given to the state. Its principal slogan was '*Ek desh mein do vidaan, ek desh mein do pradhan nahin chalega*' (meaning 'two constitutions, two flags, and two heads of state in one country are totally unacceptable'). [5] It was this movement along with the rise of communalism in other parts of India that compelled Abdullah to rethink as early as in 1952 about the issue of accession.

The turning point came when a popularly elected Sheikh Abdullah, the then Prime Minister of the state, was arrested and kept in detention for almost two decades without any trial. This event remains etched in the memory of people of Kashmir as the mark of the denial of democracy even though Abdullah family has lost much of its goodwill. The post-1953 period politics of Kashmir, which was constantly monitored by a hegemonic centre, added weight to such perceptions of Kashmiris.

Repeated violation of the democratic rights of the people to representation who were ironically promised constitutional autonomy at the time of accession not to mention the right to self-determination, reaffirms the contention that if there has been a Kashmir policy of the Indian state all these years that 'has been based implicitly on the theory that all secular and what are called pro-India forces'. [6] Working on such assumption, the centre encouraged the homogenisation and hegemonization of the local politics leaving no space for opposition or dissent. The state politics, for all practical purposes, had a long stretch of one-party dominated politics till the 2002 assembly elections.

That Kashmiri people have been forced to remain mute observes to the political events taking place in the state can be clearly explained with reference to the case of the constitutional integration of the state with India. Such a constitutional integration giving way to extension of constitutional provisions beyond the original scope of Article 370 and the Delhi Agreement of 1952 has had hardly any concurrence of the people of Kashmir with the puppet governments endorsing them (Anand, 1998: 106). Most of the constitutional changes leading to the process of integration took place during 1953-1975 period when the governments were considered puppets of the centre. Such a dubious kind of integrationist approach naturally undermined the legitimacy of the basis of accession.

In understanding the impact the impact of politics of 'integration' on the issue of identity in Kashmir, it is important to note that it was the federal context of India that was more relevant to the Kashmiris rather than its 'nationalist' context. Having the pragmatic and functional reasons for preferring India and to Pakistan, the Kashmiri leadership was emphatic on maintaining the distinctiveness of Kashmir. Autonomy as guaranteed under Article 370 of the India's Constitution, therefore, had special significance for the people of Kashmir as endorsed by the Supreme Court ruling in Prem Nath Kaul versus state of Jammu and Kashmir. It not merely symbolized a 'special status' but also the basis of the federal 'contract' which the state had with the Indian State.

People of Kashmir had entered into a social and political contract with Indian state that was in their views, 'sacrosanct' and 'enviable', radiating a sense of parity and negotiability. The widespread alienation among the people in Kashmir that followed emanated from the post-1953 happenings, mentioned very briefly above. The fragility of the democratic structures, especially those capable of channelling the discontent in the legitimised political space, like elections had much to do with the emergence of extra-constitutional form of politics based on violence. [7]

Among the various factors that account for the accumulating discontent in Kashmir has been the failure of the successive regimes to pay attention to the increasing expectations and demands upon the system in the economic arena. It was in the initial period of politicisation of Kashmir that their expectations were raised. Much before the transfer of power to the political elite of Kashmir, the *New Kashmir Manifesto* had promised the reorganization of the economic structure keeping in view the interests of the class of the landless peasantry and the artisans. Such a promise was given a concrete shape in the period between 1948 and 1953 when the most radical land reforms were pursued in the state by Sheikh Abdullah government (Ladejinsky, 1952: 183). There was a definite change in the socio-economic structure of Kashmir both at the levels of legislation and implementation as the landless peasantry got empowered.

The land reforms programme, however, despite its initial success soon ran into serious difficulties at the stage of implementation itself as the loopholes in the laws were exploited by the influential elements. It became a source of aggrandizing the political and other ambitions of the politicians and bureaucrats especially under the Bakshi Ghulam Mohammad government that succeeded Abdullah government. The Union Government's opposition to these radical measures on the ground that taking away of the surplus land from the Hindu landlords without compensation was raising communal passion in Jammu did not help either.

Spread of education over the years has resulted in the emergence of a new generation of Kashmiris-better educated than their predecessors, more conscious of their political rights and prerogatives. It has also led to the emergence of a middle class that has thrown up a new set of political leadership different from the traditional political elite in the valley.

The growing asymmetry between the 'mobilization success' of Kashmiris on the one hand and the non- fulfilment of their aspirations, however, has come into sharp focus due to the perennial nature of crisis of governance. While modernization has exposed young Kashmiris to the possibility of alternative futures, the actual politics chokes off such opportunities (Ganguly, 1997: 30).

The stunted growth of agriculture as well as industry, the lack of adequate job opportunities in the administration, public and private sectors, a high level economic mismanagement and political nepotism over the years has contributed in a significant manner to the process of alienation among the youth (Prakash, 2000: 2051). Today, there exists about 1,50,000 educated unemployed youths in the state. It is from this group that many of the today's Hurriyat leaders and the militants have come up. By one estimate about 20 percent of the educated unemployed youth are joining the militant movement. It may be argued that the most effective strategy to combat militancy in Kashmir to create more opportunities for higher education and better employment in diverse fields for youth. As per the Economic Survey 2006-2007, for Jammu and Kashmir, the unemployment rate in the state is at 4.21 percent, which is higher than national average of 3.09 percent.

Jammu and Kashmir, being a land scarce and labour abundant state having a very low level of development, has remained one of the union's ten special category states. In fact till 1970's the centre funded state's five-year plan expenditure to the extent of 90 percent. Even now it follows an aid policy of 30 percent grants and 70 percent loans. Such a policy of economic appeasement rather than winning the confidence of the masses has had, however, adverse implications for the beleaguered economy of the state. First, it failed to give the state an impetus to valorise its own resources for economic growth and fostered economic dependence in the form of highly subsided transfers from the centre that has been both degrading and counterproductive.

At present the state's revenue covers only 25 percent of its expenditure. The ratio of central transfers to the total revenues, which is 78.6 percent for the state, is twice of that for all other states at 38.5 percent. Then more than 50 percent of the state's revenue goes towards servicing debt. Second, the policy of heavy subsidization primarily in the form of unproductive expenditure has turned Kashmir into a 'high cost economy'. Way back in December 2005, Ghulam Nabi Azad, the then

Chief Minister claimed that 50 percent of the 2,73,508 government employees 'had no work to do'. Ironically, the parties contesting 2008 assembly elections promised to fill vacancies running at 23,000. Third, the privileged strata of society became the sole beneficiary of Centre's funding and subsidies as corruption got institutionalised. Fourth, it has failed to release the entrepreneurial initiative of people or provide sufficient benefit to the targeted groups.

The fact that as per the admission of the then Chief Minister of the state, by 2006 as much as two million canal or 2,50,000 acres of state land had been encroached upon by the private parties can illustrate the crisis of governance. The failure of the governance is also apparent when one considers that the state with identified potential of 16,200 MW of hydroelectric potential has been able to tap only 1,481 MW.

The indirect way in which militancy has hit the land scarce state's economy is clear in the manner the fertile land and orchards to the tune of 170 square kilometre have been occupied by more than 6,00,000 armed forces (as per the government records presented in the Parliament in 2003) considering that agriculture and horticulture are the main sources of income. Another critical economic sector that has been hit due to militancy is the tourism sector, which has been identified as the 'backbone of the state economy'. In this respect the successive governments have been dithering on the issue of land lease to the private investors who are non-state subjects and are interested in tourism sector due to the fear of possible peoples protest against 'selling out'.

It is obvious that a 'reformist long-term development strategy-to raise growth, increase employment, reduce poverty, and improve factor use efficiency' in the strife torn state is directly linked to the 'conflict resolution and prevention, and peace through economic reconstruction'.

The emergent alienation in the valley fuelled the communalisation process. The role of the Islamic schools, the *madarsas*, mainly set up by a Saudi financed organization,

Ahl-e-Hadis, which had mushroomed in the rural Kashmir valley in the seventies contributed a great deal in concocting a lethal 'combination of *Kashmiriyat* and Islam'. The mosques re-emerged as 'the key political arena for the campaigns of the new Islamic groups' (Hewitt 1995: 15) providing outlets to the dissident population (Tremblay and R. Chowdhary 2002: 573).

The defining moment that had 'profound impact of eliminating any major democratic outlet of Kashmiri Muslims' (Kohli, 1999: 123) was the arbitrary dismissal of the National Conference government of Farooq Abdullah in 1984 followed by an unholy electoral alliance in 1986 between same Farooq Abdullah and Rajiv Gandhi which saw the massive rigging of the assembly elections in 1987, denying the electoral gains to resurgent Muslim United Front, an umbrella organization of the Muslim groups. The elections marked a watershed in the turbulent history of the valley as people lost all the faith in Indian democracy and for a considerable period of time politics in its formal form became irrelevant in the valley. It is only now after the periodic holding of the elections since 1996 that the political parties have been able to recapture their legitimacy as well as relevance in the state politics.

What Needs to be Done: The Autonomy Argument

The above account of the social, political and economic bases of the formation of the distinct ethno-regional identity in the valley also and the causes of the wide spread alienation makes it clear that in order to achieve a credible and lasting peace in the valley, it is imperative that the people of Kashmir are allowed to exercise their democratic rights to participation, representation and self-government. As discussed above any other option that is statist in nature burdened by the consideration of national interest is neither feasible nor would be acceptable to the people of Kashmir.

That the basic issue in Kashmir still remains the right of the political community to determine its own political future is evident from the 2008 assembly elections in which a significant number of the Kashmiri people participated despite the call for boycott by the separatist Hurriyat Conference, the indigenous umbrella political group and threat posed by the militant organizations.

The successful holding of the recent elections also showed that Indian state, being a democratic state unlike military dominated Pakistani state, has the ability to allow the formal as well informal structures to mobilise the disgruntled masses to articulate their grievances and aspirations. The elections in the recent years on a regular basis in a democratic manner have definitely provided an opportunity to the Indian state to come out with a comprehensive Kashmir policy that can fulfil the quest for autonomy/*azadi* of the people of Kashmir.

End Notes

1. Moreover Kashmir has also figured in the genesis of China-India boundary dispute, Kaur, Amar Jasbir (1992).
2. Lamb has supported Pakistan's contention by arguing that the Maharaja did not sin the instrument of accession on October 26, 1947, a day before the Indian armed forces entered Kashmir to liberate it from the control of the tribals from the North-West province of Pakistan. In other words, Lamb questions the legal validity of the accession and suggests that the accession was the product of a conspiracy entered into by the Congress leadership, the Kashmiri government and the senior army officers including some British (Lamb, 1993). Jha provides a direct rebuttal to Lamb's recounting of the events by quoting from counter historical material and testimonies. For Jha, however, the timing of the signing of the instrument of accession [whose wordings were the same as that of others signed by the other princely rulers at the time of their accession to India] is of no great significance (Jha, 1996).
3. Wirsing (1998), Another formulation for peace that can be traced to the talks between the then foreign ministers of India and Pakistan namely Sardar Swaran Singh and Z.A. Bhutto in 1965 has been that the Right Bank of Chenab should go to Pakistan and the left Bank to India. Accepting this idea would mean that the entire valley would go to Pakistan without taking into consideration their view. It has been well argued that only a

minority of the Kashmiri people would wish to join Pakistan even if the option of *azadi* is denied to them (Bajpai, 1995).

4. Given the regional heterogeneity of the state there is need for negotiation with credible representatives of the regions of Jammu and Ladakh also that there can be a 'permanent institutionalisation' of autonomy for the whole region. In fact Jammu and Ladakh's discontent against the dominant Kashmiri leadership has often been used by New Delhi, to force the pace of constitutional integration of the state with Union (Puri, 1992). An integral regional and inter-ethnic dialogue should precede any dialogue with Pakistan or the Kashmir militants or Kashmiri leadership. Such a grant of substantial autonomy to each region would be logical extension of the demand for restoration of original status of 'limited accession' (Government of Jammu and Kashmir, 1999). Autonomy to each region would most likely 'act as a unifying force between peoples of regions' (Puri, 1999). Pertinently long ago in his address to the Constituent Assembly, Sheikh Abdullah had pledged to give 'maximum autonomy for the local organs of the state power which are the ultimate source of authority in the state while discharging obligations as a unit of the federation' (Government of Jammu and Kashmir (1999:1). The formation of the autonomous development councils for Leh and Kargil has been welcome steps in this regard. Then there are ethnic groups within these regions like Gujjars, Gaddis, Paharis, and Baltis who have their distinct identities and demands. The Kashmiri Pandits who after leaving the valley have been languishing in the camps and scattered all over India have been asking for the creation of Panun Kashmir as their separate homeland in the valley. It follows that institutional and permanent measures are to be evolved to reconcile the ethnic urges on regional basis.
5. In the words of Sheikh Abdullah: 'It is said that Sheikh Abdullah is a friend of Pandit Jawaharlal Nehru. Yes, I admit that I feel honoured that such a great man claims me as his friend. And he happens to belong to my own country; he is also a Kashmiri. Blood is thicker than water' (Abdullah, 1949).
6. The implications of the application of Article 370 have been as follows: It extended the state within the Indian Union. Second, the Parliament's legislative power over Jammu and Kashmir was to be restricted to three subjects: defence, external affairs and

communication. This was confirmed in Article 152 of the 1956 version of the Constitution where it was specified that the expression state 'does not include the state of Jammu and Kashmir'. The obvious interpretation being that the state was an autonomous polity under Indian Protection (Kaur, 1992).

7. The constant denial to the people of the state of their fundamental right to change, choose and oppose the Government and the political party in power through electoral process "merely remind them that they are less than full citizens of India" (Puri, 2000). The electoral manipulation evident in the form of the number of candidates 'elected unopposed' has been highest in India: 'The number are startling: In 1951, 73 out of a total of 75 seats were won by National Conference uncontested, in the 1957 elections, 43 candidates out of 75 were elected unopposed; 70 candidates were returned unopposed in the 1962elections. In 1967, nomination papers of 118 opposition candidates were rejected to have 39 out of 75 assembly constituencies returned candidates unopposed!' (Editorial, Economic and Political Weekly, 1999).

References

Abdullah, Sheikh Mohammad, (1993), Flames of Chinar (translated by Khuswant Singh), Vikas, Delhi, p. 33.

Abdullah, Sheikh Mohammad (1977), Introduction in New Kashmir, New Delhi, Kashmir Bureau of Information, p. 5.

Abdullah, Sheikh Mohammad (1949), Kashmir Appeal to World Conscience, Government of India Press, New Delhi.

Alavi, Hamza (1972), "The State in Post-Colonial Societies: Pakistan and Bangladesh", *New Left Review*, No. 74, p. 52.

Anand, A.S. (1998), "The Constitution of Jammu and Kashmir: Its Development and Comments", Jammu, Jay and Kay Publishers, p. 106.

Balagopal, K. (2003),'What Will They do to Kashmir Now?' *Economic and Political Weekly*, June 21, p. 24.

Balagopal K. (1996), Kashmir: Self- determination, Communalism and Democratic Rights", *Economic and Political Weekly*, November 2, p. 29.

Bajpai, Kanti (1995), "India and South Asia: Community, Order, Cooperation", *Seminar,* 425, January, p. 51.

Bazaz, Prem Nath (1954), The History of Struggle for Freedom in

Kashmir: Cultural and Political, New Delhi, Kashmir Publishing Company, p. 83.

Bose, Sumantra (1992), The Challenge in Kashmir: Democracy, Self- Determination and a Just Peace, Sage Publications, New Delhi, p. 115.

Chowdhary, Rekha (2000), "Autonomy Demand: Kashmir at Crossroads", *Economic and Political Weekly*, July 22, p. 2603.

Chowdhary, Rekha and Ashutosh Kumar (2000), "Regional Autonomy Committee Report for Jammu and Kashmir: A Critique", *Mainstream*, August 12, p. 3.

Dhar, P.N. (1951), "The Kashmir Problem: Political and Economic Background", *India Quarterly*, Vol. VII, No. 2, April-June, p. 143.

Editorial (1999), "Kashmir: The Negative Vote", *Economic and Political Weekly*, September 18.

Ganguly, Sumit (1997), The Crisis in Kashmir: Portents of War, Hopes of Peace, Woodrow Wilson Press and Cambridge University Press, Cambridge, p. 30.

Gias ud-Din, Pir (1997), The Historical Destiny of the Kashmir Insurgency, Jay Kay Publishers, Jammu, p. 80.

Government of Jammu and Kashmir, State Autonomy Report (1999), Government of Jammu and Kashmir Press.

Harshe, Rajen (1998), "South Asian Regional Co-operation: Problems and Prospects", *Economic and Political Weekly,* May 8, p. 37.

Hewitt, Vernon (1995), Reclaiming the Past? The Search for Political and Cultural Unity in Contemporary Jammu and Kashmir, Portland Publishers, London, p. 15.

Jalal, Ayesha (1999), Democracy and Authoritarianism in South Asia: A Comparative and Historical Perspective, Cambridge University Press, Cambridge.

Jha, Prem Shankar (1996), Kashmir 1947: Rival Version of History, Oxford University Press, New Delhi.

Kaur, Amar Jasbir (1992), "More on Kashmir Dispute", *Economic and Political Weekly,* January 18, pp. 94-95.

Kohli, Atul (1999), Can Democracies Accommodate Ethnic Nationalism?: The Rise and Decline of Self-Determination Movements in India' in Amrita Basu and Atul Kohli (eds.) *Community Conflicts and the State in India*, Delhi, Oxford University Press, p. 123.

Kumar, Ashutosh (2001), "Communal Trifurcation of Jammu and Kashmir", *Economic and Political Weekly*, April 21, p. 16.

Ladejinsky, W.I. (1952), 'Land Reform Observations in Kashmir' in Ladejinsky (ed.): *Agrarian Reforms as Unfinished Business: The Selected Papers of Wolf Ladejinsky,* Oxford University Press, New York, p. 183.

Lamb, Alastair (1993), Kashmir: A Disputed Legacy, Oxford University Press, New Delhi.

Mattoo, Amitabh (2000), "Towards a Peace Process", *Seminar*, 496, December, p. 87.

Mehta, Pratap Bhanu (2003), "India-Pakistan: The Enduring Stalemate", *Economic and Political Weekly*, May 24, p. 201.

Mohammad, Bakshi Ghulam (1947), Kashmir Today: Thru My Eyes, Bombay, Bombay Provincial Congress Committee, p. 2.

Navlakha, Gautam (2008), "Jammu and Kashmir: Winning a Battle Only to Lose the War?", *Economic and Political Weekly*, July November 8, p. 47.

Navlakha, Gautam (2001), "Ceasefire in Kashmir: Some Critical Issues", *Economic and Political Weekly*, March 3, p. 8.

Navlakha, Gautam (2001), "Kashmir: Some Issues", *Economic and Political Weekly*, March 3, p. 726.

Navlakha, Gautam (2000), "It's Never Too Late To Do the Right Thing", *Economic and Political Weekly*, July 29, p. 27.

Navlakha, Gautam (1998), Invoking Union: Kashmir and Official Nationalism of Bharat in T.V. Satyamurthy, (ed.), *Religion, Caste, Gender and Culture in Contemporary India,* Vol. 3, New Delhi, Oxford University Press, p. 95.

New Kashmir (1977), 'With an Introduction by Sheikh Mohammed Abdullah', *Kashmir Bureau of Information*, New Delhi, pp. 28-49.

Prakash, Siddhartha (2000), "Political Economy of Kashmir since 1947", *Economic and Political Weekly*, June 10, p. 2051.

Puri, Balraj (2008), "Independence, Autonomy and Freedom in Kashmir?", *Economic and Political Weekly*, March 22, p. 20.

Puri, Balraj (2001), "Sovereignty, Territorial Integrity and Right to Self-determination", *Economic and Political Weekly,* January 27, p. 263.

Puri, Balraj (2000), "The Farooq Doctrine: Kashmir's Relations with New Delhi", *Economic and Political Weekly*, Vol. 35, No. 26, June 24-30, pp. 2218-2219.

Puri, Balraj (1999), "How Government Scuttled Regional Autonomy", *Economic and Political Weekly*, Vol. 34, No. 23, June 5-11, pp. 1400-1401.

Puri, Balraj (1995), "The Vitality of Kashmiri Identity", *Contemporary South Asia*, Vol. 4, No. 1, p. 60.

Puri, Balraj (1992), "Ominous Portends from Jammu", *Economic and Political Weekly,* Vol. 27, No. 38, September 19, pp. 2020-2021.

Puri, Luv (2003), "India-Pakistan Relations: Towards a Softer Border", *Economic and Political Weekly*, May 31, pp. 16-21.

Ramesh, Jairam (1999), "Yankee Go Home, But Take Me with You: Yet Another Perspective on Indo-American Relations", *Economic and Political Weekly*, December 11, pp. 35-37.

Raza, Maroof (1996), Wars and No Peace Over Kashmir, New Delhi, Lancer Publishers.

Stein, M.A. (1979), Kalhan's Rajatarangini: A Chronicle of the Kings of Kashmir, Delhi, Motilal Banarasi Dass, p. 30.

Sufi, G.M.D. (1949), Kashmir: Being a History of Kashmir (From the Earliest Times to our Own, Lahore University Press, p. 25.

Tremblay, Chowdhary Reeta (2002), "Kashmir Conflict: Secessionist Movement, Mobilization and Political Institutions", *Pacific Affairs*, Winter, p. 573.

Wirsing, Robert G. (1998), India, Pakistan and the Kashmir Dispute: On Regional Conflict and its Resolution, St. Martin Press, New York.

Younghusband, Francis (2000), Kashmir As it Was, Rupa Paperbacks, New Delhi, pp. 127-175.

Zusthi, U.K. (1986), Emergence of Political Awakening in Kashmir, New Delhi, Manohar.

4

Globalization, Democratic Decentralization and Inclusive Growth

S.N. Sangita

Introduction

The policies and developments in many countries including India are influenced by the globalization. Globalization is not only a movement of ideas, information, capital, people, technologies, goods and services, and labour across the nation-states but also has serious implications on social, economic and political sphere of life. Now, global economic integration is presented as the best, the natural and universal path towards growth and development. This can be achieved by the application of neoclassical free market principle as well as liberal political philosophy. In this, the role of the market (rather than the state) has to be increased through liberalisation of trade, finance and investment. Along with this, the political liberalisation (participatory democracy, political economic and cultural rights, and good governance) has also been advocated for developing countries to protect the rights of the people.

India has globalised its economy with the liberalisation of trade and investment in 1990s. There is many fold increase in foreign capital and trade. Disinvestment has taken place in a big way in the public sector. Unlike other developing countries, India took several initiatives to counter the negative implications of globalisation and protect the rights and livelihood of disadvantaged particularly from the rural and backward regions. The Plan allocations for social security, health, education and so on have gone-up since the onset of liberalization. Programmes like Mahatma Gandhi National

Rural Employment Guarantee Scheme (MGNREGS), National Rural Health Mission (NRHM), Sarva Shiksha Abhyan for universalisation of education, National Missions for drinking water and sanitation, and Jawaharlal Nehru Urban Renewal Mission (JNNURM) have been initiated.

The eleventh plan aims to promote inclusive growth. It has aimed to revive dynamism in agriculture and build necessary infrastructure in rural areas, expanding access to health and education. A three-tier structure of local self government at the district, taluk, and village level came into existence in late 1990s by the 73rd Constitutional amendment to empower the rural people. The Right to Information Act that came into existence in 1996 brought transparency in governance. This Act is being used by the rural people to fight corruption in administration.

This paper examines the role of decentralized governance in promoting inclusive growth in the context of globalization. The implications of globalization on local, state, society and economy particularly on disadvantaged groups and regions have been examined. The empowerment and capacity building of the people through decentralization has been discussed at the length. The paper also deals with the provisioning of services through decentralised governance in an efficient and equitable manner. The final section emphasizes the role of State and civil society in the success of decentralization.

Globalization means integration of economies and societies through cross country flows of capital, finance, information, ideas, technologies, goods, services, and people. Globalization is the "inexorable integration of markets, nation-states and technologies to a degree never witnessed before—in a way that is enabling individuals, corporations and nation-states to reach round the world farther, faster, deeper and cheaper than ever before". Anthony Giddens (1990) describes globalization as 'the intensification of worldwide social relations which link distant localities in such a way that local happenings are shaped by events occurring many miles away and vice versa'. Globalization is 'accelerating interdependence' and time-space compression (Harvey, 1990: 13). Globalization means no world state-or to be more precise, world society without a world state and without world government (Giddens, 1990: 12-24.).

Many expressed concern about the consequences of global change for the well-being of various groups, the sovereignty and identity of countries, the disparities among peoples, and the health of the environment (Hirst and Thompson, 1996: 167-169.). According to Srinivasan (2003), globalization improves people's lives by making new products and ideas universally available, breaking down barriers to trade and democratic institutions, resolve tensions between old adversaries, and empower more and more people (Mickelthwait and Wooldridge, 2000).

Globalization provides opportunities for development. It is a positive force for sustainable development (Barro, 1991: 403-43; Mankiw, Romer and Weil, 1992: 22-24; Sachs and Warner, 1995:65). Per capita income in Africa had grown by about 0.8 percent per year over a period of 20 years since the opening up to the global economy (Atardi and Martin, 2003:10).

Globalization has been linked with increased income inequality among the people and regions. It helps dominant states and multinational companies to pursue material interests by exploiting new technologies to shape a world in which they can flourish. Globalisation leads unsustainable consumerism, deforestation, loss of plant cover and water pollution. Globalization allows developed countries to export their "dirty" industries to the developing world. Trade is the major source of invasive species being introduced into local environments.

Globalisation widens the gap between the rich and poor, and mounts the debt of developing countries (Atardi and Martin, 2003: 10). The World Commission report found unequal distribution of the growth and disparities across the nations and increasing unemployment and poverty. According to the report, the per capita income of the 20 richest capitalist countries went up to 121 times during 1985-2001, while in 16 countries inequality remained static and only in case of 9 countries it declined. The UNDP and the ILO studies found an increase of unemployment.

Poverty and inequality had registered sharp increase in the globalization period in many developing countries in Latin America and Africa. However, China and some countries in South Asia had improved their economic growth and social development.

Globalization constrains the authority and autonomy of the state. Free trade limits the ability of states to set policy and protect domestic companies. Capital mobility makes generous welfare states less competitive; global problems exceed the grasp of any individual state; and global norms and institutions become more powerful. Globalization leads to cultural homogeneity and there by diminish difference. Global norms, ideas and practices overtake local mores. Cultural flows such as news and entertainment reflect exclusively the western interests and hegemony. The cultural imperialism of the United States leads to the global spread of American symbols and values (Hamelink, 1994: 98).

Decentralization and Inclusive Growth

Decentralized governance can contain the negative implications of globalization on polity economy and society to some extent. Globalisation removes decisions from the local and national stage to the global sphere. Decentralization on the other hand brings decision-making back to the sub-national and local levels. Devolution of powers deepens democracy and enhances the legitimacy of political system. It facilitates people's participation in decision making and reflects their needs and preferences. It promotes representative and responsive grass root level leadership. It generates incentives for people to own the local government, since newly assigned responsibilities and resources promote their wellbeing. In decentralised governance, citizen finds it easier to hold government accountable through voter information, participation, and monitoring. It promotes legitimacy, transparency and accountability. Devolution of powers, responsibilities and resources to local government facilitate better service delivery.

Democratic decentralisation tends strongly to enhance speed, quantity and quality of responses from government institutions. Local governments have both authority and resources to respond quickly to problems and pressures from below without waiting for approval at higher levels. It helps to mobilize both human and financial resources as well as it contains corruption and ensures accountability. Decentralised governance has more and better information regarding their constituents and better able to enforce and coordinate policies and programs (Bardhan, 1996: 28). Thus, the decentralisation promotes expected improvement in allocative efficiency, welfare and equity through increased participation, transparency, empowerment, responsiveness and accountability.

Economists tend to frame their analysis in terms of costs and benefits of decentralisation, while other social scientists and practitioners are generally concerned with the democratic process and aspects of the processes. In this paper, the expected outcomes from democratic decentralisation in the context of globalisation are studied. Decentralisation Process brings about empowerment and autonomy of local people and ensuring political stability and social harmony. The second dimension is the provision of various public services to the people efficiently and equitably. The provision of affordable, accessible and appropriate services to all categories of a population in equal measures is a universal standard (efficiency) but a social justice perspective on service provision privileges the benefits that directly accrue to economically and socially marginalised groups. Democratic decentralisation does not affect the outcomes—provision of service in terms of quantity, quality or equity—directly but through its process variable like participation, empowerment, responsiveness and accountability.

Democratic Decentralisation in India

India is one of the few developing countries which have

been experimenting with the democratic decentralisation to promote development since its independence. A major initiative has been taken with the introduction of three tier structure of local self-government known as Panchayati Raj Institutions (PRIs) at the district, taluk and village level in late 1950s. The third tier of government (along with the central and state governments) for rural and urban areas with independent powers and resources have been constituted in 2000s with the 73rd and 74th Constitutional Amendments.

After the Constitutional Amendments, PRIs are emerging as units of local self-governments for promoting the development. PRIs enjoy political, administrative and financial autonomy in many respects. Firstly, all major responsibilities along with resources (central and State plan schemes and other resources) are transferred to PRIs. Many centrally sponsored programmes have been transferred to PRIs in many states.

PRIs can prepare plans for subjects like agriculture, animal husbandry, primary and secondary education, public health, rural roads and housing, women and children, social welfare, public distribution, public libraries and so on. Gram Panchayats can undertake regulatory functions such as issue of licenses, approval of building plans, and maintenance of common properties, assets and buildings. They can provide basic services such as drinking water and sanitation and maintain village roads, buildings and streetlights. The elected heads of PRIs are entrusted with the executive powers and control over officials. The State Election Commission is entrusted with the responsibility of holding free and fair elections. State Finance Commissions are constituted to devolve financial resources to the PRIs.

Democratic decentralization empowers the people to articulate interests and improve the livelihoods. People are also mobilized through other democratic movements (civil society/ political parties) to counter the negative implications of globalization. Democratic decentralization makes participation easier and makes empowerment more feasible at the local level than it would be at the national level, especially for minorities and vulnerable groups. Firstly, democratic decentralisation enables the people to participate in country's governance. The establishment of small decentralised governance structures/units like Village Panchayats nearer to the people (6,000 and 400 population for GP and ward respectively) and regular elections motivates people to participate in the election of responsive leaders and selection of relevant policies (responsiveness). High turnout in PR election reflects this trend.

Secondly, the mobilisation of people through elections (contesting, campaigning, and voting and so on) brings awareness among the rural people about their rights, and entitlements. Elections also bring information about the leaders and political parties and their programmes and policies. Even Gram Sabha (Village Assembly) and Ward Committee meetings enable people to know the information about the relevant schemes and resources available with PRIs to take correct decisions. As a result of this, poor people's dependence on rural rich has come down. This is evident from the people's assertion and articulation in defeating the sitting members and incumbent regimes in PR elections. Even the poor are raising their voice if their needs are not fulfilled.

Thirdly, decentralization has also opened a wider political space for disadvantaged to occupy leadership positions in PRIs. Reservation enables the selection of disadvantaged groups to the higher level positions. For instance, around 36-38 percent of women, 17-20 percent SCs, and 7-11 percent STs got elected to the positions in village panchayat, taluk panchayat and zilla panchayat respectively.

This representation has helped the disadvantaged to improve their administrative skills and articulative capacity in local governance. For instance, women's association with PRIs has brought transformation in terms of empowerment, self-confidence, and political awareness. Some studies highlighted that the women who reluctantly entered into politics showed great maturity in outlook, enthusiasm, increasing political consciousness and increasing perception of their role and responsibility.

Most of the women who got elected for the first time

without political experience started asserting control over resources and officials and challenging male authority and supremacy. Initially, many of the women who are first timers and illiterate depend upon their men folk (husbands and other male representatives) for conducting the panchayat activities and to shield them from the PR officials. Gradually, they become independent and exercising control over officials. Even this has also resulted for a change in the power relations between husband and wife.

Besides, the women from the lower caste take much interest in PRIs than the higher cast women. Studies found that the participation of weaker sections (SCs/STs, women) in meetings and in decision-making is quite satisfactory (Litvack et al., 1998; Klitgaard, 1988). It was reported that about 80-90 percent of women particularly from lower income attend the PRIs meeting regularly. Even women are responsible for changing working culture in PRIs and articulating issues related to women. Chattopadhyay and Duflo (2001) found that the women leaders of village councils concentrate more in infrastructure that is relevant to the needs of rural women (drinking water, fuel and roads). The weaker sections' power over resources has increased through PRIs.

Studies also pointed out that reservation has improved the perception levels of women and it has created an urge in them to participate in the governance. Twenty five percent of the women members found visible change in their status within the family after they have been elected. About 60 percent of women said that they would encourage women to contest election. The same percent is contemplating to contest election (PRIA, 2000). In an all-women Gram Panchayat of Mydolalu in Karnataka it was found that the women were performing better than men in promoting all round development. Interestingly, all women in this Gram Panchayat got elected for the first time and had no previous experience. Similar observations are offered regarding other disadvantaged groups such as SCs/STs/OBCs.

Village Panchayats (VPs) Resent Mega Projects

Many VPs have raised their voice against multinational companies (MNCs) and mega projects which have been come up as a result of globalisation. For instance, the Perumatty Village Panchayat in Plachimada, Kerala raised their voice against Coca Cola for exploiting ground water. Even some VPs opposed the acquisition of land for special economic zone (SEZ). Similarly, many VPs in Goa have raised their voice against mega projects. Gram Sabhas have passed resolutions for cancellations of licences for housing projects obtained by fraudulent means. Expert committees were appointed to scrutinise the licences given to the builders. Even demands are made for investigation by vigilance commission in the dealings with the builders. VPs have also gone to the courts for cancellations of mining. VPs have also succeeded in securing compensation for the loss of agricultural crops from the mining companies.

Many civil society movements have come into existence to take-up the issues relating to poor and environment in the context of globalization. People are mobilised against the SEZs in regard to acquisition of land and compensation to the farmers. For instance, Singur, Nandigram, Narmada and many other movements can be mentioned in this regard. Farmers in Maharashtra voted against the acquiring of land for SEZ by Reliance. Similarly, the farmers in Singur and Nandhigram in West Bengal stalled the Tata's small car project and SEZ respectively. In AP, the notification of acquiring land for Coastal Corridor in between Kakinada and Vishakapattanam was cancelled following the movement launched by the opposition parties. As a result of these movements, a new rehabilitation package policy protecting the interests of the farmers has come into existence.

Besides, political parties are also mobilising people against the negative implication of globalisation. Competitive politics compelled the political parties to promote welfare schemes in their government plans, budgets and programmes and election manifestos as well. In recent times, both DMK and AIDMK in Tamil Nadu and Congress and Telugu Desam parties in Andhra Pradesh announced popular schemes like waiving of loans and free electricity for farmers, ₹ 2 per kg. of rice, houses, pension, health care and insurance to win the elections. For instance, Congress party introduced popular schemes like MGNREGS, NRHM, and so on to promote inclusive growth. Political parties are going slow on economic reforms (labour laws, FDI in banking and insurance sector, disinvestment in PSUs and so on) due to fear of losing people's support. Reform regimes under Vajpayee at the centre and Chandra Babu Naidu, S.M. Krishna and Digvijay Singh in states got defeated in 2004 elections.

Decentralization, Service Delivery and Allocative Efficiency

Democratic decentralization not only generates allocative and productive efficiency but also accelerates better service delivery. Allocative efficiency is high in decentralised governance rather than the higher level government. It facilitates perfect match between resources and needs. Local information and needs can be ascertained by local governments more accurately and there by identify project/schemes which have maximum utility or welfare gain. Selection/location of projects/members is very effective, whenever they are selected by the local people. The involvement of Gram Sabha has brought down the selection of wrong persons. This is more so where needs are more diversified.

For instance some village needs water facility rather than road. In such situation the utilisation of the former is more than the latter provided by the higher level government through uniform policy and guidelines. Many centrally sponsored rural development programmes in the past have failed due to wrong priorities, design and location. Infrastructure facilities like roads, school building, hospitals, water and field channels provided were not effectively used as they were not strategically located to the needs of people. Similarly, many hand pumps were out of order, since people never had the feeling of owning them. Ultimately, maintenance and sustenance of such projects and schemes under decentralised governance appears to be very high (Sangita, 2002: 101-104). It is found that many assets created under various central schemes were under utilized.

Decentralization, Service Delivery and Productive Efficiency

Productive efficiency is also high in decentralised governance due to people's participation. Firstly people's involvement in formulation and implementation results in reduction of transactional cost (such as administrative costs, salaries, complex procedures, waste, leakages and corruption). It is estimated that only 15 paisa out of one rupee spent reaches the poor through various anti-poverty programmes.

Decentralisation contributes towards better compliance and enforcement with low cost, since decisions regarding selection of schemes and design of projects are taken in consultation with the various stakeholders. This is particularly so in the management of common property resources like forests and water where law enforcement and punitive regulations are minimal.

Peoples monitoring contributes to minimise wastages and leakages. Their close observation prevents the procurement of substandard inputs like goods and materials. Close monitoring by PRIs helps to improve the attendance of teachers and doctors in schools and hospitals respectively. Regular monitoring by elected representatives (monthly review and surveys) help to assure that the policies and programmes serve the intended purposes. Further, the increased transparency and accountability that result from the civil society oversight enhances efficiency by decreasing the potential for diversion of resources due to patronage or corruption (Brinkerhoff, 2000: 604).

The productive efficiency also increases due to transparency and accountability in delivery of services. Regular PR election has become a powerful mechanism for ensuring accountability. This is because if the elected leaders do not work devotedly for the upliftment of rural society, they will not be able to win the election next time. The defeat of large number of sitting members in PR elections reflects this trend. Studies even mentioned that the accountability of officials to the elected representatives has increased.

Responsible officials (like PHC medical officer, agricultural and veterinary officer etc.) can be asked for their presence in the PRIs meetings. In the meeting an officer may be asked/questioned for his/her performance. Productive efficiency can also be improved through social auditing and monitoring. Social audit *(Jamabandhi)* through Gram Sabha (GS) and Ward Sabha in Karnataka has enabled citizen to monitor the progress of works and ensure administrators' accountability for the entrusted tasks and responsibilities (Sivanna, 2004: 123).

Productive efficiency can be achieved through reduction of corruption. Study shows that decentralised governance enhances greater transparency and reduces the incidence of corruption. Another study found that corruption among PRI functionaries was minimal where media and civil society were effective. The rent seeking is more in areas where institutions like grama sabha, media and civil society organisations are non-functional.

Productive efficiency can also be improved in decentralised governance by mobilising additional resources (voluntary contribution like land, capital and labour) for promoting rural development. Such contributions accounted for 20 to 40 percent of the expenditure of the community development blocks in 1950s. Many villagers donated lands for construction of schools and hospitals. Even instances such as repair of field canals and tanks, and construction of buildings and roads were evident. Even peoples involvement has also helped to manage village common property resources. People's involvement is also resulted in improvement in collection of levies and user charges. For instance, PRIs functionaries and Representatives in Belandur and Kinnigoli

GPs have taken many innovative measures in mobilising local resources and promoting development. [1]

Decentralisation has improved the public provision of the service in sectors like education and health. It was observed that there was a significant improvement in the area of medical and public health facilities and the supply of drugs in Karnataka. The attendance of doctors and paramedical staff improved considerably under the constant monitoring of local leaders in many PHCs and hospitals. VP leaders played a positive role by exerting moral pressure on the staff not to skirt their regular duties. Availability of doctors and para-medicals in medical centres are 74 percent and 93 percent, respectively. About 31 and 26 percent of households were satisfied with the behaviour of doctors and teachers respectively. The utilisation of resources which has been transferred to the PRIs is much better than it used to be under line departments. Developmental works are being executed more speedily under PRIs (Meenakshi Sundaram, 1994: 99).

Decentralisation, Service Delivery and Equity

Decentralised governance ensured effective delivery of services like poverty elimination programmes. It is more sensitive to poverty and unemployment according to World Bank (2002) and John (2000). According to these studies, PRIs in India have done remarkably well in respect of devolution of power, implementation of the centrally sponsored employment generating and anti-poverty programmes (NREP, PDS, and IRDP) especially in Karnataka, West Bengal, Andhra Pradesh, Madhya Pradesh, Rajasthan and Kerala and so on.

Westergard's (1986) study suggested that NREP had considerable success in providing employment of the rural poor. Dreze (1990) also found that IRDP had overwhelmingly benefited landless labourers. Swaminathan (1990) has also noticed similar success while comparing the state performance in implementing IRDP in West Bengal and Tamil Nadu. Webster (1992) found that the benefits under the employment generation programme and IRDP had gone to the poor and improved their living condition.

Leakages and wastages have come down under PRIs in implementation of poverty alleviation programmes. Bardhan and Mookherje (2000) in their study on IRDP and Agricultural mini-kits during 1978-98 in West Bengal found that the proportion of Gram Panchayat seats secured by landless doubled (10 percent to 20 percent). Distribution of IRDP leakage rate to the medium and large landowners was quite small (less than 4 percent) as against 87 percent of benefits for small and marginal farmers.

State and Civil Society for Success of Decentralisation

The success of decentralisation depends upon the commitment of the central and state governments and the support of civil society organizations and movements as well. Political regimes (parties and leaders) with strong commitment towards decentralisation and development are responsible for devolving adequate powers and resources to local governments. For instance, the PRIs have come into existence with the initiative of Congress Party under the leadership of Nehru and S.K. Day in late 1950s. Similarly, PRIs received enhanced attention by Rajiv Gandhi in 1990s which ultimately resulted in according constitutional status to PRIs. Janata Party Chief Minister, Ramkrishna Hegde along with dedicated brand of bureaucrats was responsible for devolving major powers along with resources to PRIs in 1980s in Karnataka.

Leftist governments in Kerala and West Bengal have provided supporting legislations along with the resources to strengthen PRIs for reducing poverty and promoting social development. At the same time, the civil society organizations and movements are instrumental in mobilizing the people for devolving powers and resources to PRIs. Reform minded political parties in Kerala and West Bengal created opportunities for collective action from below by mobilising the small and marginal farmers and landless to take advantage of the benefits from PRIs and anti-poverty programmes.

Even civil society organizations and movements have mobilized the people to devolve powers and resources to PRIs. Some of them have empowered PRIs by protests, advocacy, capacity building and so on. In recent years, NGOs in Karnataka have fought for the rights of the PRIs, when State government was trying to dilute the powers. Similarly, Kerala Sastra Sahitya Parishad has played a significant role in shaping and implementing the people's campaign for decentralised planning in the late 1990s (Crocker, 2008).

Conclusion

It is evident from the above review, that the democratic decentralisation along with civil society organisations can play a significant role in empowering the disadvantaged to raise their voice against the negative implications of globalisation. The intensive electoral battles among the candidates and parties for positions in PRIs have liberated the rural poor from the influence of traditional leaders and rural rich and enabled them to elect the leaders of their choice. Even the leaders who got elected in PRIs from the disadvantaged groups through affirmative action are also effective in taking decisions independent of their mentors.

Many women leaders (who initially depend on their male household members and administrators) are started asserting their control over local governance and influencing policies. Many of these leaders particularly representing VPs are opposing the mega projects (including MNCs) which affect the livelihoods of the local people. PRI leaders along with civil society organisations are preventing over exploitation of natural resources and protecting the rights of the disadvantaged.

Democratic decentralization is also promoting inclusive growth by effective provisioning of public services meant for the rural poor. Wastages have come down in major social security programmes initiated in the context of globalisation. Major efficiency gains have been noticed in the delivery of health, educational and other services. Thus, democratic governance institutions, along with civil society organisations and movements have acted as catalysts in protecting the interests of the disadvantaged groups. The benefits of globalisation can be harnessed and spread evenly. The negative shocks associated with globalisation can be prevented by effective implementation of social welfare policies and antipoverty programmes. Positive effects of globalisation on growth and equity can be found when institutional conditions are characterised by participatory, democratic, transparent, and accountable mechanisms and to manage social, economic and political conflicts arising out of globalisation.

End Note

1. **Experience of Belandur Village Panchayat (VP) in Bangalore District:** The Belandur is the most successful VP with the income of more than 1.7 crore and 100 percent tariff collection. It has underground drainage system and garbage collection facilities. It has provided mini water schemes with 5 overhead tanks to every ward. GP has made bye-law for fair delivery of water to all households. A penalty of ₹ 2,000 can be levied for illegal water connection or the regular connection may be disconnected for a period of six months. About ₹ 25 lakh has been spent for the construction of drainage system. Toilets are being constructed for all the households, including those living below the poverty line. There is no evidence of open defecation in the panchayat area. In 2001-02, about 365 toilets were constructed in this panchayat under different schemes. GP took a mandatory decision that it will construct more than 40 latrines in a year. Factors that play crucial role for the success of the VP are many. However, the important factor is the quality of leadership as provided by the president of the panchayat and his team (Source: Nayak, Bhargava and Shubha, 2004).

   Experience of Kinnigoli VP in Dakshina Kannada: This VP demonstrated that water supply schemes can be maintained successfully by collecting tariffs from the households. The scheme comprises a bore well as the sources of water that feeds 5,000 litres capacity overhead tank. There are nearly 100 pipe connections to individual houses. The total cost of the scheme was estimated at ₹ 7 lakh of which 10 percent was contributed by the villagers. The VP ensured regular water supply to all the households. The VP expected to levy and collect a one time advances charge of ₹ 1,000 for each connection but failed to collect the water charges. It was decided to levy a higher rate on higher incremental consumption. A new tariff formula was devised for the *Guttakaadu* scheme based on monthly consumption (₹ 50 for 3-10 Kls, ₹ 100 for 15-30 Kls, and ₹ 350 for above 30 Kls. Water meters are fixed for all 133 house pipe connections. separate electric meter is fixed for submersible pump to keep a proper account of electric power consumed. The system is working very well and the cost collection is 100 percent (Source: Deccan Herald, April 19, 2003).

References

Artadi, E.V. and Xavier Sala-i-Martin (2003), "The Economic Tragedy of the XX Century: Growth in Africa", *NBER Working Paper, No. 9865.* Cambridge: National Bureau of Economic Research, p. 10.

Bardhan, Pranab (1996), 'The Nature of Institutional Impediments to Economic Development', *Working Paper No. 1041,* U.C., Berkely: Institute for Business and Economic Research, p. 28.

Bardhan, Pranab and Dilip Mookherjee (2000), "Capture and Governance at Local and National Levels", *American Economic Review*, 90(2): 135-39.

Barro, J. Robert (1991), "The Economic Growth in a Cross Section of Countries", *The Quarterly Journal of Economics,* 106(2): pp. 403-443.

Brinkerhoff, D.W. (2000), "Democratic Governance and Sectoral Policy Reform: Tracing Linkages and Exploring Synergies", *World Development,* 28(4): 601-615.

Chattopadhyaya, R. and E. Duflo (2001), Women as Policy Makers: Evidence from an India Wide Randomized Policy Experiment, (Unpublished), Cambridge University, Mass.

Crocker, A. David (2008), Ethics of Global Development: Agency, Capability and Deliberative Democracy, Cambridge University Press, New York.

Dreze, Jean (1990), "Poverty in India and the IRDP Delusion", *Economic and Political Weekly,* 25(39): 95-104.

Gidden, Anthony (1990), The Consequences of Modernity, Polity

Press, Cambridge.

Hamelink, C.J. (1994), The Politics of World Communication: A Human Rights Perspective, Sage, London.

Harvey, David (1990). The Condition of Post Modernity: An Enquiry into the Origins of Cultural Change, Blackwell Publishing, New York, p. 13.

Hirst, Paul and Grahame T. Thompson (1996), Globalization in Question: The International Economy and the Possibilities of Governance, Polity Press, Cambridge, pp. 167-169.

Manor, James (1997), The Political Economy of Decentralisation, The World Bank, Washington DC.

Klitgaard, E. Robert (1988), *Controlling Corruption*, California University Press, Berkley.

Litvack, Jennie, Junaid Ahmad and Richard Bird (1998), Rethinking Decentralization in Developing Countries, World Bank, Washington DC.

Mankiw, G., D. Romer and D.N. Weil (1992), "A Contribution to the Empirics of Economic Growth", *Quarterly Journal of Economics,* 107(2): 407-427.

Mittleman, J.H. (1996), The Dynamics of Globalization in James H. Mittelman (ed.), (1996), *Globalization: Critical Reflections*, Lynne Rienner, Boulder.

PRIA (2000), Programme for Strengthening Panchayati Raj Institutions: Narrative Report, New Delhi: PRIA.

Sachs, Jeffrey and Andrew Warner (1995), "Economic Reform and the Progress of Global Integration Harvard I.E.R.", *Working Paper, No. 1733,* Harvard: Harvard Institute of Economic Research, p. 65.

Sangita, S.N. (2002), "Administrative Reforms for Good Governance", *The Indian Journal of Political Science*, 63(4), December, pp. 101-104.

Sangita, S.N. (2007), "Decentralisation for Good Governance and Service Delivery in India: Theory and Practice", *The Indian Journal of Political Science,* Vol. LXVIII (3), July-September, pp. 447-484.

Schiller, Otto (1969), Cooperation and Integration in Agricultural Production Concepts and Practical Application: An International Synopsis, London: Asia Publishing House, p. 54.

Sivanna, N. (2004), 'Panchayat Jamabandhi in Karnataka: A Case of Transparency and Accountability in Good Governance', No.

142, ISEC, Bangalore, p. 123.

Srinivasan, N. (2003), Federalism, Decentralization, Globalization and Economic Reforms: Some Issues by Centre for Research on Economic Development and Policy Reform', *Working Paper, No.158,* Stanford University: Centre for Research on Economic Development and Policy Reform.

Sundaram, Meenakshi (1994), Decentralisation in Developing Countries, New Delhi: Concept, p. 99.

Webster, Neil (1992), Panchayati Raj and the Decentralisation of Development Planning in West Bengal, Calcutta: K.P. Bagachi and Company.

Westergaard, Kirsten (1986), 'People's Participation, Local Government and Rural Development: The Case of West Bengal', *CDR Research Report.*

World Bank (2000), 'Decentralisation: Rethinking Government', *Entering the 21st Century World Development Report 1999/2000*, Washington, 107-124.

World Bank (2002), 'Decentralizing Indonesia: A Regional Public Expenditure Review', *Overview Report East Asia*, Washington DC: World Bank.

Micklethwait John and Adrian Wooldridge (2000), *A Future Perfect*, New York, Random House Business Books.

5

Right to Information: A Paid Right in Neo-liberal Politics

Biju B.L.

Freedom of information in the present-day discussions draws together three different, interrelated definitions. The first is its definition as a passive right of citizens to be informed, and voluntary disclosure of information by public and private authorities because of moral responsibility or public good. In the second definition, freedom of information means the legal/constitutional right authorising the citizens to know, and the mandatory obligation of the state to respond to the applicant's request for information. Third definition of freedom of information is based on the positive appraisal of the impact of information and communication technologies in human relationship. In such a view, technological development is the main facilitator of freedom of information.

Therefore, adaptation of state and society to the technological changes indicates a positive sign of realizing freedom of information. The freedom of information laws in various countries, the methods of implementation, and the demands from civil society movements endorse the three definitions in various proportions. The three ways of defining freedom of information have a common objective—creation of an open and transparent society. The open society shall be considered as the reference point to examine the utility of freedom of information laws and the meaning of the dominant discourse of right to information.

Freedom of Information

Freedom of information became a subject for international

discussion in 1946 when the UN General Assembly declared freedom of information a human right and the touchstone of all the freedoms [Tomasevaki 1987: 1]. During the Cold War period, this right became a weapon in the hands of western democratic states to criticise those communist countries which were cautious to maintain iron curtain in governance and decision making. There was a UN conference held on this right in Geneva in 1948, in which the liberal democratic states challenged the unwillingness of the communist bloc to endorse the freedom of press. USA had the privilege to convincingly defend press freedom because the first amendment to the US federal constitution had already provided that the Congress should make no law...abridging the freedom of speech or of the press. [Keane, 1991: 128] Communists threw back at liberal democrats a valid, but different question, 'If the press is under the control of capitalist business groups, how it can ensure free and fair information to the citizens?' The conference was plunged into misery due to the cold war politics [Whitton, 1949]. Tomasevaki says:

"[T]he enthusiasm continued into 1948 when a large-scale conference on freedom of information was held and where three draft conventions and forty-three resolutions were adopted. One of the drafts—concerning international right of correction—became a convention, but without much effect, if any. The other two drafts, purporting to regulate freedom of information in a legally binding instrument, never moved further than drafts". [Tomasevaki, 1987: 1]

In the UDHR also, freedom of information became a controversial item. Article 19 of the International Covenant on Civil and Political Rights (ICCPR) provides for freedom of expression and information. In different contexts and time, freedom of information was used to serve different purposes. 'Freedom of information has been called a weasel-word noted for its protean meaning; the contents can be emptied and the shell filled by something different, and the terms can still be applied to it' [Tomasevaki, 1987: 2]. The evolution of debates over freedom of information since 1980s proves this point.

Freedom of information assumed significance in the international discussions in the 1980s, when the OECD donor states declared that administrative transparency should be a condition for the economic aid for African countries. Following this, other multilateral lending agencies also decided the same. Proper documentation and open access to the data held by governments were of great significance for the lenders to prevent the misappropriation of foreign aid by the autocratic regimes in the recipient countries. The development economists associated with lending agencies also believed that the lack of information or knowledge for the donors and recipients was the main reason for failure of foreign aid to actually target and achieve the desired effects [Williamson, 2010:18].

Information: Neo-liberal Economic Functions

There is a vital relationship between the demands for free flow of information and the evolving global free market economy. The relationship shall be noted for both causation and simultaneity. The Mont Pelerin Society founded in 1947 brought together economists like Friedrich Hayek and Ludwig von Mises (who were opposing the interventionist state and socialism) and philosophers of 'open society' like Karl Popper. This intellectual club soon became the hatchery of neo-liberal economic and political thought [Harvey, 2005: 20-21]. [1] Hayek warrants the role of information in the free market economy in the following way:

"What is the problem which we wish to solve when we try to construct a rational economic order?...If we possess all the relevant information and if we can start out from a given set of preferences and if we command complete knowledge of available means, the problem which remains is purely one of logic...This however is emphatically not the economic problem which the society faces" [Hayek, 1945: 519].

Hayek applied this insight in order to challenge the state monopoly over information in welfare democracies and socialist states. Following his view, neo-liberals argued that centralized planning could never achieve widespread wealth because neither one person nor a group of persons [at the top level of political leadership and economic planning] hold all of the information necessary to successfully coordinate an economy. Such arguments of neo-liberals were accepted by the public policy makers of western democracies, while the welfare state and Fordist management of capitalist economy were facing crises in the 1970s. In the post-Fordist management of globalising capitalism that replaced the previous Fordist management which met with accumulation crisis, free flow of information across the globe had catalysing effects.

Free flow of information, information revolution and network society became crucial terms and concepts for the neo-liberal intelligentsia primarily to facilitate accelerated globalisation of capitalism. Information revolution became a metaphor of globalisation. A group of sociologists led by Manuel Castells and Anthony Giddens have done important critical research about the rise of informational society after the post-Fordist shift in management practices of capitalism. [2] Castells concurs: "All societies are affected by capitalism and informationalism, and many societies are already informational, although different kinds, in different settings, and with specific cultural/institutional expressions" [Castells, 2010: 20]. He continues: "...[following the economic crisis of 1970s] To open up new markets, linking in a global network valuable market segments of each country, capital required extreme mobility, and firms needed dramatically enhanced communication capabilities. Deregulation of markets and new information technologies, in close interaction provided such conditions" [Castells, 2010: 96].

The relevance of information for the post-Fordist management of globalising capitalism is worth analysing. The information(s) that flow freely across the globe carry out the following basic economic functions in the neo-liberal economy.

1. Coordinator of 'Decentralization': Post-Fordist management gives emphasis to decentralization of production, marketing, and management. [3] Capitalism steadily spread out its operations in the globe, both horizontally and vertically. Therefore, effective channels of global communication and unhindered flow of information are of great significance. The successful expansion and penetration of capitalism depend on continuous and uninterrupted flow of information across the chains of production, consumption and marketing.

Post-Fordism is a unique system of decentralization which envisages a procedural framework for devolution to the units. Along with devolution, it helps the existing centre(s) to wield power for greater command and control over the units. In fact, replacement of Fordist management by Post-Fordism does not mean the total abolition of centres of political and economic regulation. It may be noted that decentralization of management in post-Fordism seldom resulted in de-concentration of resources and power.

By decentralization, it only implies the creation of a procedural framework for discretionary devolution, and disciplined and flexible accumulation. Even though it provides functional autonomy to the units of production or to the lower tiers of the administration (sub-national and local), chances for using this autonomy against the dynamics and logic of the capitalist system are cautiously checked. To put it differently, the decentralisation provided by post-Fordism only confirms, not contradicts the unity of functions and objectives of capitalist economy.

The decentralization is organized in such a manner that it must not radically alter the centralizing dynamics of capitalist economy, for instance, persistent concentration of accumulated surplus, otherwise known as profit-making. To be precise, global information channels are essential to facilitate the 'decentralised' capitalism and to impart standardization of actions from top to bottom. Decentralisation through post-Fordism, in fact, imparts market discipline on the lower tiers.

[4] But, by mistake or due to their deliberate intellectual faith in the self-regulatory mechanism of free market, the neo-liberals regard free flow of information tantamount to decentralization. They are also extolling its potentials to realise citizens' freedom through participatory governance. This intellectual mistake is shared by academics and large number of civil society activists who pay little attention to the unique way of concentration of wealth and power in the post-Fordist capitalism.

2. Rectifier of Malfunctions: In addition to becoming the main facilitator of global spread of capitalism and providing it with means of regulation to ensure flexible accumulation, free flow of information performs the functions of a rectifier in the globalizing market economy. The post-Fordist management of decentralized production, widespread marketing and global consumption chains face the challenge of making accurate choice/decision. Uninformed and misinformed choices lead to erroneous decisions and cause market failures having global impact. This complexity actually elevates the status of free flow of information to a rectifier in the globalizing capitalism. The free and authentic information is one among the crucial externalities of the globalizing capitalist economy.

However, the information technology was proved to be no effective as a regulator within a short period of informatisation of economy and politics. It failed in early detection of the quick flow of financial capital and prevention of frequent stock market crises. It shows that in globalizing capitalism, the dynamism of financial capital has surpassed the most advanced technological capability. Globalising capitalism actually diminished the potentials of technological progress.

3. Information as a Production Segment: In the early 1970s, liberal economists described the extensive application of information technology and large scale off shoring of skilled jobs from North to South as the beginning of third industrial revolution. [5] Due to the emergence of information industry in the advanced stage of industrialization of their economies, the capitalist countries were relatively better accustomed to its impacts on socio-political life. But concerted attempts were needed to pervade its currents into the developing countries in which the level of industrialisation was not sufficient to generate domestic demand for the use of skilled technology.

At the same time, the skilled but cheap labour available in certain developing countries was useful to reduce the cost of informatisation of western companies and their IT suppliers. By the end of 1980s, when the developing countries officially declared economic liberalisation, information industry was regarded as the powerful engine of economic growth. The growth of service sector in the global and national economies and the IT boom were mutually enforcing developments, and became the most visible changes contributed by economic globalisation.

The policy makers were quite convinced about the potentials of information and allied technologies to establish a separate domain of production in the global economy as well as in the emerging capitalist countries of the developing world. However, the initial enthusiasm of developing countries in information technology did not show any consistent presence in the future. Compared to other sectors of the domestic economy, the IT jobs in developing countries continue to be very much vulnerable to the change in external demand.

Tragedy of Techno-enthusiastic Scholarship and Civil Society

Frank Webster [2002] criticizes the techno-enthusiasts of information society for two reasons. First, this view of scholarship (for example, Daniel Bell who first wrote about post-industrial society, and Alvin Toffler) is under the trap of 'presentism', the conceit that one's own times are radically different from those that went before. The second reason is that accounts which insist that the information society is a new era readily pressure others to accept and accede to the here and now. 'Claims that we have entered a new society fit comfortably with the view that we can do nothing about change, and that we ought accordingly to adopt and adjust to the realities'. [6] Against this, accounts which trace historical antecedents and lay stress on continuities can draw attention to ways in which the present has emerged from a past that, having been humanly made, can also be remade. [7] [Webster, 2002: 267]

Even though the primary objective of informatisation was flexible accumulation, it was always hidden; and the magnified effect on democracy was propagated as the benign intention of information revolution. Consequently, the incongruity between the democratic idea of freedom of information and the accumulative neo-liberal economic order was obscured by the neo-liberal theorists, their sponsor institutions and a large number of philanthropic civil society activists who have been mobilizing people in every country with the demand for freedom of information. A sizeable number of them are influenced by technological determinism. [8] Such determinism infects their analysis. Their suggestions are consonant with this flawed analysis. Therefore, a critical examination of freedom of information is essential now. Such an analysis shall be considered as part of efforts to redefine and appropriate freedom of information for radical democratic purposes.

Right to Privacy/Secrecy versus Freedom of Information

In the liberal theory, certain rights always contradict each other. The enduring philosophical debates to determine the relative priority of liberty and equality is the best example. Right to information also contains a similar problem. It is at friction with another liberal right-right to personal privacy/secrecy. [9] From an extreme liberal point of view (libertarianism), in the present information society 'the right to be let alone' is at risk [Wacks, 2010]. In India, this contradiction was noted recently, when Ratan Tata approached the Supreme Court with a complaint against the media and government about leaking his conversation with a corporate lobbyist Nira Radia.

His advocates argued that it was a violation of his right to privacy. This incident proved that secrecy is no longer the prerogative of state alone. For private businessmen also, commercial confidentiality is almost like a legitimate right in the capitalist economy. As a solution to Tata's complaint, the Central Government quickly agreed to introduce a right to privacy/data protection bill in the monsoon session of Parliament in 2011.

India is an example of countries, where the demand for right to privacy has been a matter of long neglect. Right to privacy was not directly included as a fundamental right in the Indian constitution, though it shall be argued that it is part of right to life. [10] In the western democracies, where individualism had deep roots in citizen's life, freedom of information is easily conceived as a potential threat to privacy.

Therefore, their legislations for freedom of information are followed by the enactment of data protection laws. In the Indian society, where meaning of privacy has not been expanded beyond probably one's (secret) sexual affairs, the contradiction between freedom of information and right to personal privacy has not been widely noted yet. Most interestingly only in Section 8 (1)(j) of the Right to Information Act 2005 the term privacy is directly mentioned. The exemption from the freedom of information on the ground of privacy in the Act shall be read as: [I]nformation which relates to personal information the disclosure of which has no relationship to any public activity or interest, or which would cause unwarranted invasion of the privacy of the individual unless the Central Public Information Officer or the State Public Information Officer or the appellate authority, as the case may be, is satisfied that the larger public interest justifies the disclosure of such information [Government of India, 2005: 8].

Definition of privacy based on 'larger public activity or public interest' is undoubtedly making the act vulnerable to lawyers' expertise. It is difficult to arrive at a universal definition about what is private and public, much like what is obscenity and not. But this public-private distinction by allocating a larger share in the private is indispensable for the existence of liberal democratic political life.

Following the precedence of western freedom of information laws, India's RTI act in section 8(1)(d) exempt 'information including commercial confidence, trade secrets or intellectual property, the disclosure of which would harm the competitive position of a third party, unless the competent authority is satisfied that larger public interest warrants the disclosure of such information' [Government of India, 2005: 8]. It shall be argued that the existing exemptions from Right to Information law under personal privacy and commercial confidentiality are not very effective because of the clause for disclosure based on a formless view of public interest. Therefore, the Indian businessmen now find that the right to privacy must be a fundamental right. In fact, they indirectly require protection for their private property under the expansive fundamental right to privacy.

It is more important because the right to private property, which was originally a fundamental right, is now only a legal right. The full turn of the consequence of this demand is yet to be visible. The urbanising middle class population of India has also been slowly realising the value of privacy, and now they give support to a demand of businessmen for strong legislation to protect their secrecy. Interestingly, it was the same group that gave moral legitimacy to the civil society's demands for right to information in the past.

Like other liberal rights, the right to privacy is noted for the different utility for the rich and the poor, in practice. Such a class division is evident from the greater publicity for the legislation on right to privacy in the English media, compared to the vernacular. [11] The rural-urban difference in the perceptions of right to privacy prevents nation-wide debate. The right to information is not yet a fundamental right, only a legal right. Therefore, the right to privacy as a fundamental right (if the government follows the demand of Tata which has been approved by the urban middle class) is going to be the hardest fetter for right to information.

Exclusion of Private Business and NGOs

Freedom of information, like other liberal democratic rights, is mainly defined vis-à-vis the authority of state. Not to the surprise, it completely excludes private business groups and nongovernmental agencies such as NGOs and religious institutions from its direct effect. Majority of FOI legislations do not require mandatory disclosure from the private sector. Among nearly 85 countries which had adopted comprehensive Freedom of Information Acts till now the Acts of only 19 countries apply to information held by government as well as private bodies, whereas the others apply to government information only. Only in three capitalist economies—US, UK and France—the laws cover private sector, though partially [Siraj, 2010:211-12]. In the post-liberalisation period, the private sector is performing many public functions that were conventionally performed by the state. In spite of this fact the substantial amount of information held by the private sector is now placed outside the scope of legal right for access to information. While defining the public, India's freedom of information law also uses source of funding and ownership as the criteria instead of the functions of an agency. [12]

The reluctance of neo-liberal governments to directly include private firms under right to information laws causes violation of consumer rights and environmental rights. [13] It has already been proved that the private sector is unwilling to follow norms of transparency under moral compulsions. They may fall in line, only if there is adequate pressure from either the laws of the state or the consumer market. The growing awareness of consumers about the environmental issues has indirectly become compulsion for the private companies to adopt green technology and to emphasize environmental concerns in their business advertisements.

This example of corporate environmentalism is widely

cited to prove that market compulsions are sufficient to make private firms accountable and transparent. But, the success of the consumer market to persuade private companies for transparency and accountability are a few; failures are many more. For example, there is little evidence to show that the compulsion from the consumer market for fair business practice was helpful to improve the labour rights and to resolve gender injustice in the privatising economy.

In spite of all these valid arguments for inclusion of private sector under the freedom of information laws, most of the countries prefer either total exclusion or only targeted mandatory disclosure. Archon Fung and others rightly point out that in public policies relating to freedom of information there is no such thing as full disclosure (in both public and private sector)—only varying degrees of partial transparency that may or may not serve the public's needs [Fung et al., 2007: xii]. Russell Stevenson suggests [Stevenson, 1980] that there may be a corporate freedom of information act under which companies will be obliged to divulge information unless they could show that disclosure is not in the public interest. This will encourage regular company disclosure and reporting to minimize the cost of ad hoc requests for information [Henriques, 2007:161].

Even though there is a global consensus between policy makers, think-tank academicians and legal experts about the common framework to be followed by the legislations related to freedom of information, and about the permissibility of exemptions to be provided to the public authorities, such a consensus has not evolved about the application of transparency policies to the private sector. Until now, it has not become the main demand of the Global NGOs that combat corruption. For example, Global Corruption Report, 2009 prepared by Transparency International with a special focus on 'corruption and private sector' does not adequately analyse this point.

The contributors to the report suggest only routine

solutions such as corporate ethics and responsibility, as well as greater awareness for the investors and consumers about the 'risk in market economy' (not to say fraud) to deal with rampant corruption in the private sector (For example, see: Enderle, 2009: 11). Their therapeutic suggestions are weighed with those related to cure more than those aiming at prevention. From the beginning, no liberal political suggestion has ever seriously challenged the basic existence of capitalist economy, and the rules of private property and accumulation. Therefore, by using the liberal language, it is difficult to articulate right to information as a radical demand vis-à-vis the privatising economy.

Inadequate Definition of Authority

In the modern left perspective, human rights become politically meaningful, when they are defined vis-à-vis concrete authority (agency, structure or both) that shall be the violator of rights. The definition of right against authority is effective to remind the beneficiaries about the previous struggles required for securing the right, and to demand for perpetual vigilance to safeguard it from potential infringements. In this respect, the dominant authority that violates freedom of information deserves special attention.

The neo-liberal defenders of freedom of information are tempered with government monopoly of information. For the neo-liberals, it is an arduous task to define the right against market and private agencies. Therefore, they consider right to information as an access code for the citizens (and for private entrepreneurs) to the state monopoly of information. Recall the conviction of Hayek and other neo-liberals about the compatibility between free information and market economy, and their refusal of state led planning on the ground of scarcity and lack of coordination of information to manage economic activities. Following his line of argument, the obligation should be placed only on the state. In the neo-liberal perspective, the state is the sole violator of citizen's freedom.

The narrow definition of authority of violation of right to information spares the market economy and the market forces from the direct impact of the civil society struggles. [14]

Availability versus Authenticity of Information

The technological development has increased the content of information and the access levels of citizens to such information. The proliferation of information has also resulted in decreasing authenticity of information. Freedom of information laws have also not been able to resolve this information paradox emerging from the information overload.

The prime purpose of freedom of information laws is to make the information available to citizens. The onus of verification of information is not specified in such laws. In this respect it seems that the laws for freedom of information are following the liberal logic related to media freedom—'Provide the citizens with different news (or views?), then let them judge'. [15] It is exactly what the free market economy also suggests, "let different agencies provide them with all sorts of goods and services and let the consumers make an informed choice". Due to the fundamentalist faith of neo-liberals in market laws, the possibilities of distortion of information and misinformation are glossed over.

Economic liberalisation also paved the way for permitting the private agencies to undertake financial rating and accounting jobs related to private companies and government. Outsourcing of these functions causes further challenge to the reliability of information. The financial accounting of private firms done by private professional rating agencies is taken for granted by the neo-liberal governments and the citizens. The reliability and legitimacy of these private professional rating agencies became an issue, when the investors who made choice following the estimate prepared by such professional rating agencies lost money in stock market crashes in the last one decade in many parts of the world. The most recent financial meltdown known as sub-prime crisis started from

USA also points out the negative role of credit rating agencies. The Financial Crisis Inquiry Commission appointed by the US government to find out the reasons of the crisis says in its report:

"The three credit rating agencies [Moody's Corporation, Standard and Poor and Fitch Ratings] were key enablers of the financial meltdown. The mortgage-related securities at the heart of the crisis could not have been marketed and sold without their seal of approval. Investors relied on them, often blindly. In some cases, they were obligated to use them, or regulatory capital standards were hinged on them. This crisis could not have happened without the rating agencies. Their ratings helped the market soar and their downgrades through 2007 and 2008 wreaked havoc across markets and firms" [Federal Government of USA, 2011: xxv]. [16]

The mismatch between the data from accounting done by the government and by the international private rating agencies related to financial status, and the different criteria used to measure standard and quality is another factor that brings confusion about the authenticity of information, though information(s) is plenty enough.

First, the citizens become paying consumers to benefit from a human right. Second, the state starts to provide human right on the basis of purchasing power of the citizens. Third, the right becomes a commodity. It is the finest example of penetration of political life by commercial values. [17] Political life is gradually being colonised and commodified by extensive and intensive spread of 'business civilisation'. It is tantamount to what Frank Webster presents more emphatically: 'enclosure of the earth by business practices; the incorporation of activities once outside into the routine of business realm' (Webster, 2002: 269).

If the quantity of demand for information is greater; for example, if an applicant requires a document containing larger number of pages, the applicants have to pay higher fees than for the normal. In certain countries, the governments are preventing the citizens from seeking for information by including data collection and processing charge within the application fees, which would make the information more costly. The price to be paid for this right will likely be escalating, if the private firms are placed under the freedom of information law. If the state, a democratic entity, provides this right for reasonable fees, what is wrong if the private firms decide to charge a price higher than that?

Increasing State Surveillance in Citizen's Life

Many of us consider right to information a device to place the state under the citizen's surveillance. But, there is another side of this claim. Freedom of information provides the state with tremendous opportunity to collect data about citizens. Though it is documented and made accessible to citizens under the freedom of information laws, it increases the capability of the state to exercise greater surveillance over the citizens. The laws to enforce the third generation human rights occasionally tend to increase the state power.

Remember, the right to education legislation in India contained a provision for punitive action against the parents who are unwilling to send their children to schools. [18] The western states, which guaranteed right to information earlier than the developing countries, have already been proved to become powerful radars in their citizens' life. Compulsory Identity Cards were already introduced in eleven European states, which are by usual standards democratic governments [Wacks, 2010: 18]. The fear about increasing state power and the possible misuse of personal data by the state and private agencies actually necessitated data protection laws and constitutional guarantee of privacy in these countries. [19]

Demand for Media News about Secrets of Power albeit Right to Information

The continuing relevance of media as the main source of information about the hidden practices of governments contradicts the blissful enthusiasm of techno-globalists and neo-liberals about information society. A look into this issue would also help us to understand the real meaning of information society. The current popularity of Wikileaks is a case in point.

WikiLeaks has been widely appreciated for leaking the political, military and bureaucratic secrets from the inner circles of power. The great significance of this new age journalism leaves before us three arguments related to the existence of information society and the efficiency of freedom of information laws.

Argument I: The global popularity of WikiLeaks and the extensive circulation of its news are possible only because of the existence of a global information society. The quantum leap in information and communication technologies helped the efforts of Wiki to expose political conspiracy, corruption and violations of human rights, and to gain the public support across the globe. Media has proved to be an effective whistleblower and guardian of human rights in the information society.

Argument II: Why Wikileaks becomes so important and the secrets has a great demand from the public, if the information society is truly an open society? High market value of secrecy is incompatible to the style of open society. It shows that the increasingly interconnected global information society is nothing more than a highly mediated communicative society. Information society is not an open society governed by the norms of transparency in politics, society and economy. Information society is only a global space, where you can carry, sell and purchase information. Open society is qualitatively different from the current information society. The capitalist information society which appears as open society deceives us, the spectators.

Argument III: If the policy framework and the legislations hitherto passed by national legislatures were so efficient and met their objectives, why the contemporary public have to depend on the new age media as the reliable source of information. [20] The increasing opaqueness of government and politics in spite of freedom of information laws is a reality.

In the mainstream analyses of the relation between media freedom and open society, there is a customary effort to justify their complimentary features rather than exploring the contradictions. Arguments in support of the complementary existence of free media and open society have a history that goes long back to the period of origin of freedom of information as the freedom of press in liberal democracies. The liberal democratic tradition extraordinarily privileged the media the guardian of open society. Unfortunately, in such a narration, the commercial character of media is disregarded. In fact, the commercial media helps to convert the secrets into news, which is now ready for consumption as a commodity. Really, an open society can hardly cater to the commercial needs of the media by secrets.

Even though the media was initially considered as effective to reveal the secrets of power, it was not able to help the creation of an open society. The metamorphosis of public media from a political device into a commercial instrument for profit happened during the relatively shorter history of modern democracy. The professionalization of journalism was gradually measured using the standards of market economy. If the news about secrecy is the main source of profit, how the commercial media can sincerely stand for an open society without becoming self-destructive?

The economic compulsions and moral commitment are intertwined in the greater media interest in political news about the secrecy of the state. [21] In fact, the commercial media, which survives on the profits from the news about the secrets, has parasitic relation with secretive society. Depoliticization and commercialisation fasten the bond between the commercial media and the secretive society that is really a challenge to freedom of information and open society. The commercial media can stand for freedom of information, and can justify it, only if its publicity is useful to increase the circulation. The differential attention that the diverse sorts of secrets receive from the media indicates the structural limits of commercial media.

The common journalistic trend of prioritisation of different news items shows that the higher commodity value of news about political, military and bureaucratic secrets is the cause for the predilections of the media for such news. Media reports related to unruly business practices are occasional, and do not have any follow up from the journalists compared to the media focus on party politics and corruption.

In addition to this, the media reports of corporate corruption and fraudulent practices of capitalism do not cause any demand from the public for legal and structural changes, if compared with the media impact of political news. This trend of reporting has already produced a peculiar consumption pattern, both of which are mutually enforcing. In fact, the secrets, which appear in the media in the form of fragmented stories and news about incidents, are only the symptoms of structural secrecy. Slavoj Zizek rightly argues this point in the case of WikiLeaks.

'What Wikileaks threatens is the formal functioning of power. The true targets here weren't the dirty details and the individuals responsible for them; not those in power, in other words, so much as power in itself, its structure. We shouldn't forget that power comprises not only institutions and their rules, but also legitimate (normal) ways of challenging it (an independent press, NGOs etc.). The aim of WikiLeaks revelations was not just to embarrass those in power but to lead us to mobilise ourselves to bring about a different functioning of power that might reach beyond the limits of our representative democracy' [Zizek, 2010].

A quick look at the modern history of usefulness of media for various social movements shows that the media activism promoted larger number of social and political struggles against political dictatorships than those against the exploitations structurally linked to the economy. [22] The help from the media was mostly for the movements aiming at regime change, rather than those bringing about structural change. It shall also be argued that the commercial media activism is more interested in placing the political enemies as the target, rather than the economic powerhouses even in reporting political corruptions.

There are four reasons to think that the new age journalism is not harbinger of freedom of information. First, Wikileaks was following the prioritisation set by the mainstream media about the publication of secrets related to polity and economy, and the liberal values of modern journalism. The military and diplomatic secrets, involvement of bureaucrats and politicians in corruption etc. came to light much faster and in greater quantity compared to the news about the backstage affairs of the corporate world. Wiki has not challenged the established production-consumption pattern of media news. The Wiki might be following the liberal distinction between public and private to turn its focus away from the economy. The motto of this whistle blower website—"Keep us Strong; Help WikiLeaks Keeps Governments Open"—affirms its attraction to the conventional state-centric definition of freedom of media. The economy, for the liberal media, always fits into the category of the private sphere.

Second, Wiki Leaks was using the data about the secret affairs of the corporate financial institutions and private business groups, mainly as a deterrent to safeguard itself. In the first month of 2011, Julian Assange in certain press conferences declared that Wiki would reveal the data about corporate world including Bank of America and other dominant bankers. Subsequent events proved that it was only a blackmail to tame the governments, which had taken legal action against him and blocked access to his website; and those banks and credit card companies, which had frozen the financial transactions of Wiki. Dirty news about corporate world was only a deterrent in the hands of the WikiLeaks, not a prime target of attack. So far, the people did not receive anything substantial from the Wiki in this respect.

Third, even though the freedom of information was originally considered as media freedom, there are plenty of examples of media seeking for protection/exemption from this right by citing both professional and economic reasons. Many times, Julian Assange was challenged by his opponents to reveal the sources of funding for his non-profit media. He used to give vacillating answers. In the end, he said that it was met by a charitable foundation in a European country. Interestingly, the foundation was under exemption from revealing its donors' details according to their national freedom of information law. This event shows that the whistleblowers are also seeking self-protection with the help of the exemptions from freedom of information. The secrecy is necessary to fight for open society. It is yet another irony of freedom of information in the neo-liberal world. [23]

Finally, the new age global media also leaves a question about the ways to assure accountability of the whistleblowers. Even though the new age media persuade the national governments to a great extent and the private business to a very lesser extent to be accountable and transparent, there is no serious thought about how to bring the commercial and non profit media firms, NGOs and religious/spiritual organisations under a global mandatory disclosure system. Here also, the liberal notions of private/public distinction prove to be a hindrance. The liberal political philosophy has not clearly specified the exact location of civil society - in public or private.

Conclusion

I would suggest that we need a comprehensive definition of freedom of information to realise its democratic objective. For this purpose, instead of limiting our criticism against the state and pointing out certain technical flows in its implementation, we should pay attention to the inherent contradictions of this new generation right by contextualising it in the market economy and the changing state-citizen relationship. Instead of being fascinated by the idealistic images of right to information and contended with the magic paradise of information society, one must set the open society as its radical objective. Thus, we can hope that the right to information would transcend its liberalist limitations, and transform its present day appearance of a paid right. Civil society that demand for transparency should also aim at identification of structural issues and promotion of structural changes, instead of its present focus only on certain agencies of formal institutions of political power.

End Notes

1. Later academic manifestations of neo-liberal thought shall be found from institutions such as Chicago School of Economics and Department of Political Science in University of Rochester. The exchange of ideas between neoclassical economics and quantitative analysis in political studies led to certain conclusions—'market can make better choice than the ballot boxes do'. The persuasion for democratic politics to adopt the rationality of free market was the summary of their academic projects. Milton Friedman et al. were the leading figures from such institutions that exercised greater influence over policy making institutions in the West since mid-1970s. For an informative discussion on the interrelationship between contemporary liberal philosophy and neo-liberal economic thought see: Mirowski and Plehw (2009) and Olssen (2010).
2. For a comparative review of theories of information society and a brief review of works of Daniel Bell, Manuel Castells, Herbert Schiller, Anthony Giddens, Jurgen Habermas and Zygmunt Bauman on this topic, see: Webster, 2002.
3. For the analysis of causal relation between the shifts in capitalist management (from Fordism to post-Fordism) and the changing pattern of political governance (from centralised bureaucratic state to decentralisation and network state) see: Chandhoke, 2003. The causation/explanation resembles the analysis by the Regulation theorists.
4. Stephen Gill's analysis of the disciplinary effect of neo-liberalism is worth mentioning here. He says: "Although the governance of this

market civilization is framed by the discourse of globalizing neo-liberalism and expressed through a combination of market discipline and the direct application of political power…When we introduce the issues of power and justice into our examination of neo-liberal forms of globalization, what is emerging is a politics of supremacy...rather than a politics of justice...[T]his supremacist bloc can be conceptualised as commensurate with the emergence of a market-based transnational free enterprise system, which is dependent for its conditions of existence on a range of state-civil society complexes. It is both inside and outside the state...thus in my sketch of the power structures of global politics with significant local variations a transnational historical bloc is outlined, with its nucleus largely comprising elements of G-7 state apparatuses and transnational capital (in manufacturing, finance and services) and associated privileged workers and smaller firms (e.g. small and middle sized business linked as contractors and suppliers, import-export business, and service companies, such as stock brokers, accountants, consultancies, lobbyists, educational entrepreneurs, architects and designers)...thus policies are cast within a neo-liberal discourse of governance that stresses the efficiency, welfare and freedom of market, and self-actualisation through the process of consumption" [Gill, 1995: 399-401]. In addition to the managerial control through the information channels, common standards for states' public policy formulation, uniform fiscal and monetary rules and globally standardised trade, environment and labour laws have also evolved throughout the period of decentralised capitalism. All these aim at decentralisation with discipline.

5. There is a difference of opinion about the event and the time to specify the origin of third industrial revolution. For example, Marxist economists like Ernest Mandel points out the invention of nuclear energy and increasing growth of energy generation in 1940s as the beginning of third industrial revolution. See: Mandel, 2008: 605.
6. This kind of logic always brings certain amount of conservatism, though they obviously intend to justify technological progress. The view of such scholars that is at the edge of criticism by Frank Webster shall also be found in certain academic justifications in favour of capitalism by contravening egalitarian imaginations. Regarding the feasibility of a society where human beings can realize their species self without the mediation of private property

and money, the neo-liberals (otherwise known as neo-conservatives) follow more or less same approach. They used to defend private property as a basic reason for the progress and prosperity of hitherto history of mankind. Sharing and collectivism would only bring about lethargy and end of progress and prosperity. But, those who energetically try to justify private property and knowledge patents hardly remember a fact. If the first individual who invented the technique of fire making had not shared his/her knowledge with others and if they had taken patent, the entire progress of human civilization would have been blocked. It is a philosophical question related to the prime reason behind progress – sharing or accumulation of wealth and knowledge? Production, sale and purchase of knowledge in the market, for a competitive and cost effective price is the common answer of neo-liberals to this question. They may have us to believe that the free market, which is relatively recent in origin in human history, is natural institution; and it is the model for the future. Moreover, the free market claims that it represents the basic human self.

7. "In Herbert Schiller's work we get a recurrent insistence that it is capitalist characteristics which predominate in the origination and current conduct of the informational realm: it is the primacy of corporate players, of market principles and inequalities of power which are most telling" [Webster, 2002: 266].
8. "With those who assert that we are witnessing the emergence of an information society, then high on that list of shared principles is technological ... determinism" [Webster, 2002: 272].
9. "In any event, it is clear that at the core of our concern to protect privacy lies a conception of the individual's relationship with society. Once we acknowledge a separation between the public and the private domain, we assume a community in which not only does a division make sense, but also an institutional structure that makes possible an account of this sort. In other words, to postulate the 'private' presupposes the 'public' [Wacks, 2010: 31].
10. The omission of right to privacy from fundamental rights shall be regarded as a deviation of India from the liberal constitutionalism. However, it requires a comparison with the inclusion of property, another liberal right which was originally part of fundamental rights in the constitution.
11. But even though the right to information has been a popular topic in the vernacular press, its mediated expression is not free or radically

different from its liberalist moorings in the English media.

12. Section 2(a) of the Right to Information Act, 2005, states: "Appropriate Government' means public authority which is established, constituted, owned, controlled or substantially financed by funds provided directly or indirectly by central government, state governments or union territory government".

Section 2(h) elaborates the meaning of public authority which states: "public authority means any authority or body or institution of self-government established or constituted: (a) by or under the constitution, (b) by any other law made by Parliament, (c) by any other law made by state legislature, (d) by notification issued or order made by the appropriate government and includes any: (i) body owned, controlled or substantially financed; (ii) non-Government organisation substantially financed, directly or indirectly by funds provided by the appropriate Government".

Interestingly, Section 8(d) leaves the task for definition of 'public interest' at the discretion of competent authority (information officer, information commission or the appellate authority.

Two issues are involved in the definition of 'public' and 'private'. First, is related to the diffusion of state funding across the society and the benefit of private agencies from the subsidies, infrastructure, land and tax exemptions provided by the state. In such a view, they are no longer fully funded private agencies based on the source(s) of income. It leads to the possibility of inclusion of private agencies under the act. But the clause 'substantial' funding is a problem, because the exactly recorded data is not available regarding the indirect state funding for private firms. Second is related to the definition of public agency in Section 2(h) that follows the criteria – agency constituted by government law rather than operating under the government law. It may lead to the exclusion of private agencies from the law. These careless definitions of public authority in the act provide many escape routes for the private agencies, and make the 'public interest' depend on the discretion of the adjudicators. It was not an issue for the NGOs that were demanding for right to information in the formative stages of the act; and even now not many of them consider it as a serious lapse in the Act. We can understand the intention of the neo-liberal government to restrict the meaning of public. But, what actually prevents the NGOs and civil society activists from taking a common approach towards the inclusion of the private sector under the RTI act?

13. For more examples of violation of freedom of information by private companies and its consequences on the public (customers, investors and citizens), see Siraj, 2010:119-20.
14. The Third National RTI Convention (March 10-12, 2011) organized by the National Campaign for People's Right to Information (NCPRI) in its Shillong Declaration on the Right to Information (Item No. 7) states: "public private partnerships, the private sector, political parties, trade unions, NGOs, and cooperative societies are all under the purview of the RTI Act. Rules and procedures need to be defined to ensure that information from them can be easily accessed." However, the opinion of NGOs regarding the inclusion of non-state agencies varies. Note the omission of religious bodies from the list of NCPRI.
15. Media impact on democracy shows that the commercial media is able to 'mediate' even the process of citizens' judgement of media news.
16. However, after the subprime crisis the credit rating agencies which gave triple 'A' grade to junk securities and misled the investors escaped from the responsibility by stating that they expressed opinions only. There is every market participant may decide if he follows this or not.
17. Colin Leys by citing an example from his life, points out the transition from citizen to customer in the following way: "I recently received a circular from the local authority of the district in London where I live, which addressed me as a 'customer'. I should really be inured by now to neo-liberalism's relentless penetration of the 'life world', but it took me aback all the same. I don't buy anything from my local council; on the contrary, it is supposed to represent me. I elect it, and it spends my taxes. But in the mind of the official who wrote the circular it is evidently more like a corporation with something to sell: satisfaction, perhaps" [Leys, 2008: 1].
18. Recall the criticism raised by Flavia Agnes against the usual demand by the Indian civil society groups for enactment of another law by the state to deal with the violation of human rights of women. She says: "Instead of empowering women, the laws serve to strengthen the state. And a powerful state conversely means weaker citizens, which includes the women. The weaker the women, the more vulnerable they will be to male violence" [Agnes, 1997: 524]. Such a tragedy may also be awaiting freedom of information laws. The increasing obsession of the neo-liberal state

with data collection about its citizens shows such a development. Its differential benefits to the marginalized sections and the dominant groups certainly deserve serious attention.

19. The principle of data protection was first enshrined in West German and Scandinavian legislation in the early 1970s...The European Convention on Data Protection, which came into force in October 1985, provides an international legal framework for individual countries to adopt [for details see: Keane, 1991:133-134]. The ascending significance of right to privacy in the West seems to be simultaneous to the emergence of neo-liberalism.
20. The role of media as a whistleblower and defender of right to information has not been proved beyond doubt because 'recent leaks [by the WikiLeaks] seem to fill a vacuum not only in the simple volume of information they reveal, but also in the desire of the consumer to know more than the obvious' [Gupta, 2011: 10].
21. Recall the famous comment by Rupert Murdoch: "It's a libel to say that I use my newspapers to support my other business interests. The fact is, I haven't got any other business interests".
22. In his analysis of media and democracy, John Keane highlights the drawbacks of this old American and European heritage of defining liberty of press (and freedom of information) vis-à-vis state alone. [Keane, 1991: 123-124].
23. The Wikileaks episode aroused contrasting responses. For example, Noam Chomsky very positively appreciates the performance of Wiki [Goodman 2010]. Slavoj Zizek (2011) and Giri (2010) follow a middle path, though they suspect the potentials of the secrets revealed by WikiLeaks to gain a subversive effect on the system. The most scathing criticism came from Michael Chossudovsky (2010) who argued that the Wiki Leaks had signed agreement with five corporate media groups and granted exclusive permission to the latter for publishing the secrets including the privilege for censoring the details. In this way, WikiLeaks also was part of the media game to manipulate the information.

References

Agnes, Flavia (1997), 'Protecting Women against Violence?: A Review of a Decade of Legislation, 1980-1989' in Partha Chatterjee (ed.), *State and Politics in India*, New Delhi: Oxford University Press, pp. 521-565.

Castells, Manuel (2010), *The Rise of Network Society*, London:

Blackwell Publishing.

Chandhoke, Neera (2003), "Governance and Pluralisation of the State: Implications for Democratic Citizenship", *Economic and Political Weekly*, 38(28), pp. 2957-2968.

Chossudovsky, Michel (2010), 'Who is Behind Wiki leaks?', *Global Research*, December 13, http://www.globalresearch.ca/index.php?context=va&aid=22389, retrieved on 18th August, 2011.

Enderle, Georges (2009), 'Beyond Profits and Rules: The Moral Case for Business to Fight Corruption Globally' in Transparency International, *Global Corruption Report 2009*, Cambridge: Cambridge University Press, pp. 11-12.

Federal Government of USA (2011), 'The Financial Crisis Enquiry Report- Final Report of the National Commission on the Causes of the Financial and Economic Crisis in the United States', January, http://fcic-static.law.stanford.edu/cdn_media/fcic-reports/fcic_final_report_full.pdf, retrieved on August 10, 2011.

Fung, Archon et al. (2007), Full Disclosure: Perils and Promise of Transparency, New York: Cambridge University Press.

Gill, Stephen (1995), "Globalization, Market Civilization and Disciplinary Neo-liberalism", *Millennium-Journal of International Studies,* 24(3), pp. 399-423.

Giri, Saroj (2010), 'Wikileaks Beyond Wikileaks?' *Culture and Politics after the Net,* December 16, 2010, pp. 12-39, http://interactivist.autonomedia.org/node/13857, retrieved on 18th August, 2011.

Goodman, Amy (2010), 'Interview with Noam Chomsky-WikiLeaks Cables Reveal Profound Hatred for Democracy on the Part of Our Political Leadership', *Democracy Now,* November 30, http://www.democracynow.org/2010/11/30/noam_chomsky_wikileaks_cables_reveal_profound, retrieved on 18th August, 2011.

Government of India (2005), *The Right to Information Act 2005,* http://righttoinformation.gov.in/rti-act.pdf , retrieved on 10th August, 2011.

Gupta, Manobina (2011), "The Radia Tapes, Wiki Leaks and Insurgent Media", *Economic and Political Weekly*, 46(04), pp. 10-12.

Harvey, David (2005), A Brief History of Neo-liberalism, New York: Oxford University Press.

Hayek, F.A. (1945), "The Use of Knowledge", *American Economic Review,* 35(4), pp. 519-530.

Henriques, Adrian (2007), Corporate Truth: Limits to Transparency, London: Earthscan.

Keane, John (1991), Media and Democracy, Cambridge: Polity Press.

Leys, Colin (2008), Total Capitalism: Market Politics, Market State, Gurgaon: Three Essays Collective.

Mandel, Ernest (2008), Marxist Economic Theory, Vol. II, Delhi: Aakar Books.

Mirowski, Philip and Dieter Plehwe (eds.) (2009), The Road from Mont Pelerin: The Making of the Neo-liberal Thought Collective, Harvard: Harvard University Press.

National Campaign for Peoples' Right to Information (NCPRI), http://righttoinformation.info/ retrieved on 12th September, 2011.

Olssen, Mark (2010), *Liberalism, Neo-liberalism, Social Democracy: Thin Communitarian Perspectives on Political Philosophy and Education*, New York: Routledge.

Shrivastava, K.M. (2009), The Right to Information: A Global Perspective, New Delhi: Lancer Publishers.

Siraj, Mazhar (2010), "Exclusion of Private Sector from Freedom of Information Laws: Implications from a Human Right Perspective", *Journal of Alternative Perspectives in Social Sciences*, 2(1), pp. 211-226.

Stevenson, R.B. (1980), *Corporations and Information: Secrecy, Access and Disclosure,* Baltimore, MD: Johns Hopkins University Press.

Tomasevaki, Katarina (1987),'Freedom of Information: A History of Failure(s)', Paper presented at the conference, An Interdisciplinary Inquiry into the Content and Value of the so-called New Human Rights in May 1987, Oxford. http://repository.forcedmigration.org/show_metadata.jsp?pid=fmo:349 retrieved on 10th August, 2011.

Transparency International (2009), *Global Corruption Report 2009 – Corruption and Private Sector,* Cambridge: Cambridge University Press.

Wacks, Raymond (2010), Privacy: A Very Short Introduction, Oxford: Oxford University Press.

Whitton, J.B. (1949), 'The United Nations Conference on Freedom of Information and the Movement against International Propaganda', *The American Journal of International Law,* 43(1), pp. 73-87.

Webster, Frank (2002), *Theories of the Information Society,* London: Routledge.

Williamson, Claudia R. (2009), "Exploring the Failure of Foreign Aid:

The Role of Incentives and Information", *The Review of Austrian Economics,* 23(1), pp. 17-33, http://www.springerlink.com/content/v1h1h44713554920/fulltext.pdf, retrieved on 10th August 2011.

Zizek, Slavoj (2011), 'Good Manners in the Age of Wiki leaks', *London Review of Books*, 33(2), pp. 9-10, http://www.lrb.co.uk/v33/n02/slavoj-zizek/good-manners-in-the-age-of-wikileaks, retrieved on 18th August, 2011.

6

Globalization to Global Governance

B. Ramesh Babu

Reflecting on the global scene in the Cold War era, Walter Lippmann observed that the "central drama of our age is how the western nations and the Asian peoples are to find a tolerable basis of co-existence." Since then the Soviet Union, the bipolar world, and the Cold War have passed into history. Communism, i.e. the centrally planned command economy, lost its credibility as a model of development. We now live in the post-Cold War era of globalisation along liberal capitalist lines under the hegemonic leadership of the United States of America. However, in the wake of the global meltdown of 2008 and the continued disarray of the West, the early euphoria of capitalist globalisation has eroded irretrievably. Be that as it may, the central drama of our age now (and for the near future) is how the West and "the Rest" are to find a tolerable basis of coexistence, I think.

The primary requisite for any such *modus vivendi* to be durable and viable is the macro equation between the West and the Rest should essentially be non-exploitative and move quickly towards increasingly greater justice (social, economic, and political) for all the people all over the world. It is equally important that it is so perceived by the weaker partners, who constitute the overwhelming majority of the people and the nations in the world.

Though the compulsions to move forward in that direction may not seem reciprocally equal, the West and the Rest have to learn to live together and work together amicably. In the ultimate analysis mankind has no other earthly choice! Humans, animals, trees, and all the other living and non-living inhabitants of the planet have no other home, at least as of now.

There are global MNCs and some of them bigger, richer, and more powerful than many sovereign nation states. However, there is no global union of workers, nor a world federation of farmers or agricultural labour. There are no global citizens either. But, we have an abundance of 'super patriotic' leaders of nation states (big and small) masquerading as world leaders. Some of them even harbour planetary pretensions. Unfortunately, we do not have 'truly global' leaders, who are genuinely concerned about the welfare of all the people all over the world. Even if some exceptional individual leader of a nation state dares to stray beyond the shackles of patriotism, the extant international system –a legacy of the West—will not allow him to rise above his country's "narrow", "parochial", and "short-term" nation state interests.

The UN and the elaborate system of global governance set up after the Second World War is obsolete beyond redemption. The multiple revolutions underway since mid-1980s have transformed *Inter-national Politics* into *Global Politics*. A new web of loyalties and identities (parallel and hierarchical) is in the making. Over time a new architecture of jurisdictions structuring power and authority in tune with the altered framework of loyalties (and identities) will have to emerge. This will happen sooner than we think. Whether such a new "basis of co-existence" will emerge peacefully or not is the fundamental issue of our times. If the disjunction between the emerging loyalties and jurisdictions strays beyond the (retractable range of) elasticity of the extant institutions of governance (at the local, national, or global levels), there would be disorder, chaos, and violence. Reforms will not be enough. We need new forms of governance straddling and transcending today's 'not so sovereign nation states'!

The contemporary phenomenon of globalisation is to be seen as the continuation of the historic, secular, and uneven transition of the world from *Inter-National Politics* (i.e. politics among nations) to *Global Politics*. The role and reach of this transformation have grown during the past three or four decades on an unprecedented scale in human history. All major (and many not so major) issues and challenges confronting each and every nation today have become global and demand global solutions.

Yet, there is no genuine global response, let alone a globally agreed framework or approach to deal with global challenges like the current economic meltdown, climate change, ecological balance, security of persons, national security, poverty, destitution, domestic violence and international terrorism. Sadly, the way our world is constituted today, comprehensive, and truly global solutions are not possible, not even conceivable, as will be elucidated below.

There are global MNCs and some of them are bigger, richer, and more powerful than many sovereign nation states. However, there are no global unions, nor world federations of farmers or agricultural workers. There are no global citizens either. But, we have a plethora of 'super' patriotic leaders of nation states (big and small) masquerading as global leaders. Some of them harbour even planetary pretensions.

Unfortunately, we do not have 'truly global' leaders, who are genuinely concerned about the welfare of all the people all over the world. Even if some individual leaders dare to stray beyond *the extant inter-national system,* (a legacy of the West) will not allow them to rise above their country's 'narrow' and 'parochial' national interests. The leaders are expected and duty bound to further their national goals and objectives at the expense of other nations, welfare of the mankind, and world peace. At the most some grudging concessions are made in the direction of enlightened self interest, if and when national interests of the other states involved converge. Such pretence of global governance is not merely inadequate, but could be positively dangerous for the future of the planet.

Furthermore, in operational terms, even this narrow and

parochial national interests approach does not encompass the welfare of all the citizens of the country concerned. The rich and the powerful in all the countries (i.e. 'the establishment') utilise the State and the Flag to advance their own private and personal interests at expense of the masses, the poor, and the marginalised, who constitute an overwhelming majority of the citizens of the State. It must be added that such inequity and injustice are universal and pervasive in the rich as well as poor countries.

Greed, graft, corruption (corporate, governmental, and private), and nepotism, discrimination, and racial prejudice of all hues, and aggrandisement of the powerful (local, national, and global) rule the roost. Ironical as it may seem, the good old question "whose interests are national interests?" has become doubly pertinent today. Yet, the juggernaut of the liberal capitalist globalisation rolls on spewing misery, despair, destitution, resentment, and terrorism at home and abroad, even as it achieves measurable economic growth. The recent economic meltdown worldwide has put the capitalist fundamentalists on the defensive. Free market and unregulated capitalism have lost their euphoric edge. The classic 'growth versus development' quarrel is back to the front burner.

This indeed is the most fundamental and overarching crisis confronting mankind in the 21st century. There is a wide and cruel gap between the representational legitimacies and the extant structures of governance at all levels, local to global. Our focus in this essay is on global governance. The UN and the entire Bretton Woods system of the Second World War era had their innings. They are inadequate to cope with the greatly transformed world today. A paradigm shift has been underway in global affairs, especially since the mid-1980s.

A new web of identities and loyalties (parallel and hierarchical) is in the making everywhere. Over time a new architecture of jurisdictions structuring power and authority in line with the altered framework of loyalties (and identities) will have to emerge (Babu, 2004). This will happen sooner than we think. Whether such a new equation/engagement between loyalties and jurisdictions stretching from local to global will be arrived at relatively peacefully (or not) is the fundamental issue of our times. [1]

This is the most crucial challenge confronting mankind today and in the immediate future. It is important that we build on the emerging global web of governance and keep it in step with the pace and extent of globalisation taking place in finance, commerce, communications, culture and most other spheres of our lives.

If the disjunction between the emerging loyalties and jurisdictions strays beyond the (retractable range of) elasticity of the governing institutions in place (at the national and international levels), there would be violence, disorder and chaos. Reforms are not enough. We need new forms of governance and newer combinations of jurisdictions (territorial and functional) and a creative mix of the two.

Consumerism and Conflict

The propensity of man to grab what all he wants, whether he needs it or not, i.e. consumerism, is certainly one of the most subversive legacies of the West that is threatening the planet earth with exhaustion and possible extinction. The liberal capitalist western mindset, which insists on the rights of the individual and his entitlements against the State and society without giving equal importance to his concomitant obligations and duties to the community and the nation, is fundamentally flawed. Such self-centred and essentially selfish (bordering on the greedy) and atomistic conceptions of society became the engines of achievement and 'progress' in modern times. In the globalising world of ours such notions of progress and modernity are exercising enormous magnetic influence all over the world. The revolutionary advances in IT and communications have greatly magnified "the international demonstration effect" of consumerism and are raising popular expectations sky high all over the world. I have called this phenomenon "imperialism of attraction", which is popularly and mistakenly dubbed as the "Americanisation of the world" (Babu, 1994).

This is not to deny or decry the phenomenal achievements of man in every walk of life during the last four centuries under the leadership of the modern West. A lot more is expected of the West in the future as well. However, the western legacy like so many others in history has overreached itself and is threatening the very humanity of man. Some perceptive minds (including in the West) are questioning the very concept of progress as it is understood and advocated till now.

Mere material advancement without the redeeming humane values and spirituality do not and cannot lead to real progress. It is time to curb the excesses of logic/rationality and return to sanity, common sense and above all to moderation. 'To shun too much' of everything (even logic and goodness) should become the guiding principle for mankind at this juncture. An ancient Sanskrit axiom enjoins man to eschew excess in everything and everywhere, *athi sarvatra varjayet!* However, I concede that how much is too much is not an easy rubric to cross. But, the ravages of too much are easy to see, unless we choose to be blind to the excesses around us.

Terrorism: The New Menace

International terrorism spearheaded by Islamic fundamentalists is the latest combustible added to the already explosive global situation. India has been the earliest of the victims of cross border terrorism. But, it is only after the tragically spectacular attack of 9/11 on the US, international terrorism upgraded into a serious menace of global dimensions. Instead of going after the terrorists who attacked their country, the 'neocons' led by President Bush and Vice-President Cheney went on a unilateral rampage. The US launched the so called global war on terror.

By all accounts the war in Iraq degenerated into a big

misadventure, transformed international terrorism into a bigger threat than before, which has virtually destabilised the whole region (from Istanbul to Islamabad and Riyadh to Rawalpindi). Pakistan, the epicentre of terrorism, is itself in mortal danger of being over taken by the Taliban. Ironically, it is Pakistan that nurtured the Taliban in Afghanistan with the active connivance of the US and its allies in the West, and above all by Saudi Arabia. In the bargain the Pakistani Army and the ISI worked closely with the Taliban and other Islamic fundamentalist elements culminating in the talibanisation of Afghanistan and Pakistan.

History tells us that those who ride the tiger can dismount the beast only at their own peril, as the current offensive of the Pak Army against the Taliban indicates. One need not be surprised if this cracking the whip turns out to be a drama enacted to keep the multi- billion dollar American aid flowing in. Pakistan could always return to business as usual and be back on the fast track of a failed state! This is a prospect whose implications to regional and world peace are too dangerous to contemplate, leave alone to contend with and contain.

What is the Way Out?

I believe that a return to Gandhi, 'Gramodaya,' Green, God, and Green Peace and above all, to common sense and fair play is the need of the hour. My fervent plea for a return to Gandhi should not be misunderstood. I am not advocating a return to the obscurantisms of the past, nor to blind acceptance of everything the Mahatma stood for and preached. I am alluding to the essence of his philosophy of life: truth, non-violence, peace, and self-sacrifice. The Mahatma was an ardent advocate of simple living and service to fellow human beings. He declared that '*Manava Seve*' is '*Madhava Seva*' (serving man is the only way to serve God).

For example, the Mahatma urged people to cut down their needs and wants to the barest minimum. He practiced what he preached. A loin cloth, two dry *rotis* and a cup of goat's milk was all he ever needed. Nobody could ask for a more simple living by example—the very opposite of the consumer culture that is driving humans mad and the planet earth to exhaustion. Power is to be seen and used as a trust and the more endowed among us have a greater obligation to work for the benefit of the masses, he insisted. He proclaimed that all policies and actions of the State must pass the ultimate test—whether they enhance the welfare of the poorest of the poor (*antyodaya*) in the remotest villages and hamlets of the country (*gramodaya*).

Today's economic reforms in India and the world over (*i.e. liberalisation, privatisation and globalisation*) are far from meeting the Mahatma's test. On the contrary, the rich and powerful are gaining more and more even as the marginalised millions are left out, nay, excluded mercilessly. Yet the rich and the upper classes are demanding and extracting more and more benefits for themselves, often at the expense of the poor and the hungry masses. Greed and callousness of the ruling elite are driving community after community and country after country around the world to protests, direct action, insurrection, revolution, and violence in sheer desperation. Welfare State has yielded place to a callous State.

A return to Green refers to the famous philosopher Thomas Hill Green, who conceived rights of individuals as arising from obligations fulfilled. The Mahatma always insisted that all rights are contingent on and derived from duties. In fact he was so adamant on this score that he refused to endorse the Universal Declaration of Human Rights because it did not include a corresponding list of 'Duties of Man'.

Rights and entitlements should not get precedence over citizens' duties and obligations to the State and society. Rights and duties should forever be 'balanced.' Obviously, a healthy balance between them is never static. Each generation must work for and find its optimum balance between rights and duties. It is my contention that this balance is skewed too much in favour of the individual and against the community in the modern era, especially in 'the advanced' countries of the West.

Anxieties of freedom in 'open societies' (á lā Karl Popper) are as problematic as anxieties of frustration in 'traditional societies', I would like to point out.

A plea for a return to God in the age of '*secularism*' and '*knowledge society*' may sound old hat. But, it is my contention that it is not. The modern western concept of secularism is sullied by a strong inherited prejudice of being anti-religion and even anti-God. Separation of the Church and the State in Europe then was a historical necessity for survival. The religion of the kings was forced on their subjects. Religious toleration did not grow because of faltering convictions or erosion of religious zeal. It emerged because the very survival of the kingdoms and the people in Europe was at stake. It may not be out of place to add that King Henry's anxiety to add one more wife 'sanctioned by the Church' to his harem had played not so minor a part in the separation of the State and Church in England! Over time this practice evolved into a doctrine of sorts and became one of the cardinal principles of western society much later.

Be that as it may, the West and the rest of the world have moved far from the sterile and obsolete notions of isolating religion from the other dimensions of people's lives. Today, it is widely accepted that religion is an integral part of man's very being, his life and culture. In fact, in some western nations a return to faith is being perceived as an antidote to anomie, violence, and declining moral values. What needs to be done is to emphasise the spiritual dimension of religion and de-emphasise its dogmas and rituals.

One of the central doctrines of the *Sanatana Dharma* is that reason and faith are not antithetical to each other. Reason gradually leads one to faith, the Hindu scriptures assert and the lives of sages of ancient India are a testament to the coexistence of the two for mutual enrichment. In this short essay, I cannot discuss this phenomenal transformation of the perception of religion in the post modern society. It is adequate for our purposes here to recognise the commonalities of all living religions of man: humanity of man; equality of all people before God; acceptance of differences in faith as natural; to be at peace with oneself, one's own God and fellow men. These are among the eternal values of life on earth. The rapidly globalising world of ours urgently needs the formulation of truly universal norms and values shared across cultures and continents. Otherwise planet earth will be engulfed in disorder, chaos, and wars.

My plea for a return to '*Green Peace*' is an all inclusive term for the restoration of global ecological balance. Environmental pollution, global warming and all the other related threats to the future of man on earth are included. I extend this concern for the well-being of all the other living beings and non-living things that share the planet with us. Hinduism asserts that man has no superior claims or right of precedence over the other living and non-living inhabitants on the resources of the planet earth. In fact, being endowed with more intelligence and knowledge, man has greater responsibility to act as the trustee of the lesser beings, the Hindu scriptures ordain.

Globalisation and Globalism

It is appropriate at this juncture to distinguish between globalisation and 'globalism'. The former is a process of supra-national integration and sub-national disintegration occurring simultaneously and reinforcing each other, especially since the 1990s. This dual transformation is leading to an inchoate restructuring of the architecture of global power structure. However, the extant post-Cold War globalisation can be seen as a phenomenon of integration of the major national economies into a liberal capitalist global 'free market' led by the US and the West. As such it is hegemonic, exploitative, unjust and unacceptable, especially to the Third world as well as the poor and marginalised millions in the advanced countries of the West. Globalism, on the other hand, conceptually envisions the whole world as one unit and is concerned with the welfare of all people everywhere and the planet earth as a whole.

An effort is made here to conceptually bridge the gap between the extant institutions of global governance and their representational legitimacies. There is a huge democratic deficit, which needs to be acknowledged first. Then the will to undo the inherent injustice should follow. If there is a will, there is a way. Then we have to come up with new forms of governance which are capable of institutionally steering the globalisation underway since the mid-1980s forward from hegemony to genuine global governance. This calls for a new philosophy of globalism that is valid across cultures and continents. [2]

Finally, humans must advance (or is it return?) to conceptions of authority as trust, i.e., power with a moral purpose. In short, we must return to idealism. I firmly believe that power without a redeeming social purpose is a curse. Rampant consumerism of here and now must yield place to a healthy balance between the present and the past, and the present and the future. The present generation has no right eat into the rights of the youth and the claims of future generations on the resources of the planet. Earth should have the time to replenish itself. Nature must be allowed to catch its breath, so to say. Here again, the Western urge to tame and conquer nature is in contrast with the tradition of living in tune with nature ordained by Hindu scriptures.

Parochialisms of the whites, blacks, browns and yellows; the rich and the poor; human rights activists, and feminists (in a planet shared by the other living beings and non-living things) must be given up. Even at their best these seekers of justice for their kind are advancing the cause of the few, who constitute a small segment of mankind on earth, which itself is no more than a speck in the cosmos (*Brahmand*). Need not greed should be the basis of all human endeavour on earth. Mother earth has enough for everyone's need, but not for his greed, as the Mahatma observed wisely.

Peace on Earth: India's Dharma?

As pointed out earlier, a paradigm shift in the global power structure is underway. The centre of gravity of the world is moving from the Atlantic to the Asia-Pacific. The US and the West are constrained to share power and authority with the Asian nations. India, China, and ASEAN nations are happy at the prospect of becoming partners in global governance. But, in order to define the contours and modify the content of the emerging new world order, it is not enough for Asia to enhance their share of power (economic and strategic) in global governance. They have to earn it and even more important, they have to deserve it on merits. Towards this end the Asian leaders have to come up with a vision for the world that is inherently superior and more just than what the West had offered over the last four centuries. It is absolutely crucial that the Asian "vision, mission and agenda" is more democratic, egalitarian, and just, and therefore more peaceful than the hegemonic liberal capitalist globalisation underway since the 1990s.

Towards this end, I cannot resist the temptation to place before you, the Hindu concept of *shanti*, a comprehensive and composite vision of peace on earth and the place of man in the cosmos, *brahmand*. For this we have to go back to *Bharat*, to our roots and our ancient legacy. Today's India is totally inadequate to the challenge because it is conceptually colonised, intellectually imitative, and routinely reactive. The country's elites are easily co-opted and its leaders are conveniently corruptible. I firmly believe that the *Sanatana Dharma*, cleared of its cobwebs of obsolescence—i.e., rituals, obscurantisms, entrenched anti-egalitarianisms (like the caste system, and downgrading of women), is a better candidate for illuminating a path towards a new *philosophy of globalism*, which the globalising world of ours requires urgently.

The vision of *shanti* in the Hindu scriptures rightly begins with man himself. They proclaim that man must be at peace himself and his God. Then he has to be at peace with his family, which in turn has to be at peace with the community, community with the village, the village with the mandal (region) and so on till the consuming desire to seek peace (*Shanti Kamukata*) covers the whole planet earth. The concept of *shanti* does not stop there. It is extended to the five elements (*Pancha Bhootanam*) the earth, water, wind, fire and the firmament. Man has to live in tune with nature. Taming, conquering and abusing nature (the western precepts and practices) are against the very spirit of Hinduism. The urge to seek peace is extended to the sun-centred universe of ours and the cosmos beyond (*Brahmand*). Vedic dharma desires peace at all times and everywhere.

द्यौः शान्तिरन्तरिक्षँ शान्तिः पृथिवी शान्तिरापः शान्ति-
रोषधयः शान्तिः । वनस्पतयः शान्तिर्विश्वे देवाः शान्तिर्ब्रह्म
शान्ति सर्वँ शान्तिः शान्तिरेव शान्तिः सा मा शान्तिरेधि ॥

(यजु० ३६ । १७)

May the sun and the sky be peaceful? May the earth and the outer space be peaceful? May all trees and forests be peaceful? May all the learned souls and animate elements, all the enlightened Gods of the world and the Vedas shower peace on us. May all the inanimate things in the world be peaceful? May I have that peace which bestows peace on the whole world—the all encompassing peace, only peace and nothing but peace?

In order to make such a peaceful world possible, Hinduism offers the following foundational principles of human conduct—truth, non-injury, *dharma*, peace, sacrifice and suffering. Without the spirit of sacrifice and accepting suffering and pain as integral to life, peace is not possible on earth, according to Hindu scriptures. A word about the Hindu concept of *dharma* is appropriate here. *Dharma* is a composite and an organic concept encompassing rights, duties and justice. Man earns his rights and claims over fellowmen, society and State, only after he performs his duties and if he acts justly (in accordance with his *dharma*). Everyone is bound by *dharma* and when all act in accordance with *dharma*, justice and peace will prevail everywhere, it is postulated.

Finally, prayers and invocations are integral to the Hindu way of life. Prayers said sincerely, aloud and uttered perfectly (in their diction, phonetically and in tonal purity) have impact on the man and also on the Gods and the natural forces whom they address. And all Hindu prayers end with the following final invocation (*Swasti Vakyam*).

सर्वे भवन्तु सुखिनः सर्वे सन्तु निरामयाः ।
सर्वे भद्राणि पश्यन्तु मा कश्चिद् दुःखभाग् भवेत् ॥

May all be happy; may all be free from illness and disease; may all be safe and secure; may all be protected from sorrow and difficulties. This invocation encompasses all people all over the world. Let me end by invoking the sagely mantra from *Hitopadesa*, inscribed on the first gate of the Parliament House:

अयं निजः परोवेति गणना लघुचेतसाम् ।
उदारचरितानां तु वसुधैव कुटुम्बकम् ॥

(शार्ङ्गधरपद्धति

This is mine that is another's; such reckonings are for the narrow minded. For the noble hearted, *the whole world is one family*. From such a global perspective, further research and reflection on the key constituents of a new *Philosophy of Globalism* in the making is called for, I submit humbly: That, ladies and gentlemen, is going to be the focus of the old man's next intellectual adventure.

Om, Shanti, Shanti, Shantireva Shanti

End Notes

1. The current tussles over Telangana, Vidarbha and the armed struggles of the Naxalites and other extremist groups around the country are classic examples of the ongoing flux in identities and loyalties of people. Similar mass struggles and passionate demands

for justice and fair play are going on elsewhere in South Asia (Nepal, Pakistan, and Sri Lanka) and around the world (Palestine, Iraq, Indonesia, Philippines, Spain, Yugoslavia, Malta, Brazil, Argentina, Chile and sub-Saharan Africa, etc.).

2. For an example of the inter-civilisational dialogue. See: Hu Yeping, 'Asian Civilisational Dialogue between India and China,' *World Affairs*, Vol. 8, No. 4 (October-December 2004), pp. 82-95.

References

Babu B. Ramesh (2004), 'Glocalisation' and the Indian Nation State: Jurisdictions and Loyalties in Flux, New Delhi: South Asian Publishers.

Babu B. Ramesh (1994), "Americanisation of the World: Myth and Reality", *Freedom First,* 422 (July-September), pp. 23-27.

Yeping Hu (2004), "Asian Civilisational Dialogue between India and China", *World Affairs*, Vol. 8, No. 4 (October-December), pp. 82-95.

7

Civil Society and Public Policy

V. Anil Kumar

Introduction

Civil society is defined in various ways. [1] The term has been so overused that it is on the verge of losing its core meaning namely, the organizations and associations that are non-governmental and are in the realm of civic associations with considerable distance from the state and the party system. There are numerous definitions of civil society. In political theory there are three broad streams through which civil society can be studied. First is the L-stream, that is, the Lockean notion of state of nature as civil society. Many civil society protagonists take cue from this in mentioning that society is prior to state to mean that civil society is prior to state or political society.

The second is the M-stream; the Montesquieu-de Tocqueville stream which focuses on the importance of civic associations and associational life particularly as it obtained in America at the time of de Tocqueville's study. [2] Here, civic associations are strength for civil society as well as the democratic political culture. The third strand that can be discerned is that of Hegelian tradition from which also follows the Marxian theorization. Hegel defines civil society as the realm between the family and the state. Marx includes the market and economic realm also in the definition. [3]

When we speak of civil society the one important aspect that we can not forget is that the current theorization on civil society is significantly informed by the 1989 events of the collapse of Berlin wall and the collapse of the erstwhile Soviet Union. As Kennedy and Galtz [4] (1996) write about the then actually existing socialism, the velvet revolutions have crucially brought in the questions of spontaneous and voluntary assertion of civil society over authoritarian states.

The debate of democratization in the third world during the 1980s also drawn heavily from the above historical circumstances and have made civil society as one of the chief supports for democratic governance. Therefore, the debate in the third world not only revolved around establishing democratic polities and societies as in the terms of old modernization theory, but has also focused on broadening the frontiers of democratic processes and deepening their reach to cover and include those who are hitherto have been left out from its purview.

As Shinchi Shigetomi [5] writes, the origin of developmental NGOs is most often owing to the failure of either state or market or community or all three. The NGOs also are officially non-political but their work has considerable influence and implications for political systems. They can work on development issues and attempt to have policy advocacy wings that constantly engage the state at different levels.

The civil society is supposed to influence governance process through influencing public policy. [6] This relationship is what is examined in this study. We try empirically to interrogate whether such a relationship has actually become a prominent relation between the state and civil society. Whether civil society succeeds in influencing public policy or not? What are the empirical ways and means through which civil society succeeds or fails in this process? This is the central theme of this study.

This study argues that the concept of civil society is a political concept since it is often defined contra state and family. Empirically too, civil society, as is often argued, does not limit itself to non-political aspects but explicitly or implicitly concerns itself with various aspects of politics and related aspects. Also in this context how 'the political' is defined also matters enormously. A broader definition of politics means that many aspects of the civil society activism can be considered as political aspects. For example, in the case of policy advocacy and civil rights, the questions raised by NGOs are openly and directly political, and these deal with power and the powerful.

The concept of governance became prominent after the collapse of the Soviet Union and the state-socialist societies. The structural adjustment programmes in the late eighties and early nineties too made a rethinking on the state necessary. [7] The argument was that the state needed reform: the big government and provider state have failed. The state needs to be rolled back from its role in general and that of economy in particular. What was advocated was a diminished but efficient state that can operate as a facilitator for capital.

This also led to the theorization as to what are the emerging circumstances and, what the state and its functioning—governance—should be. This theory on the state was not just the making of academic political scientists but was also largely propagated by the Bretton Woods institutions to suit their lending policies. It was more than academic theory. The theory of neo-liberal 'good governance' is also related to this change.

The neo-liberal good governance also focuses on aspects of governance such as public-private partnerships, outsourcing public sector tasks to private sector, privatizing the public sector and liberalizing the economy. The neo-liberal governance reforms accompany the neo-liberal economic reforms. Indeed the partnerships with the civil society are also often termed as public-private partnerships; though this is not a fully agreed idea by civil society. The definitional battles on civil society overshadow this particular way of characterizing civil society. However, neo-liberal governance reforms do view civil society as one of the hand maidens of neo-liberal governance.

In fact Munshi, Abraham and Chowhduri [8] clearly say in their review of the criticisms of the concept of good governance that: 'The discovery of *institutional* elements in market reforms led to a concern for good governance to make the neo-liberal economic programme efficient. A close look at the programmes supported by the World Bank under the heading 'good governance' shows that they are meant to shrink the state and make it more efficient and at the same time shift the balance of power in favour of private individuals and groups' (Italics in the original) (Munshi, Abraham, Chowdhuri: 2009: 12-13).

This is in addition to focusing on 'development management' and focusing on governance principles that are devoid of political content which the above authors call '*politics without politics*' (pp. 20-21). This involves fundamentally applying management principles for development and administration without considering the political aspects of governance that is, basically viewing state and developmental processes as apolitical or non-political in their essence.

Role of Civil Society in Governance

One view of the relationship of civil society to governance invokes the same arguments of velvet revolutions in the context of developing countries as well. And this approach sees the state as inadequate to meet the demands of the time. For this, civil society and market are to fill the gap that state has evacuated. These arguments view the situation of the state itself in the present context. For example, Ezra Mbogori and Hope Chigudu [9] say in their 'Civil Society and Government: A Continuum of Possibilities' that:

'The state is no longer the final arbiter of all decisions, and brute force is yielding to an enlightened approach those values the continual engagement of citizens. Even in the more democratic states, many people expect more from democracy than simply the right to enter a voting booth every five years' (pp. 111-112).

These protagonists of civil society often hold that in the context of changed constellation of circumstances the role of civil society is prominent in governance. That civil society holds state, and, to a lesser extent market, accountable; and intervenes in policy making; advocates new policies; or holds in abeyance the policies that are not in favour of public good; and finally helps state in implementing its policies. This view sees the state as not just collaborating with the governments but also locked up in contestation when and where necessary. For example two quotations from the above authors Mbogori and Chigudu say this quite clearly:

'Civil society makes a unique contribution to the democratic process through advocacy campaigns and, on occasion, outright opposition to government. In the past two decades, civil society has played an essential role in literally toppling governments from Philippines and Panama to South Africa and Czechoslovakia' (pp. 115-116).

As mentioned, this paper focuses on the relations between civil society and public policy. This is done by taking two empirical instances, where we attempt to see whether civil society can influence public policy. This can be through collaboration as well as through contestation. Civil society influence on government need not be that of cooperation and collaboration alone; civil society organizations can employ a repertoire of processes of which contestation and conflict too are significant.

Karnataka

Historically, NGOs developed in Karnataka out of religion-based institutions and the freedom movement. [10] While there are many religion-based organisations, there are also a number of Gandhian NGOs that are involved in constructive work and are working on illiteracy, Dalit upliftment and welfare and on poverty eradication. Religion and freedom movement, much like in many other parts of the country are two sources of voluntarism and NGO work in Karnataka.

So far as NGO's relationship with the State governments is concerned, the relation evolved tangentially with that of the approach of the central government in plan documents.

However, Karnataka has a special place in that relationship in the sense that the GoK was the first to enter into equal partnership with bilateral donor Swiss Development Agency and one of the oldest and most highly respected NGOs of the state Myrada. [11] This happened as far back as 1986, when the discourse on civil society and state and the relation between them not yet reached Indian shores. The NGOs in Karnataka largely work around three aspects: development, social service and health; and geographically a majority are situated in Central and South Karnataka.

There is a lively discourse on the partnership between government and NGOs in the literature on Karnataka. The Karnataka Human Development Report of 2005 has an entire chapter devoted to the NGO-government partnerships and is upfront about the advantages as well as limitations of such partnerships. In the first place, the Report acknowledges that there is a role for partnerships in the human development of the state, while noting that Karnataka was the first state to enter into such partnerships in the country.

There are at least two views regarding the Government NGO partnership in Karnataka in the related literature these are: firstly by Rajasekhar and Birader (2004) [12] which see the NGO-GO partnerships as 'reluctant partnerships'; and the second view by Kudwa (2008) [13] which conceptualizes these collaborations as 'uneasy' and fluid. One interesting fact Kudwa notes is that while most of the NGOs in Karnataka focus on rural areas, the focus is not limited to rural areas alone. Of late there is a burgeoning sector of NGOs focusing on urban issues. Many of them—for example NGOs such as CIVIC and Janaagraha—are concentrated in Bangalore, the urban issues in other cities in the state too are becoming agendas for NGO action. Kudwa while presenting a case of diversity of NGO sector in Karnataka thinks that it is not fruitful to categorise NGOs in Karnataka either as adversarial or as collaborative. According to Kudwa both are possible simultaneously. Below we consider the more specific case of

MYRADA in Karnataka.

MYRADA: Myrada [14] (Mysore Resettlement and Development Agency) was founded in 1968. Myrada is one of the biggest, most longstanding and highly respected NGOs of Karnataka. Myrada works in three States of Karnataka, Andhra Pradesh and Tamil Nadu; in total in 20 backward and drought prone districts in these three States. In 2010, Myrada had total staff strength of 231. [15] Initial work of MYRADA was focused on resettlement of Tibetan Refugees in Karnataka. Later work focused mainly on building self-help groups for women in rural areas and watershed and natural resource management work in rural areas of Karnataka and close by districts in Andhra Pradesh and Tamil Nadu. Myrada's approach towards rural development is unique in the sense that Myrada believes that building institutions of poor people is the most important aspect for poverty alleviation and rural development. For this, Myrada invests all energy towards building micro finance, natural resource management and gender empowerment institutions in rural areas. Its focus being as mentioned Myrada sees itself primarily as field based NGO.

While focusing on building the institutions of poor people Myrada sees itself primarily as an 'actionist' NGO in contrast to 'activist' NGOs or NGO activism. Myrada also works with PRIs but this is largely in order to provide governance linkage between public health, primary education and AIDS/HIV issues vis-à-vis PRIs. Myrada works with sex workers and their struggles toward dignity and rights. Poverty eradication, natural resource management and gender are the three core areas around which most of the work of Myrada is concentrated. Myrada carries out its actionist strategy by creating sustainable institutions of the poor in the areas of thrift and micro-finance, sustainable watershed and natural resources management and gender. [16] Influencing public policies towards the benefit of the poor in the areas mentioned is also one objective of Myrada.

Senior officials of Myrada say that Myrada is working

with government since 1979; Myrada is engaged with NABARD since 1987. Myrada and NABARD have a strategic partnership with RBI since 1987. They feel that it is not possible to effect policy change by advocacy alone. Field experiences lead to policy advocacy. Two aspects are important in this regard: (a) concrete ground level experience; and (b) credibility of NGOs pursuing advocacy.

Higher officials of Myrada feel that policy advocacy is often a matter of power game. They say that Myrada influences government through the grassroots work of its network of institutions. Policy pertaining to grassroots can be advocated if the NGO in question is able to articulate policy change by demonstrating its grassroots work. They feel that Myrada can influence government sector-wise in sectors such as primary education. Thus sector-wise advocacy in which the NGO is working is possible rather than affecting macro or national policy of the India state. It is even difficult not only at national level but at the State level too.

Another point they mention is that governments understand their own language and they do not often understand the language of grassroots NGOs. In this context, the intervention by middle level NGOs such as Myrada can be helpful. But regarding overall attempt to advocate policies to the government the Myrada officials are sceptic and feel that 'policy advocacy is difficult'. They feel that successes in effective policy advocacy by NGOs such as the enactment of Right to Information Act was possible more because of the individual linkages between the NGO sector and the political elites rather than through a standard well-laid out policy advocacy.

Officials of Myrada say that they are 'actionists' on ground and while conducting advocacy. They think that activists only do action while 'actionists' develop institutions to do activism as well as lobbying. [17] The officials of Myrada also feel that political parties at the State level do not matter in this regard; ideologies too do not matter. For Myrada, it is the local politicians at Mandal and Zilla level that matter. It is local politicians, politicians and contractors –broadly the local political elite—at Zilla level and downwards that matter. This particularly since Myrada believes in building institutions at local level. It is ground level politicians and street bureaucrats that matter.

According to this view, Myrada is not really worried about the higher level politicians or bureaucrats. The officials of Myrada say that they have good relations with higher level politicians and bureaucrats—for instance, the Executive Director of Myrada is a retired officer from the Indian Administrative Service (IAS); and most of the more progressive IAS officers have worked with Myrada at one point or the other. [18] The IAS officers are happy with Myrada because the organization delivers on the commitments taken from the government. [19]

Given the above situation of Myrada, there is need to consider some of the aspects of NGO's relationship with the state. The KHDR insists on the need for the partnerships between the two actors on the principle of mutual respect. The argument is that the state should not attempt to see the NGOs as contractors but as equal partners. The Report for instance says quite clearly that if NGOs become contractors of the state's programmes they lose the critical capacities to question the content and meaning of the programme being implemented. Not all NGOs do have the ability or capacity to question the state and therefore the questioning NGO requires to have: (a) credibility, (b) requisite scale and reach, and (c) ability to negotiate the differences and manage confrontation. All these do not exist always. Of all the questions of ability to influence policy is most important and NGOs can not do this if they are reduced to be contractors; or, rather they should not reduce themselves to contractors and enter a bidding process for government programmes.

The autonomy and independence of civil society in the form of NGOs is not only circumscribed by the state but is also limited by the increasing competition for donor funds. This competition 'squeezes out the smaller NGOs'. In addition to this the expectations of the donors in terms of deliverables are often qualitatively different from that of governments and sometimes perhaps of the concerned NGOs themselves. All the above can lead to the question of the mandate and accountability questions of the NGOs. In this context, the KHDR says that 'NGOs must be very clear about whom they derive their mandate from and to whom they are accountable' (p. 283).

Senior officials at Myrada [20] say that so far as policy advocacy is concerned, there are three cases in which Myrada has been successful. These are:

1. SHG policy of the Union and State governments.
2. The watershed policy of the Union and State governments.
3. Appointment of Panchayat Development Officers (PDO) at Gram Panchayat level by the State government and acceptance of the same policy by the Union government.

Senior officials at Myrada have taken all the initiative to make this policy advocacy success at the State level and now the policy of appointing PDOs is being taken up for implementation all over India by the Union government. The main approach of Myrada was that PRIs are not just implementing agencies but rather 'institutions of governance'.

Myrada was successful in the above three instances because there were officials from government who also had interest in general and Myrada work in particular. These officials were also associated with Myrada and other NGOs in different capacities. Therefore, success regarding the above mentioned aspects because of the support of the selected set of officials of the government that helped advocate these policies.

Andhra Pradesh

As part of the experience of civil society in influencing public policy in Andhra Pradesh we consider the efforts of one civil society organization namely, Centre for World Solidarity.

Centre for World Solidarity was founded in 1992 as a public trust and has its headquarters in Hyderabad. Centre for World Solidarity is modelled after the Berlin-based Action for World Solidarity and its vision and principles of action are prepared following the Action for World Solidarity. [21] It is an intermediate level civil society organization that works in more than two States namely in Andhra Pradesh, Odisha, Jharkhand and Bihar. The organization works on a range of issues from child rights, women's rights to rights of Dalits, and the forest based communities and of minorities. The organization also works on decentralization, panchayati raj institutions (PRIs) and broader governance issues. Centre for World Solidarity works mostly through its network of grassroots NGOs and provides thematic, financial and advocacy support for the network of NGOs.

Besides working on its own, the CWS has also found very active and influential solidarity organizations that work on watershed (WASSAN: Watershed Support Services and Activities Network) sustainable agriculture (CSA: Centre for Sustainable Agriculture) and on forestry (CPF: Centre for People's Forestry), Dalit network called National Dalit Forum (NDF) and Centre for Adivasi, Dalit Bahujan Initiatives (BODHI). These solidarity organizations work on their own and are separate institutional entities on their own right, though they are founded by, and operate in solidarity with, CWS.

It is useful to take the perceptions of the NGO sector regarding policy involvement at the very outset before stating the specific cases; before moving on to the specific cases we may take an overview of the interaction of CWS with government and policy making. [22] When asked whether he thinks the policy making in AP is open to interventions by NGOs the founder and Honorary Secretary of CWS said that the answer is a 'qualified yes'. He felt that the GO-NGO committee of the GOAP headed by a senior administrator is meant precisely for this. He said that the Programme Monitoring Committees of different development departments and the social audit for programmes such as Comprehensive Land Development Programme and also involvement in programmes such as NREGA are examples of the openness of government in AP to the NGO interventions. [23]

Answering to a question on what is the interaction of CWS with government, the higher functionaries of CWS say that their involvement is mostly through the particular bureaucrats in the government, who involve NGOs in development programmes and invite them to participate. Sometimes however, the initiative is also taken by NGOs themselves. CWS continuously seeks to interface with the government and attempts to avail the opportunities in the direction of having such interface. [24]

Regarding the aspect as to whether there is common agreement among the network of CWS partner grassroots NGOs on working with government, the higher officials of CWS say that the grassroots NGOs, even if they are of small scale, cannot be taken for granted; and while they participate in networking and solidarity building, the process is not easy; this is particularly true for intermediary level organizations such as CWS. The officials of CWS feel that the working with a network of NGOs is of mixed experience both fascinating and frustrating. [25] Broadly, CWS higher functionaries feel that the state for various reasons at times articulates things which they can not take exception to. CWS tried to work around or with these spaces and persons in the state. For WASSAN and CSA [26] there was specific favourable constellation of circumstances that favoured their coming into existence. [27]

CWS higher functionaries feel that both 'person and policy' should be favourable to civil society in order to work with any government toward any policy. They believe that there are spaces within the state and spaces within the policy. For example regarding WASSAN's coming into existence in 1994 the ground work on watershed was already done; watershed policy was already enunciated and some ground work was also ready for the watershed work. The CWS higher functionaries feel that generally, government and civil society view each other with suspicion; but the presence of powerful individuals with connections to state and in support of civil society allays such suspicion.

CWS Work Related to Panchayati Raj Institutions [28]

CWS programme on PRIs began in 2000 and since then the organization has been working with 13 out of 23 districts of Andhra Pradesh with the help of 15 grassroots NGOs. CWS feels that the PRI policy advocacy is most frustrating because MLAs (Members of Legislative Assembly) and political leaders are opposed to the promotion of PRIs. This is despite the same party in government at the state level and the Union level. Out of 29 items in the 11th Schedule of the Constitution, the devolved items are only nine by the first term government of Late Y.S. Rajasekhara Reddy (i.e., 2004-2009). This also is because elections were round the corner in 2009. PRIs are an electoral issue. From 2004 to 2009 nothing was done. APARD (Andhra Pradesh Academy of Rural Development) has done activity mapping for different tiers of PRIs long ago but the G.O.s related to devolution of powers are not in tune with the activity mapping.

Currently CWS is nodal agency for implementing PMEYSA (*Panchayat Mahila Evam Yuva Shakti Abhiyan*) of the Government of India. As part of this programme, CWS holds meetings of women representatives of about 500 from all the three tiers of PRIs. One of the major demands of the CWS was that within six months of the PRI elections, all the women representatives should be provided capacity building trainings. And CWS was successful in this and separate trainings were imparted to women representative from all over Andhra Pradesh. The Andhra Pradesh Academy of Rural Development has conducted one session of trainings for all the elected representatives coming from all parts of the State and has conducted separate trainings for women representatives from all over the State. CWS considers this to be one of its success stories vis-à-vis government. The scale at which trainings are required inevitably needs the government to take up the work.

Another success story of CWS in influencing government has been vis-à-vis PESA [29] (Panchayat Extension to Scheduled Areas) draft rules. The advocacy for this began when CWS held a long meeting of 1,000 tribals on PESA, which was attended by senior State level officials. Advocacy for pro-tribal PESA rules began with this meeting. Finally, the rules were accepted by the government of AP.

Draft Rules, as of 2010, have been sent by the GoAP to all the Departments and now they need to be finalized after the inputs from all the concerned departments. This work brings to notice the point that in the case of PRIs the advocacy is difficult, arduous, painstaking and slow; the results are not dramatically visible and the role of civil society does not come out clearly in the final instance. Third aspect of successful work of CWS was the restoration of power to issues cheques by Panchayat Sarpanches. In this case the Sarpanches Association along with CWS made protests, sit-ins (*Dharnas*) and demonstrations and as a result of this the cheque issuance powers were restored to elected representatives.

Summing up, we should say in the first case the CWS has been successful to get the women elected representatives trained in PRI laws and rules by the Andhra Pradesh government. In the second case CWS has considerably influenced the PESA rules of Andhra Pradesh government. This was done with the help of a partner NGO called *Laya* [30] and taking professional legal help. In the third instance of PRI work, the advocacy was regarding restoring the power to Gram Panchayat (village council) Presidents to issue cheques. Though these three successes appear small successes, given the context of Andhra Pradesh policy environment, they are major successes. But overall, CWS perceives PRI advocacy as extremely difficult because it directly deals with political power. PRI policy influence is 'the toughest nut.'

Centre for Sustainable Agriculture (CSA) [31]

Work on WASSAN (Watershed Support Services and Activities Network—a solidarity institution founded by CWS) and work on Centre for Sustainable Agriculture (CSA) also started from CWS and then the work branched out into full organizations. CSA was born out of Non-Pesticidal Management work at CWS. The work which began in CWS as NPM desk in 1989 branched out as CSA in 2002. The initial work showed that limited work on one single crop was not enough and the work had to be extended. Later, organic agricultural production as well as marketing of organic agricultural product was taken up. The CSA's work evolved in the following stages:

1. Promotion and advocacy for non-pesticidal management (NPM) of farming.
2. Promotion of organic farming and marketing of organic farming produce.
3. Advocacy of changes in seed policy of the Union government.

One crucial fact about the work of CSA is that it has not only been aimed at changing government policy but also aimed at educating public; and raising public consciousness about the positive outcomes of organic agriculture, and negative impact of GM foods. These both went hand in hand so far as the work is concerned. The advocacy on Bt.Brinjal had become very popular. The attempt of CSA to raise the level of public reason on specific issues related to the above aspects was considerable. And it must also be noted that the CSA made its advocacy after having conducted field trials of non-pesticidal management of agriculture; after experimenting with organic agriculture; and after sowing and examining the growth patterns of GM seeds. [32]

Another important point is that the engagement of CSA with the governments at the State as well as union levels has not just been that of collaborator. It has been that of critic of the government policies too. CSA is opposed to GM crops and chemical and pesticidal agriculture; and in this context it is continuously engaged in battles with agricultural and environment ministries of State and Union governments. Therefore, it is wrong to assume that the civil society role is always playing second fiddle to the government. Besides being critical about government policies the CSA has also been opposed to the multi national corporations that produce and sell GM seeds such as Monsanto, Cargill, Mahyco and others. These seed companies have been at the forefront of promoting GM seeds in the sectors on non-food crops such as Bt.Cotton and food crops such as Bt.Brinjal.

Discussion

The study of two civil society organizations shows that while Myrada adopted a more conciliatory approach to the state, CWS in Andhra Pradesh adopted both conciliatory and adversarial approaches. These NGOs engage the state at various levels. The CWS approach vis-à-vis PRI-empowerment brought the organization directly into a combination of conciliatory and conflicting role.

At the same time, CWS and CSA's approach towards genetically modified food and non-food crops held the centre-state and the local state quite at loggerheads. The point is also that CSA's approach has also been critical towards multinational seed companies such as Monsanto, Mahyco and Kargill. Therefore the question is in the context of globalisation and supposedly prominent role of civil society, how effective are they? The point however is that they still happen to be subsidiary partners in the paradigm of 'governance-through-networks'. Major influence on public policy still happens to be in the hands of the multinational donor organizations as well as multinational companies.

End Notes

1. A useful review of these definitions can be seen in Elliott 2003, Jayaram 2005, Carothers and Brandt, 1999-2000.
2. For the discussion of L-stream and M-stream in civil society study see: Misztal, 2001.

3. See for an update on the research in political science on civil society and the state: Chambers and Kopstein, 2006.
4. Kennedy and Galtz (1996); In the aftermath of the velvet revolutions the interest in Marxism has dissipated in Eastern Europe. Kennedy and Galtz, for example, wrote:
   'It is difficult to see socialism as an empirical or positive reference or Marxism as theoretical tradition alive in East European intellectual debate today. Sometimes Marxism is discussed by East European scholars to demonstrate its ideological rigidity and inflexibility...More often it is ignored.' (pp. 448-449) and they write:
   'There are occasions when Marxism is engaged, but these attempts often appear as part of bygone era, when the Communist Party still mattered to Marxism. Konrad Weiss [East European scholar] felt obliged to address Marxism only when asked to discuss the survival of utopias; and though he still identifies himself as a socialist, he believes Marxism could only inevitably degenerate into dystopia...In Russia, specifically, which is so often located as both the heart of communism and the heart of its failure, vibrant academic engagement with Marxism is all but dead in any discipline...' (pp. 449-450). Of course Kennedy and Galtz also quote Michael Burawoy as saying, "...Marxism still provides a fecund understanding of capitalism's inherent contradictions and dynamics...[Thus], the longevity of capitalism guarantees the longevity of Marxism" (Buroway, 1990: 792).
5. Shigetomi (ed.) 2002, pp. 1-32; Shigetomi says: 'When the systems of market, state and community fail to perform their resource-distributing functions properly, there is room for NGOs to emerge as fourth category of agents to distribute resources on their own or to interfere with the existing distribution systems, making up for or correcting their shortcomings' (Shigetomi: pp. 10-11).
6. Various definitions of public policy and the non-positivistic usage of the term are amply explained in Wedel, Lathrop 2005.
7. Hyden, Court and Mease, 2005.
8. Munshi et al., 2009, pp. 1-25.
9. Mbogori and Chigudu, 2005.
10. KHDR, 2005 and Aloysius, 2004.
11. Government of Karnataka, 2005.

12. Rajasekhar and Birader (eds.), 2004.
13. Kudva Neema (2008); Kudwa also notes that 'Karnataka is fourth largest recipient state of foreign funds [as on 2002] with organisations located in Bangalore receiving about 70 percent of funds', pp. 136-137; First being Delhi, second Tamil Nadu and third Andhra Pradesh. Kudwa: Table 6.2-B, pp. 134-135.
14. The abbreviations *MYRADA* and *Myrada* are used interchangeably in the text.
15. MYRADA, 2010.
16. Interview with Mr. Aloysius Prakash Fernandez, Member Secretary, Governing Body of Myrada on 12-10-09.
17. Interview with Mr. Aloysius Prakash Fernandez, Member Secretary, Governing Body of Myrada on 12-10-09. He said 'you can not change policy through *bhashan* [i.e., through a lecture to the government].
18. Interview with Mr. Aloysius Fernandez at Myrada on 13-1-2010.
19. Interestingly, Neema Kudwa quotes from one of the publications of Myrada in which Aloysius Fernandez categorizes government officials into three categories: levels A,B and C. Level A officials are the IAS and IFS level officials who are often in synergistic relationship with the NGO sector; Level B official who operate at the district and taluk levels at the supervisory level, and are often uncomfortable with NGOs; and Level C officials who directly interact with the citizens and are the ones who "normally relate well with the NGO staff". Kudwa: 131-132.
20. Interview with Dr. S.S. Meenakshi Sundaram at Myrada on 29-11-2010.
21. CWS' vision is stated in the following words: '[CWS] envisions a society of resilient, inter-dependent small communities, vibrant with the consciousness of their rights and duties ad sensitive to the rights of Dalits, indigenous people and minorities, to women's rights generally and to gender equality, to the rights of children and to eco-friendly development processes that cohere with the rights of these sections' CWS: 'Partnering With People' (2009).
22. This section and also subsequent sections are based on views of individuals belonging to the organisations concerned and are absolutely important for this study as some of these individuals are founders of the institutions or are key individuals heading the

institutions; or are holding key positions within the institutions; therefore the views expressed by them represent the crystallized experience of the organizational memory and therefore of significance.

23. Interview with Shri M.V.Sastri on 26-10-2009, Hyderabad; Shri M.V. Sastri besides being the founder of CWS and all the solidarity organizations is also the doyen of the NGO sector in Andhra Pradesh and as such these views are fairly representative of the views of the broader NGO sector in AP.
24. Ibid.
25. Ibid.
26. Interview with Shri M.V.Sastri on.26-10-2009.
27. Details are given below.
28. This section is based on interviews with officials of CWS, Dr. C. Vijaya Shyamala; Mr. N. Sambashiva Rao and Shri M.V.Sastri of CWS during 20th to 26th July, 2010.
29. There are a total of 9 Scheduled districts in Andhra Pradesh namely Adilabad, Khammam, Warangal, Mahabubnagar, East Godavari, West Godavari, Srikakulam, Vishakhapatnam, and Vijayanagarm. CWS work covers all the nine districts through grassroots partners and these have also formed into a state level PESA network by CWS.
30. CWS and *Laya* have taken help of a lawyer called Mr. Trinath Rao to draft rules for the PESA Andhra Pradesh Act and these have been accepted by the A.P. government for incorporation.
31. The information on this is based on interviews with Dr. G.V. Ramanjaneyulu, Executive Director of CSA and with Shri MV. Sastri, Honorary Convener CWS and the other staff members of CSA and the documents provided by them.
32. The work of CSA has been documented in *Down to Earth, The Ecologist, Economic and Political Weekly* and the journal *Seedling* and widely in the News papers and national TV channels such as NDTV.

References

Baviskar, B.S. (2005), 'Non-governmental Organizations and Civil Society in India', in N. Jayaram, (ed.), Civil Society: Issues and Perspectives, Sage, New Delhi.

Bevir, Mark (2009), Key Concepts in Governance, Sage, London.

Blau, Judith (ed.) (2001), Blackwell Companion to Sociology,

Blackwell, Oxford.

Carothers, Thomas and William Brandt (2000), "Civil Society", *Foreign Policy*, No. 117, Winter.

Chambers, Simone and Jeffrey Kopstein (2006), 'Civil Society and the State' in: John S. Dryzek, Bonnie Honig and Anne Phillips (ed.) The Oxford Handbook of Political Theory, OUP, Oxford.

Chitlangi, B.M. (2008), "The Concept of Good Governance: The World Bank Perspective", *Prashasnika,* 35(1).

de Tocqueville, Alexis (1965) in Commanger, Henry Steele (ed.), Democracy in America, OUP, London.

Down to Earth (2006), "Out of the Trap: Andhra Farms Show the Future of Pest Management: It Doesn't Have Pesticides', *Down to Earth,* May 31.

Dryzek, John S., Bonnie Honig and Anne Phillips (2006) (eds.), Oxford Handbook of Political Theory, OUP, Oxford.

Eade, Deborah and Ernst Ligteringen (2001) (ed.), Debating Development: NGOs and the Future, Oxfam, Dorset.

Elliott, Carolyn M. (2003) (ed.), Civil Society and Democracy: A Reader, OUP, Delhi.

Ezra Mbogori and Hope Chigudu (2005), 'Civil Society and Government: A Continuum of Possibilities' in Civil Society at the Millennium, Civicus and Kumarian Press, Connecticut.

Femia, Joseph (2001), 'Civil Society and the Marxist Tradition' in Sudipta Kaviraj and Sunil Khilnani (ed.), Civil Society: History and Possibilities, CUP, Cambridge.

Fernandez, Aloysius Prakash (2002), People's Institutions for the Sustained and Equitable Management of Micro-Watersheds: The Myrada Experience, Myrada, Bangalore.

Fernandez, Aloysius Prakash (2003), Putting Institutions First: Even in Micro Finance, MYRADA, Bangalore.

Fernandez, Aloysius Prakash (2004), "NGOs and Government in Collaboration for Development", *Rural Management Systems Series,* Paper No. 39, Myrada, Bangalore.

Ghose, Bhasker (2010), "Give NGOs a Chance", *Frontline,* July 2.

Government of Karnataka (2005), Investing in Human Development: Karnataka Human Development Report 2005, Government of Karnataka, Bangalore.

Grain (2008), "Saying 'no' to Chemical Farming in India", *Seedling,* July.

Grindle, Merilee S. (1999), "In Quest of the Political: The Political Economy of Development Policy Making", *Working Paper No. 17*, Centre for International Development, Harvard University.

Harriss, John (2001), "Social Capital Construction and the Consolidation of Civil Society in Rural Areas or Public Action and Rural Development", *DESTIN Working Paper No. 01-16*, Development Studies Institute, London School of Economics and Political Science, London.

Hyden, Goran, Julius Court and Kenneth Mease (2003), "Civil Society and Governance in 16 Developing Countries", *World Governance Survey Discussion Paper 4*, Overseas Development Institute, London.

Hyden, Goran, Julius Court and Kenneth Mease (2005), Making Sense of Governance: Empirical Evidence from Sixteen Developing Countries, Viva Books, New Delhi.

Jayaram, N. (2005) (ed.), On Civil Society: Issues and Perspectives, Sage, New Delhi.

Kadekodi, G.K., Ravi Kanbur and Vijayendra Rao (2008) (ed.), Development in Karnataka: Challenges of Equity and Empowerment, Academic Foundation, New Delhi.

Kaviraj, Sudipta and Sunil Khilnani (2001) (ed.), Civil Society: History and Possibilities, CUP, Cambridge.

Kennedy, Michael D. and Naomi Galtz (1996), "From Marxism to Postcommunism: Socialist Desires and East European Rejections", *Annual Review of Sociology*, Vol. 22.

Kudva, Neema (2008), 'Conceptualizing NGO-State Relations in Karnataka: Conflict and Collaboration Amidst Organizational Diversity' in: Kadekodi, G.K, Ravi Kanbur and Vijayendra Rao (ed.), Development in Karnataka: Challenges of Equity and Empowerment, Academic Foundation, New Delhi.

Marten, Gerry and Donna Glee Williams (2007), "Getting Clean: Recovering from Pesticide Addiction', *The Ecologist*, December 2006/January 2007.

Mbogori, Ezra and Hope Chigudu (2005), 'Civil Society and Government: A Continuum of Possibilities' in Civil Society at the Millennium, Civicus and Kumarian Press, Connecticut.

Misztal, Barbara A. (2001), 'Civil Society: a Signifier of Plurality and Sense of Wholeness' in Judith R. Blau (ed.), The Blackwell Companion to Sociology, Blackwell, Oxford.

Munshi, Surendra, Biju Paul Abraham and Soma Choudhuri (2009), 'The Concept of Good Governance' in The Intelligent Person's Guide to Good Governance, Sage, New Delhi.

MYRADA (2010), 'MYRADA: Past, Present and Future: An Agency Profile', Myrada, Bangalore.

Popoviski, Vesselin, G. Shabbir Cheema, Cameron Lowry and Mark Notaras (2008), "Governance through Civil Society Engagement in Asia", *Policy Brief No. 7*, United Nations University, Tokyo.

PRIA (2002), "Invisible, Yet Widespread: The Non-Profit Sector in India", Society for Participatory Research in Asia, New Delhi.

Quinn, Aoife Gilligan (2008), "Social Capital: An Assessment of its Relevance as a Conceptual and Policy Tool", *Voluntary Sector Working Paper 9*, Centre for Civil Society, The London School of Economics and Political Science.

Rajasekhar, D. and R.R. Birader (eds.) (2004), Reluctant Partners Coming Together? Interface between People, Government and the NGOs, Concept, New Delhi.

Ramanjaneyulu, G.V. and Kavitha Kuruganti (2010), Bt Cotton in India: Sustainable Pest Management?, Mimeo, CSA, Hyderabad.

Seminar (2010), 'Karnataka Vignettes: A Symposium on Emerging Trends in Contemporary Karnataka', *Seminar,* 612, August.

Sen, Siddhartha (1999), "Some Aspects of State-NGO Relationships in India in the Post-Independence Era", *Development and Change*, 30.

Shigetomi, Shinchi (2002) (ed.), 'The State and NGOs: Issues and Analytical Framework' in Shinchi Shigetomi, The State and NGOs: Perspectives from Asia, Institute of South East Asian Studies, Singapore.

Stoker, Gerry (1998), "Governance as Theory: Five Propositions", *International Social Science Journal*, 155/1998.

Vakil, Anna C. (1997), "Confronting the Classification Problem: Towards a Taxonomy of NGOs", *World Development*, 25(12).

Van Der Zweerde, Evert (1996), "Civil Society and Ideology: A Matter of Freedom", *Studies in East European Thought*, Vol. 48, No. 2/4.

Warren, Mark E. (1999), 'Civil Society and Good Governance', Washington: Centre for Study of Voluntary Organizations and Services, Georgetown Public Policy Institute, Georgetown University.

Wedel, Shore, Lathrop Feldman (2005), 'Toward an Anthropology of

Public Policy', *Annals of the American Academy of Political and Social Science*, Vol. 600.

8

Globalization and Swadeshi

D. Jeevan Kumar

The word *globalization* is now used to sum up the contemporary world order. It refers to the integration of the world into one capitalist political economy, operating under a neo-liberal free market ideology. The trend is present in a shift from a world economy based on national market economies that trade and investments link together, to a single borderless global market economy, increasingly governed by *one* set of rules.

Globalization operates through four increasing "webs" of global commercial activity: the global cultural bazaar, the global shopping mall, the global financial networks and the global workplace. The global cultural bazaar promotes the notion of uniform cultural values and products across the world. It influences billions of people by homogenizing their tastes and preferences towards a fantasy lifestyle. Global trade has created a planetary super-market. The cultural bazaar and shopping mall intersect through the vehicle of advertising. The media has become a powerful player in the globalization process. In fact, globalization of the world has also led to the globalization of the media. The media is used to impose the culture of the North. All this proves that globalization is not a simple but a complex set of processes that operates at multiple levels—political, economic, social and cultural.

Nikhil Aziz argues that we can see globalization in different perspectives. At the political level, they reflect Western countries and global financial institutions pressurizing countries in the South to democratize (Nikhil Aziz, 1995: 23). This translates into the adoption of a Western-style liberal democratic system of governance.

This closely ties economic globalization to the political aspect in that: (i) the sources of pressure for change are the same; and (ii) close links are forged between the ideologies of free markets and free societies. Economic globalization entails countries of the South to accept—within the parameters of the dominant world capital system—the imposition of structural adjustment programmes and neo-liberal economic policies, including the wholesale liberalization of domestic economies, to allow unrestricted entry to trans-national capital. On a cultural level, globalization arises from the control of the global information and communication networks by Western media corporations, the spread of modern technologies of a consumerist nature, and Western cultural expressions as *the* global culture.

Since the concept of globalization is frequently employed, but rarely defined clearly, Arie Kacowicz (Arie Kacowicz, 1999: 54) includes the following, among the "possible definitions" of globalization:

1. Intensification of economic, political, social and cultural relations across borders;
2. The historical period (or historical epoch) launched since the end of the Cold War;
3. The transformation of the world economy epitomised by anarchy (literally defined) of the financial markets;
4. The triumph of US values, through the combined agenda of neo-liberalism in economics and political democracy;
5. An ideology and an orthodoxy about the logical and inevitable culmination of the powerful tendencies of the market at work;
6. A technological revolution, with social implications; and
7. The inability of the nation-states to cope with global problems that require global solutions, such as demography, ecology, human rights and nuclear proliferation.

Although globalization is definitely not a new concept or phenomenon, the current phase has distinctive features. As pointed out by Susan Willett, technological developments have decisively compressed the traditional barriers of time and space. Information can be transferred from one side of the world to another in real time, creating global simultaneity (Susan Willett, 2001: 67). This has enabled production to be structured in global factories, linking workers across the world. Electronic retailing has enabled 'just-in-time' stocktaking and production that transcend geo-spatial boundaries.

In the financial sector, rapid communications have linked capital markets across the world, resulting in a 24-hour global financial market. Improved air transportation allows for the physical transference of people and goods from one location to another, with unprecedented ease. The Internet enables cyber communities to flourish, creating or reinforcing trans-border identities. In the military area, 'over-the-horizon' weapons systems utilizing a combination of satellites, communication and computer systems, can hit targets on the other side of the world, breaking down territorial notions of warfare. The result is that across the spectrum of human endeavour, traditional boundaries and identities are breaking down.

Scholars like Kenichi Ohmae claim that globalization is enhanced through the subjugation of people and states to market liberalization and deregulation, privatization and economic integration (Kenichi Ohmae, 1995: 90). The global spread of capitalism reinforces the sense of an emerging global civilization defined by universal standards of economic and political organization. This global civilization is effusive with its own instruments for global governance, whether in the form of the IMF, the IBRD, the WTO or markets. These institutions promulgate the neo-liberal discourse on globalization and, via their considerable international leverage, have incorporated most of the developing world and transition economies into the post-Cold War liberal order. Accordingly, globalization is the harbinger of a radical new world order which presages the demise of the nation-state.

Sceptics such as Hirst and Thompson view this notion of

globalization as illusory; arguing that the international economy is no more integrated now than the world economy was in the 19th century (P. Hirst and G. Thompson, 1996: 102). It is however increasingly segmented into three powerful trading blocs, centred on North America, Western Europe and Japan, in which the state remains strong and highly regulatory. The benefits of globalization are concentrated in these developed and powerful states to the exclusion of the rest of the world. This sceptical position acknowledges the deeply-rooted patterns of inequality and hierarchy in the global economy. Such inequality contributes to the advance of fundamentalism and nationalism, so that, contrary to the neo-liberal notion of the emergence of a homogenized culture, the global order is fragmenting into civilizational blocs and ethnic enclaves.

Analysts such as Giddens (A. Giddens, 1990: 86) and Rosenau (Rosenau, 1998: 30) regard globalization as historically unprecedented in that states and societies across the globe are encountering a process of profound change as they adapt to a more inter-connected but highly uncertain world. The previously clear distinction between international and domestic, external and internal affairs, are breaking down on such a scale that the global order is being profoundly transformed. According to this viewpoint, where this transformation is leading is unclear, as globalization is a long historical process with many contradictory characteristics.

Nevertheless, new patterns of global stratification are emerging, in which some states and societies are becoming increasingly integrated into the global order, while others are becoming increasingly marginalized. Power, functions and authority are being re-engineered away from the nation-state and onto the international stage in the form of international law and new economic and political organizations, whose authority transcends national boundaries. Complex global systems, from the financial to the ecological, connect the fate of communities from one locale to another across the globe. In this account, globalization is associated with the unravelling of the relationship between sovereignty, territoriality and state power.

Dynamics of Globalization

There is no doubt that the trans-nationalization of economic life is an outstanding contemporary development. Proponents of the globalization thesis even state that globalization is inherently neither good nor bad! It is acceleration in the movement of information, capital, trade and labour. This leads to integration of national economies and growing interdependence between nations. It is speeding up because information technology has massively increased the speed with which information and knowledge can be moved about. Following the end of the Cold War, the global economy is less divided, and trade, investment and even labour mobility barriers are coming down. This is creating a global community not just of economics but of human concern and values. We now have more democracy than ever before. Humanity increasingly sees itself as one. If well managed, globalization enhances the prospect of eliminating extreme poverty from the world—enabling all children to go to school, giving all people access to basic health care, and providing everyone with enough for a decent life.

Opponents of the globalization thesis, however, are equally vehement that the thesis is based on misconceptions and myths that stem from a historical construction of social reality, and from plain misunderstandings about the processes and social forces that are reshaping the world economy.

A closer look at the dynamics of globalization is necessary in order to understand the arguments of both schools of thought. At the outset, it needs to be emphasized that the location of globalization in the ideological discourse is imperative. Once this is done, globalization presents itself as the process aiming at the universalization of capitalism. There is no disagreement on the fact that the market plays a very important role in capitalism, and that behind the dictates of the capital market are the three imperatives of competition—

increasing labour productivity, profit maximization and capital accumulation.

Does capitalism produce eternal growth and prosperity? Critics point out that capitalist systems experience economic instability. While they do grow rapidly and produce prosperity, capitalist economies are also accompanied by business slumps, recession and stagflation. Capitalism also creates inequalities in the distribution of wealth. Karl Marx described it as the fetishism of commodities resulting in the promotion of unbridled consumerism and the commodification of women (Edwards, Reich and Weisskopf, 1972: 12-32). Marx further branded capitalism as the ultimate dehumanization of man, because it rewards the affluent, gifted, intelligent and privileged, but penalizes the weak, the handicapped and the poor. But, by far, the most serious charge against the ideology is the promotion of colonialism in the past and neo-colonialism today.

According to Andre Gunder Frank, (Edwards, Reich and Weisskopf, 1972: 12-32) the three internal contradictions of capitalism are:

1. The polarization of the capitalist system into metropolitan centres and peripheral satellites;
2. The expropriation of economic surplus from the many, and its appropriation by the few; and
3. The continuity of the fundamental structure of the capitalist system throughout the history of its expansion and transformation.

According to Samir Amin (Amin, 1998: 45) there are two new contradictions:

1. The erosion of the auto-centred nation-state and the subsequent disappearance of the link between the arena of reproduction and accumulation, together with the weakening of political and social control, which had hitherto been defined precisely by the frontiers of this auto-centred nation-state; and
2. The erosion of the great divide: industrialized centre/non-

industrialized peripheral regions, and the emergence of new dimensions of polarization.

These capitalist contradictions have generated underdevelopment in the peripheral satellites whose economic surplus was expropriated, while generating economic development in the metropolitan centres which appropriate that surplus. The structure and development of the capitalist system on an integrated world scale creates a contradictory development which generates, at once, economic development and underdevelopment on international, national, local and sectoral levels. For the generation of structural underdevelopment, more important than the drain of economic surplus is the impregnation of the satellites' domestic economies with the same capitalist structure, with all its fundamental contradictions. This, then, is what is happening in the name of globalization, involving the operation of what Samir Amin describes as 'the five monopolies':

1. Technological monopoly.
2. Financial control of world-wide financial markets.
3. Monopolistic access to the planet's natural resources.
4. Media and communication monopolies.
5. Monopolies over weapons of mass destruction.

For a better comprehension of the process, it would be useful to take a look at the role of major actors in the process.

The *Group of Seven* countries are undoubtedly behind the globalization process, since they represent the world's leading industrialized nations which are convinced that capitalism was instrumental in their development, and that what was good for them should be good enough for the rest of the world. Through a variety of devices, the G-7 has succeeded in imposing its globalization agenda on the rest of the world, its work having been rendered facile by the disintegration of the Soviet Union, and the transition economies consequently looking to the West for material and moral support.

The G-7's globalization agenda has, and is, being imposed on the rest of the world through multilateral lending institutions like the World Bank and the International Monetary Fund, particularly through the ingenious structural adjustment programmes (SAPs), which have been applied widely through much of the Third World. The SAP menu includes devaluation of national currencies, market liberalization, elimination of subsidies, de-indexation of wages and liberalization of the labour market. SAPs also call for liberalization of trade and the elimination of protective trade barriers, privatization of state development banks in agriculture and industry, promotion of commercial agriculture, privatization of state enterprises, privatization of social programmes including health and education, and so on.

According to Michael Chossudovsky, SAPs involve a massive disengagement of human and material resources (Chossudovsky, 1997: 118). The 'economic stabilization' package produces economic disarray, destroys the endogenous base of economic development and generates fundamental dislocations in the structure of the state. More generally, the various measures—which, in theory, are intended to generate a surplus from which Third World debt will be repaid—accomplish exactly the opposite of financial solvency. The solution to the debt crisis therefore becomes the cause of further indebtedness.

Since 1995, the Bretton Woods twins have been converted to a trinity, with the establishment of the World Trade Organization (WTO). The three main functions of the WTO are:

1. To provide a framework for the implementation of GATT objectives.
2. To review the trade policies of member-countries.
3. To cooperate with the World Bank and the International Monetary Fund in monitoring and enforcing a market-based global strategy.

What makes the WTO more formidable than the World Bank and the IMF is the power it possesses to enforce its will and decisions, by a variety of means, ranging from cross-sectoral retaliation to expulsion. What is even more alarming is that its jurisdiction extends beyond the realm of trade proper. WTO's reach covers four new areas that were untouched by

GATT—agriculture, services, intellectual property rights and investments. All these are areas that have attained sophisticated levels of development in the First World, and globalization provides the key to internationalize this dominance.

Take the case of intellectual property rights (IPRs). By the conversion of a patent into an intellectual property right, the WTO has conferred monopoly rights upon transnational companies (TNCs), instead of protecting the inventor. Moreover, enlargement of patent protection to cover the product rather than the process, is clearly calculated to serve the interests of TNCs, which seek to retain monopoly control of their products. The consequences of the IPR regime on the Third World are alarming, to say the least. Not only does it freeze the North-South technology gap and make products like drugs and medicines frightfully expensive, the patents on genetic material and seeds will further impoverish peasants in the Third World.

Investment measures are not yet a part of the WTO's business, but strong efforts are being made by the G-7 to incorporate a foreign investment treaty known as the Multilateral Agreement on Investments (MAI), within the framework of the WTO. The MAI constitutes a Bill of Rights for TNCs—a *carte blanche* to go wherever they like and do business on their own terms, with practically no restrictions on their functioning.

Can developing countries afford to be naïve in dealing with TNCs? No doubt, TNCs have transformed the world economy by ushering in the Second Industrial Revolution, which perhaps prompted Henry Kissinger to describe them as one of the most effective engines of development.

But it is also true that TNCs distort development priorities in host economies. They rarely set up basic and heavy industries in infrastructure sectors. They prefer to manufacture sophisticated products catering primarily to demands of the local elites. They reinforce dualistic economic structures, exacerbate income inequalities, and worsen the imbalance between urban and rural sectors. They widen wage differentials by promoting the interests of a small number of modern sector workers. TNCs create dependence on discarded technologies. They promote inappropriate, capital-intensive technologies of production, and stimulate inappropriate consumption patterns. They suppress domestic entrepreneurship, drive out local competition, and inhibit the growth of small-scale and cottage industry sectors. No small wonder, then, that Ronald Muller and Richard Barnet describe TNCs as one of the most powerful impediments of Third World development.

Consequences of Globalization

The following consequences of globalization have been well documented (Hildyard et al., 1996: 77):

1. Globalization has created a situation where the role and importance of nation-states are becoming irrelevant. Kenichi Ohmae raises the question that in a world where economic borders are disappearing and money flows around the globe beyond the reach of governments, who, indeed, needs the nation-state? He argues that the four "I's"—Investment, Industry, Information Technology and Individual Consumers—make the traditional "middleman" function of nation-states, and of their governments, largely unnecessary.
2. A few rich or middle class people have emerged in societies where transition to market systems have been introduced. China and Vietnam are typical examples for the emergence of a *nouveau riche* class, as a result of globalization and market reforms, at the expense of the poor. These new rich and middle classes are really the products of globalization, and they provide the market for imported products.
3. Mergers and acquisitions that companies have undertaken in the pursuit of global reach are causing major job losses, even in the West. In the United States, where merger

mania in the 1980s led to massive job losses, new rounds of acquisitions are underway. In the defence industry, the 1995 merger of aircraft makers, Northrop, Grumann and Vought led to 14,000 job losses from a workforce of 53,000. The Lockheed Martin merger resulted in the closing of 12 factories and 12,000 redundancies.

4. Under globalization, for firms seeking to reduce labour costs, their objective is to relocate to those areas where labour is cheapest; for those seeking to establish retail outlets, to those areas where incomes are highest; and for those seeking to set up service industries such as advertising or banking, to wherever other service industries are already concentrated. In many countries, high technology sectors such as electronics are favoured over more traditional industrial sectors; likewise, areas of cheap or unorganized labour are preferred over areas where wages are high or where trade unions are strong. This is reinforcing regional disparities.
5. Workers and the communities, in which they live, are forced to compete against each other to attract the inward investment that will create jobs. As unemployment rises and jobs become more insecure, communities seeking to ensure that new jobs are available and to retain old ones, are vulnerable to what has been termed 'regulatory arbitrage'. To attract new investment, governments must bid and counter-bid against each other, as companies with capital to invest, play one regional government off against another, in order to gain the best overall package—the lowest corporate taxes, the weakest unions, the most flexible rules on working conditions, the most lax health and safety regulations, and so on. National governments, both in the North and South, are engaged in the same race to the bottom.
6. Globalization has adversely affected the bargaining position of labour. With capital, and companies, free to move across borders, the scope for playing workers and communities off

against each other in order to gain concessions on wages and conditions—has greatly expanded. Worldwide, capital and companies are on the move. What began as a one-way dribble of relocations in the 1950s (as Northern companies moved their manufacturing to the South) is now a steady flow, "with new locations endlessly replacing old, as new demands and new advantages emerge"? Demands for higher wages in one country are met with threats to transfer production out of the country altogether. In some cases, the threats are real; in others, they are not. Either way, the bargaining position of labour is being compromised.

7. As free market policies create a pool of "surplus labour", increasing numbers of people are forced to migrate in search of work, pricing other workers out of the market, and creating yet more downward pressure on wages. Migrant workers have long been used by capital as a source of cheap labour and a tool for driving down the rates of pay. Doubly discriminated as *aliens* and as the lowest paid workers, migrants frequently work and live in atrocious conditions and are invariably subject to racial 'scapegoating', especially during times of high unemployment. N. Harris calls them the 'New Untouchables' and describes their condition thus: *The misery of the unemployed and the low-skilled in the developed countries is painfully visible in the great cities, nearly as painful now as the poverty of the developing countries...The political establishments need easy targets in order to deflect any anger that might be targeted against them...and few governments can resist the temptation to blame the immigrant.*
8. Full employment has been abandoned as the goal of governments. Instead, to satisfy the demands of global financial markets, macro-economic policy is directed to controlling inflation, regardless of the costs in terms of jobs and social welfare.
9. In developing countries, global corporations are allowed to feast on natural resources, human resources and national

wealth. They displace farmers from their land, workers from their jobs, and communities from their roots. They are responsible for the breaking up of communities and the destruction of the environment to serve the human and raw material requirements of global production for the global market. The consequence is the collapse of our food security and the emergence of global environmental crises. Global capitalism has ensured that more than a billion of the world's people live in absolute poverty. More than 15 million people die each year as a result of poverty. At the same time, the principle of profit maximization which goes completely unchecked under the pretext of operating in a global market, threatens the world with an ecological disaster. The tropical forests, already eliminated by more than 40 percent, are disappearing "at a rate of 30,000 to 37,000 sq. miles every year", as multinational companies are having a field day under free trade and free market legislation.

Indeed, the ecological effects of globalization are strikingly catastrophic. Under the fiscal pressures imposed by capital movements, the Third World state, in particular, sells off more and more of its public resources—forests, mining regions, natural reserves and maritime resources. In this context, it is obvious that the greater the external integration, the greater the exploitation of domestic resources to fuel overseas expansion.

10. One of the main consequences of accelerated globalization has been the intensification of human insecurity. Increased economic insecurity is at the centre of the rising spiral of human insecurity. The key contributory factors to economic insecurity are intensified competition, internationalization of production, changes in the methods of production, surges of financial speculation, and rapidity of technological innovations. Even people with jobs have experienced deterioration in conditions of employment, as reflected in the decline of employment security; the

increase in casual and part-time work; the increase in work pressure from employers; and the need for constant adjustment to rapidly changing circumstances.

These sources of economic insecurity have been reinforced by changes in government policies in the field of income re-distribution and social security. Influenced by new ideologies, governments in most countries have been cutting down on subsidies on items of mass consumption, increasing charges for social services, and reducing the level and range of benefits under social security and welfare programmes.

The sources of insecurity are to be found in other domains of human activities. In the sphere of politics, the close bonds between political parties and their supporters have become loosened in recent years; workers, the unemployed and other categories of low-income groups lack confidence in the traditional parties to defend their interests.

It is not surprising to find a growing disenchantment and lack of interest in the political process. In the social domain, the weakening of community and family structures has contributed to increased personal insecurity. In the sphere of culture, the clash between traditional values and those propagated by the media and the consumerist society, has contributed to conflicts and uncertainty.

The void so created, is filled increasingly by ethnic and religious bodies. Such organizations supply material needs, cultural identity and secure values. Unfortunately, in many circumstances, these organizations also espouse extremist causes characterized by intolerance, exclusion, hatred and violence. Material deprivation and cultural crises provide fertile hunting ground for the operation of fundamentalist forces. The consequences are religious and ethnic violence.

Globalization and Human Rights

The trends and consequences of globalization need to be understood from a human rights perspective. One area where the impact of globalization on human rights is very clearly visible is industry. It would not be an exaggeration to state that globalization has resulted in the violation of the fundamental right to work. With mergers and acquisitions and the consequent restructuring of operations, TNCs, for instance, are becoming 'leaner and meaner', and generating unemployment in the process.

The capitalist *mantras* of 'privatization', 'corporatization', 'just-in-time' production, 'contractualization' and the like are producing similar consequences. Statistics from an ILO Report of 1995 document the fact that at least one-third of the world's willing-to-work population is either under-employed or unemployed.

Further, globalization has engendered or accentuated the process of casualization and informalization of labour. It is the TNC in its quest for more and more profit, and lesser and lesser accountability, which initiated the worldwide trends of 'sub-contracting' and 'leasing out' unprofitable operations. These innovations have been picked up by public sector units, and even governments, all over the world, in the name of liberalization and privatization. Consequently, it is becoming increasingly the order of the day to employ workers on part-time or short-term contracts, thereby revealing an utter disregard for their human rights.

Another fallout of globalization is the feminization of labour. As more and more women are forced to look for employment, an overwhelming majority of this labour is being concentrated in low-wage industries like textiles and footwear production. These industries are notorious for exploiting their workers by denying them job security and the right to organize, and subjecting them to long working hours, without the most basic of amenities.

Globalization has adversely affected traditional cottage industries, too. With the entry of the TNC in areas which were the monopoly of the informal sector, large numbers of artisans—"ecosystem people" in the words of Madhav Gadgil and Ramachandra Guha—those dependent on Nature and its natural resources to eke out a livelihood, like the basket maker, the potter, the village blacksmith and a host of others–are being marginalized, driven out of their occupations and converted into environmental refugees (Gadgil and Guha, 1995: 212). And at the global level, globalization has intensified the development of the phenomenon of migrant workers who face human rights violations like discrimination, low wages, absence of social security, sexual abuse and so on.

Mahatma Gandhi and *Swadeshi*

The concept of *Swadeshi* occupies an important place in Gandhian thought and programme of action. It is one of the 'Eleven Vows' formulated by Gandhi. Its practice, according to him, is essential for reaching the goal of 'Gram Swaraj'. Yet it remains one of the least studied, and perhaps the most misunderstood concept in Gandhian thought. Occupying as it does, the one end of the spectrum of development, with globalization occupying the other end, and given its potential to address the challenges and adverse consequences of globalization, it would be useful to take a closer look at the concept of *Swadeshi* and its many interpretations.

The most obvious interpretation is that of *Swadeshi* as a successful economic strategy to end the suzerainty of the British Empire over its colonies. Undoubtedly, *Swadeshi* was a key focus of Gandhi who described it as the soul of *Swaraj*.

But there is another interpretation to *Swadeshi* which is rural-based. For Gandhi, the soul and spirit of India resided in its village communities. According to him, "*The true India is to be found not in its few cities but in its seven hundred thousand villages. If the villages perish, India will perish too*"

When viewed from this perspective, *Swadeshi* avoids economic dependence on external forces that could make the village community vulnerable. It also avoids unnecessary, unhealthy, wasteful and environmentally destructive transportation. The village must build a strong economic base to satisfy most of its needs, and all members of the village community should give priority to local goods and services.

Mainstream economics believes in centralized, industrialized and mechanized modes of production, whereas Gandhi envisions a decentralized, home-grown, hand-crafted mode of production.

Mass production leads people to leave their villages, their land, their crafts and their homesteads and go to work in the factories. Instead of dignified human beings and members of a self-respecting village community, people become cogs in the machine, standing at the conveyor-belt, living in shanty towns, and depending on the mercy of the bosses. Then fewer and fewer people are needed to work, because the industrialists want greater productivity and profit. The masters of the money economy want more and more efficient machines working faster and faster, and the result would be that men and women would be thrown on the scrap heap of unemployment. Such a society generates rootless and jobless millions, living as dependents of the state or begging in the streets. In *Swadeshi*, the machine would be subordinated to the worker; it would not be allowed to become the master, dictating the pace of human activity. Similarly, market forces would serve the community, rather than forcing people to fit the market.

Gandhi knew that with the globalization of the economy, every nation would wish to export more and import less, to keep the balance of payments in its favour. There would be perpetual economic crises, perpetual unemployment, and perpetually discontented, disgruntled human beings.

In communities practising *Swadeshi*, economics would have a place but would not dominate society. Beyond a certain limit, economic growth becomes detrimental to human well-being. The modern worldview is that the more material goods you have, the better your life will be. But Gandhi said, *"A certain degree of physical comfort is necessary but above a certain level, it becomes a hindrance instead of a help; therefore the ideal of creating an unlimited number of wants and satisfying them, seems to be a delusion and a trap. The satisfaction of one's physical needs must come at a certain point to a dead stop before it degenerates into physical decadence. Europeans will have to remodel their outlook if they are not to perish under the weight of the comforts to which they are becoming slaves"* (V.G. Desai, 1957: 64-68).

In order to protect their economic interests, countries go to war—military war as well as economic war. Gandhi said, "*People have to live in villages, communities and simple homes, rather than desire to live in palaces*". Millions of people will never be able to live at peace with each other, if they are constantly fighting for a higher living standard.

We cannot have real peace in the world if we look at each other's countries as sources for raw materials or as markets for finished industrial goods. The seeds of war are sown with economic greed. If we analyze the causes of war throughout history, we find that the pursuit of economic expansion consistently leads to military adventures. "*There is enough for every man's need, but not for every man's greed!*" said Gandhi. *Swadeshi* is thus a pre-requisite for peace.

The economists and industrialists of our time fail to see when enough is enough. Even when countries reach a very high material standard of living, they are still caught up with the idea of economic growth. Those who do not know when enough is enough will never have enough, but those who know when enough is enough already have enough.

Swadeshi is the way to comprehensive peace: peace with oneself, peace between peoples, and peace with Nature. The global economy drives people toward high performance, high achievement, and high ambition for materialistic success. This results in stress, loss of meaning, loss of inner peace, loss of space for personal and family relationships, and loss of spiritual life. Gandhi realized that in the past, life in India was not only prosperous, but also conducive to philosophical and spiritual development. *Swadeshi*, for Gandhi, was the spiritual imperative.

There is yet another interpretation to *Swadeshi*. "*Swadeshi is that spirit in us which requires us to serve our immediate neighbours before others, and to use things produced in our neighbourhood, in preference to those more remote"* (M.K. Gandhi, 1947: 156). In so doing, according to Gandhi, we serve humanity to the best of our capacity. In his words, "*We cannot serve humanity by neglecting our neighbours*" (V.G. Desai, 1957: 64-68).

Elsewhere, Gandhi described *Swadeshi* as "a call to the consumer to be aware of the violence he is causing by supporting those industries that result in poverty and harm to workers and to humans and other creatures". He recognized that alienation and exploitation often occur when production and consumption are divorced from their social and cultural context—and that local enterprise is a way to avoid these problems.

Did Gandhi adopt a doctrinaire and rigid position on *Swadeshi*? Obviously not, as the following paragraph would reveal: "Even Swadeshi, like any other good thing, can be ridden to death, if it is made a fetish. That is a danger that must be guarded against.

To reject foreign manufactures merely because they are foreign, and to go on wasting national time and money in the promotion in one's country of manufactures for which it is not suited, would be a criminal folly and a negation of the Swadeshi spirit. A true votary of Swadeshi will not harbour ill-will towards a foreigner and not be actuated by antagonism towards anybody on this earth. Swadeshi is not a cult of hatred. It is a doctrine of selfless service that has its roots in the purest Ahimsa, that is, love" (Desai, 1957: 84).

Concluding Observations

It is imperative and urgent that we increasingly make use of Gandhian ideas and strategies for a global non-violent awakening, and consequent qualitative socio-economic transformation for dignified human survival. This requires the development of a new world view, a new *weltanshauung*, based on Gandhi's ideas for a better world. Such a *weltanshauung* should embody the Gandhian values of non-violence, righteous conduct, truth, peace, love, dignity of labour, self-reliance, self-control, equality, *swadeshi, sarvodaya,* sacrifice and *satyagraha.* This will seek to avoid violence which divides humankind for the well-being of some, and promote non-violence which will unite us for the well-being of all.

The challenges of globalization make it essential for us to rediscover Mahatma Gandhi and the moral imperative of his eternal wisdom.

References

Giddens, A. (1990), The Consequences of Modernity, Stanford University Press, Stanford.

Arie, Kacowicz (1999), "Regionalization, Globalization and Nationalism: Convergent, Divergent or Overlapping?", *Alternatives,* Vol. 24, No. 4, p. 54.

Smith, B.C. (1996), Understanding Third World Politics: Theories of Political Change and Development, Macmillan, London.

Edwards, Reich and Weisskopf (1972), The Capitalist System: A Radical Analysis of American Society, Prentice-Hall, New Jersey.

Hildyard, Hines and Lang (1996), 'Who Competes? Changing Landscapes of Corporate Control", *The Ecologist,* Vol. 26, No. 4.

Rosenau, J. (1998), 'Government and Democracy in a Globalising World' in Archibugi, Held and Kohler, (eds.), Re-imagining Political Community, Polity Press, Cambridge.

Kenichi, Ohmae (1995), The End of the Nation-State, The Free Press, New York.

Chossudovsky, M. (1997), The Globalization of Poverty, Third World Network, Penang.

Gandhi, M.K. (1947), Harijan, Navajivan Publishing House, Ahmedabad.

Gandhi, M.K. (1957), From Yerawada Mandir, (translated by V.G. Desai), Navajivan Publishing House, Ahmedabad.

Gadgil, Madhav and Ramachandra Guha (1995), Ecology and Equity, Penguin Books, New Delhi.

Nikhil, Aziz (1995), "The Human Rights Debate in the Era of Globalization: Hegemony of Discourse", *Bulletin of Concerned Asian Scholars,* Vol. 27, No. 4, p. 23.

P. Hirst and G. Thompson (1996), Globalization in Question: The

International Economy and the Possibilities of Governance, Polity Press, Cambridge, p. 102.

Samir, Amin (1998), Capitalism in the Age of Globalization: The Management of Contemporary Society, Madhyam Books, Delhi, p. 45.

Susan, Willett (2001), "Globalization and Insecurity", *IDS Bulletin,* Vol. 32, No. 2, p. 67.

United Nations Development Programme (1999), Human Development Report, Oxford University Press, New Delhi.

Vandana Shiva (1991), "Violence of the Green Revolution", *Third World Network*, Penang, p. 134.

9

Globalisation and Islamic Fundamentalism

K.M. Sajad Ibrahim

Implications of Islamic Fundamentalism

Islamic fundamentalism refers to a complex whole of burgeoning extremist political ideologies, which purport to be defiant of the political, cultural and economic domination of the west. It is generally viewed as a sharp reaction to the policies and attitude of the west towards countries and people of West Asia. It can be traced back from the time of disintegration of the Ottoman empires in the aftermath of the First World War. Subsequent partition of the Arab lands was viewed as the gross injustice inflicted by the west against the original inhibitors of West Asia. The creation of the State of Israel and the promotion of unpopular authoritarian regimes in Arab countries amounted to anti-western protest. The Muslim Brotherhood movement in the early twentieth century is to be viewed in this context.

Fundamentalism means something that related to the nucleus of modern faith systems. As such, fundamentalism is mainly identified with notions related to religion. It is signified in relation to faith and the process of signification is powerfully negative rather than positive. In relation to Islam, it is important to recognise that the term fundamentalism. It is not self-descriptive, but has been applied by others in their attempts to describe and understand contemporary Islamic history and politics. Islamic fundamentalists include state and non-state actors, historic societies and associations, factions, vanguards, thinkers, philosophers, authors, clerics, individuals across the globe. Islamic fundamentalists are not ethnically or geographically homogeneous—although there are some who would try and ascribe particular primordial ethnic markers to Muslims in this way.

Those who are labelled as Islamic fundamentalists are found populating the major sects of Islam (Sunni and Shia) as well as its minor sects and schismatic tendencies and are often accused of fermenting political disorder, revolution and violence. The reference point of Islam through fundamentalism consists of a never-ending catalogue of instability in the political sphere. Fundamentalism is defined as indicating certain 'intellectual stance that claims to derive political principles from a timeless divine text three separate movements are identified revivalism, reformism and radicalism' (Milton-Edwards, 2006).

Fundamentalism was identified as a key characteristic of late twentieth-century religious revivalism across the globe. Islamic fundamentalism was recognised alongside the manifestation of Hindu, Christian, and Jewish variations. In principle, fundamentalism, therefore, is equated with a rejection of modernity and its secular variant in both democratic and non-democratic societies. In reality, however, fundamentalism has been recognised as a central, if not the defining, feature of historic and contemporary Islamism. In the West, Islamic fundamentalism is often used as the primary analytical tool for the study of contemporary Islam and politics. Fundamentalism is the primary reference point of Islam in the majority of works of academics, journalists, and other writers of the west.

Muslim identity in the twentieth century was portrayed as constricted, anti-modern, anti-secular, anti-democratic, anti-globalisation, anti-Semitic, anti-emancipation, anti-feminist, anti-plural, and consisting of followers enthralled by the promise of revolution that would put Islam in charge of the state again. This desire for power, independence and control has meant that throughout the twentieth century, post-1945 in particular, Islamic fundamentalism has been conceptualised as on an inevitable crash course with secularism.

This conceptualisation has failed to understand that Islamism and Islamic fundamentalism are very much a modern phenomenon, 'no cliché is more stupefying than that which describes Al-Qaeda as a throwback to medieval times' (Gray, 2003), and the insistence that Islamism is anti-modern fails to grasp the primary motive for Muslim political action in the contemporary age. From the perspective of the secularists, Islamists make false claims on modernity. Islamists are also accused of 'cherry-picking' at the modernity project—using science and technology, but not the values that appear to go with them—in order to achieve their political goal of new state forms based on a throwback to the past. The religious and more specifically Christian values inherent to Western secularist discourse are ignored in the construction of a case against Islam and its fundamentalist majority.

Islam is not welcomed with open arms in the debates about modern society. Islamic fundamentalists have agitated against what they believe to be the deleterious effects not only of the activities of the West in their own countries whether as a legacy of colonialism, a by-product of superpower rivalry during the Cold War, or economic manoeuvring to secure energy resources in Muslim countries, but also of Western ideas and political thought on the absorption of the process of modernisation that has affected their nations.

Islam is not limited to national or racial boundaries, or to certain political, cultural or economic environments. Islam has not only spread in the Arab World, but in Nigeria, Turkey, Pakistan, Iran and Indonesia. Furthermore, its expansion has not been limited to Muslim countries, but also occurs in countries like India, the Philippines, the former Soviet Union and even some Western countries (Jabbour, 1994: 81-86).

The first wave started at the end of the 19th century, when Afghani, followed later by Muhammad Abdu, responded to the westernization process which came as a result of the strong colonialism of the 19th century. The second wave came between the two wars through Hasan al-Banna and the Muslim

Brotherhood. This was in response to the westernization process, which came with colonialism and manifested itself in openness to Western culture and education.

However, in this century, whether in the Islamic League of Afghani, the Muslim Brotherhood of al-Banna and Qutb, or others who came throughout the 1970s and 1990s, the distinct characteristic of this resurgence is the comprehensiveness of Islam. Islam is dånwa dawla (doctrine, life, and politics) and it includes all the various aspects of the life of the individual and of the nation. Economics, politics, theology as well as the judiciary system, are parts of an all-inclusive and comprehensive Islamic system (Qutb, 1987).

According to the prophet and Muslims throughout the centuries, Islam was the best economic, social, religious, legal and political system on earth. However, Muslims were totally disappointed with the real objectives of Islam and what was practiced. As such, efforts had been made to bridge this gap by charismatic leaders like al-Banna and al-Khumeini, by ideologists like Qutb and Mawdudi, and by influential Islamic writers like Amara and al-Ghazzali (Jabbour, 1994).

The people who were attracted to the Fundamentalist movement consisted of the lower middle class and the students. The basic reasons for their attraction to fundamentalism lied: (i) in their social and religious sense of despair, and (ii) in their being a class of the society that has no future. They saw themselves as marginal in their impact on the history of the nation.

The lower middle class in Egypt did not find a place of significance, either in the religious sphere, or on the social ladder; therefore, they had a pessimistic perspective on life. Significant impact on the history of a nation was made through individuals, and since the individuals belonged to the lower middle class were deprived of their rights and the qualities, then they found means of fundamentalism only through which they could reach their goals. It promised to radically change this unjust social system and gave the marginal population the opportunity to enter the heart of the history of the nation.

These groups then not only played the normal roles which they were deprived of, but they even played a much bigger role, rejecting the values and the foundations of the existing social system.

Another group of people who went through a similar set of experiences were the university students. Education was compulsory and a long span of years was required to graduate from the university. In this type of educational system which offered no motivation, except to the few who enter the faculties of medicine and engineering, students became marginal as well. Students were forced to be marginal and look to the future with anxiety and despair as there was no opportunity for employment. They readily became a social group in the society with distinct cultural values. They, along with the young graduates who found no hope for upward mobility, became open and eager to respond to an invitation of Fundamentalism, which promised involvement, significance and a role to play in making history.

Because the revolution of 1952 in Egypt made education free and available to all, lower class people were given the hope that they could join the upward movement of social mobility and reach the middle class. As a result, the universities grew, producing about half a million young men and women annually who were supposed to have become middle class people because of their education. The middle class became the huge tail on a disproportionate creature, with a small head and body. People who belong to the tail are basically the lower middle class. Many of these people came from the villages and small towns, migrating to the big cities to live in the suburbs, bringing along with them their rural culture. Many found it hard to make it in this difficult battle for survival. These disenchanted people gradually found their best asylum in promoting fundamentalism (Jabbour, 1994).

The factors which helped produce the type of environment where the youth become good candidates for fundamentalism could be political, religious, economic, social or psychological. In this vacuum, youth looked for an identity, a place of belonging and an enemy to vent his hatred. In fundamentalism, the young find their identity in following God, their place of belonging in becoming dedicated members in the various fundamentalist groups, and their enemy in Satan and the hypocrisy of the so-called "Muslim society".

The main reason for the resurgence of Islamic fundamentalism was the enormous political vacuum created by the collapse of Stalinism and the left in these societies. In the context of severe socio-economic distress, unemployment and poverty, the masses find themselves in blind alley. The arrogance and contempt of the monarchs and dictators in the Arab and Islamic world further fuelled the hatred and wrath of the masses. The corrupt and plundering democracies have increased social frustration. With no way forward some backward sections of the masses and petty bourgeoisie have started looking backward. The strategies of fundamentalism have exploited the vices of the present leaders and system and are offering the illusion of the virtues of a distant past epoch (Khan, 2000).

The hypocrisy of imperialism and fundamentalism was very reciprocal. These Islamic leaders used the anti-IMF and anti-imperialist sentiments amongst the masses to further expand their base. The massive levels of unemployment give led to severe crisis in society. This was capitalised on by the Islamic organisations, which not only provided weapons and money to these hordes of lumpish youth, but also gave them sanctuary where they were safely hidden away from the hands of the state machine.

Large sections of deprived, frustrated and bewildered youth entered into fundamentalism in the same way as many tried to find an escape in a drug dose. They could not face the challenges, hence they tried to use fundamentalism as a path into oblivion. A large number of raw youth, especially those migrating from rural to urban areas, were shocked by the social and cultural conditions they witnessed in the cities. They reverted to Islamic fundamentalism seeking piety and honesty.

They tried to find eternal peace in Islam to get solace for their souls and minds. But when these captives of faith faced the stark reality of Islamic fundamentalism it was too late. Finally, they had no other way but to become the slaves of fundamentalism, without considering its objectives.

Another factor in the rise of fundamentalism in some countries was the oil wealth of Muslim countries. It has given self-confidence to many Muslim states, which resulted in a renewal of Islamic fervour. In fact, fundamentalism was also a reaction against corrupt autocratic regimes in the Muslim world, where leaders showed little concern for their people. Fundamentalist groups offered education, jobs, health care etc. which led to popular support.

However, the most important reason for the rise of Islamic fundamentalism was the interference of Western countries. The Muslim Brotherhood gained popularity since 1980s mainly as part of the reaction to the un-Islamic trends in the so-called Islamic states, while Hamas, an offspring of Brotherhood, found its birth through the Palestinian frustration. Most recently, Islamic movements received much acceptance even in Turkey. At the same time, Islamic revolution in Iran produced another flavour of Fundamentalism in the name of political Islam. Although the West unleashed all attacks against the Islamic fundamentalism, their role for upbringing such an ideology was evident since the beginning of twentieth century (Haque, 2007).

Those Muslims who strove to establish an Islamic state could be divided in two groups according to the methods they employed their aims. The mainstream Islamists trend sought to accomplish its objectives by working within the existing rules and regulations of its respective societies. They were generally not opposed to a degree of political pluralism, to working within the system, to democratic participation, and acknowledge the interests and rights of minorities. These Islamists were generally pragmatic, as they even extend their support to a market economy.

The second category of those who espoused the concept of an Islamic state were the militant, radical and revolutionary Islamists who were prepared to use violence in their efforts to unseat existing governments. The threat of Islamic fundamentalism which was widely publicized in the west these days came exclusively from this group of Islamists. They rejected the idea of pluralism, political or otherwise, decry democracy as non-Islamic and repress ethnic, linguistic religious minorities. Terrorists' tactics were normally considered legitimate tool in the arsenal available to such groups—'Jihad' is one such term deliberately used to unleash violence.

In reality, the word 'Jihad' has no relation with violence as mentioned in Quran and Prophetic words. Jihad has the literal meaning of exerting our best and greatest effort to achieve the path of God. Quran did not call for the annihilation of non-believers. For example, Quran calls: "The truth is from Lord: let him who will, believe, and let him who will, reject it (Quran18:29). "If it had been Lord's will, they would have all have believed—all who are on earth! Wilt thou then compel mankind, against their will, to believe!" (It means men of faith must not be impatient or angry if they have to contend against Unfaith, and most important of all, they must guard against the temptation of forcing Faith...Forced faith is no faith. (Abdullah Yousuf Ali, Quran Translation: 505). At the global context, the people who were attracted to the fundamentalist movements were the lower middle class and the students.

Impact of Globalisation

In the aftermath of the terrorist attacks of September 11, the effect of globalisation on Islam has emerged as a hotly debated topic. With twenty percent of the world's population professing Islam as their religion, it is a matter of more than academic interest. A survey of the evolution of Islam in recent decades shows that *ummah*—a universal community based on shared Islamic faith and implementation of its law—has indeed become a greater reality in an ever-shrinking world.

At the same time, globalisation has also allowed divisive militancy to arise and flourish. In the years to come, the force of globalisation may lead to the emergence of multiple centres of Islam rather than the current one based in Saudi Arabia Islamic historians have credited the concept of *ummah* as an important contributing factor in the rise and development of Islam and Islamic civilization. The evidence from various studies shows that although Muslims share a sense of being part of a global *ummah*, the intensity of this feeling varies significantly across Muslim countries (Hassan, 2003).

Unlike in the past, when limitations of transport and communication technologies made it difficult for Muslims worldwide to acknowledge the cultural and social diversity of the *ummah*, the introduction of satellite television, internet, international travel, and access to books and magazines and increasing literacy is now making Muslims aware of their cultural and social diversity. The impact of colonialism and the emergence of nationalist movements, which spearheaded the struggle against it, have also served to fragment the Islamic world into over 45 Muslim countries with competing economic and political interests. Another consequence of this development for Muslims is that while they are becoming aware of the cultural diversity of the Muslim world, the new technologies are also promoting a greater *ummah* consciousness, a heightened sense of belonging to a global community of believers (Hassan, 2003).

Globalisation is prompting a reformulation of the common Muslim belief that Islam is not only a religion but also a complete way of life, which in Islamic discourse is known as the 'one religion, one culture' paradigm. Instantaneous and worldwide communication links are now allowing Muslims and non-Muslims to experience the reality of different Islamic cultures. Such experiences reveal not only what is common among Muslims but also what is different. For example, gender relations and dress codes for Muslim women are structured in different ways in Muslim countries like Indonesia, Saudi Arabia, Turkey and Uzbekistan.

In the old pattern of religious universalism, religion is the motive force, the cause, of universalization and globalization.

Globalization in its later waves, by contrast, is a much broader process. It is set in motion not by religion, but by new cultural and especially technological forces that are entirely secular. The emergence of fundamentalist movements is often attributed to the impact of globalization on the religious sphere. From this perspective, fundamentalism is, at least in part, a consequence of globalization.

As we shall see, globalization is not the only factor, and other forms of social change are important causes of the contemporary resurgence of Islam and the growth of Islamic fundamentalism. Nevertheless, the impact of globalization on Islam has its own dynamics, as it is now added on to the old dynamics of the Universalist expansion of Islam, complicating the old pattern but by no means obviating it. It can indeed be argued that the great theoretical interest of contemporary Islam stems from the intertwining of the dynamics of the old universalism and the new fundamentalism (Arjomand, 2004: 9-28).

The effects of globalization on Islam are interpreted very differently by different observers. Eickelman (1998) sees the combined effect, on the world's one billion Muslims, of globalization, the growth of education and vigorous discussion of Islam in books and in public debates in the press and the media as the making of an Islamic Reformation (Eickelman, 1998: 80-89). The Islamic reform movement of the last decade in Iran provides supportive evidence for this view, as it undoubtedly makes a radical break with the apologetic Islamic modernism of the mid-20th century (Arjomand, 2002: 19-31).

According to Eickelman, the current Islamization of social life has been far-reaching but also dispersed, lacking any focus or single thrust. For Barber, by contrast, globalization puts Islam in the front line of the 'Jihad versus McWorld'. He sees the effect of globalization concentrated in a sharply focused and vehement 'anti-western anti-universalist struggle' (Barber, 1995). In his last work, the late Ernest Gellner (1981) did not make a distinction between Islamic fundamentalism and the general scriptural Islam of the cities, and considered what he had earlier called Islamic permanent reformation the major obstacle to modernity.

Islam was in this later version a Protestantism of sorts, but its law atomized and stultified society and prevented the growth of political institutions (Gellner, 1994). Along similar lines, Barber obliterates the distinction between Islamic fundamentalism and Islam. His central chapter is entitled 'Essential Jihad: Islam and Fundamentalism'. The emphasized connective is significant: "all Islam is Jihad; fundamentalism refers to Jihad elsewhere, especially to the struggle of American fundamentalists against the global McWorld. It is Islam which 'nurtures conditions favourable to parochialism, anti-modernism, exclusiveness and hostility to "others"—the characteristics that constitute what I have called Jihad" (Barber, 1995).

Barber's view on Islam and globalization, which is widely shared by journalists and commentators, is fundamentally mistaken. Not only is there variety in Islamic fundamentalism (Arjomand, 1995: 179-198), but Islamic fundamentalism is by no means identical to all the contemporary manifestations of Islam as a Universalist religion. Urbanization, development of roads and transportation, the printing revolution, and other contemporary processes of social change, including globalization, simply reinforce trends toward expansion and intensive penetration of society that are typical of Islam as a universalist religion. These trends remain distinct, as they are not swamped by fundamentalism. One would therefore have to agree with Eickelman on the dispersion of the current trends in Islamization, whether or not one concurs with his value judgment that they constitute reformation. One important question remains to be answered, however: how does globalization affect the old Islamic universalism?

The twentieth century also gave rise to a combination of internal sub-globalization processes typical of the early modern period and externally stimulated globalization. On the one hand, the continuous improvement and declining cost of transportation since the Second World War has greatly increased the number of pilgrims to Mecca, and of missionaries from Africa and Asia to the main centres of Islamic learning in the Middle East. It should be noted that this aspect of globalization reinforces Islam's old universalism, which was institutionalized around the hajj. On the other hand, the postcolonial era has also witnessed the massive immigration of Muslims into Western Europe and North America, where sizable Muslim communities have formed. Meanwhile, there has been unprecedented global integration of Muslims through the mass and electronic media (Arjomand 2003: 28-39).

The international repercussions of the Salman Rushdie case are the best illustration of the impact of the media on a globally integrated Muslim world. The protests and burning of his Satanic Verses by indignant Muslims began in Bradford, England. Images of these protests were broadcast throughout the world, and stimulated more violent protests in Pakistan and India. In a particularly low point of Iranian post-revolutionary politics, after the book had been banned in India, South Africa, Bangladesh, Sudan, Sri Lanka, and Pakistan, Ayatollah Ruhollah Khomeini broadcast his famous fatwa condemning Rushdie, a non-Iranian writer who lived in England, to death for apostasy on 14th February, 1989 (Arjomand, 2003).

An interesting feature of globalization is the unfolding of anti-global sentiments in particularistic, variety-producing movements, which seek local legitimacy but have a global frame of self-reference. The flexibility of signing international conventions with reservations has allowed a large number of Muslim states to confirm their membership in the international community by signing such agreements while retaining their own particularity of identity and interests.

For instance, Muslim nations could sign onto the United Nations' human rights instruments, such as the 1989 UN Convention on the Rights of the Child, but insists upon significant reservations that affirmed the priority of the shari'a rules. More typically, however, global integration induces many Muslims to emphasize their unique identity within the frame of reference of their own culture, which can be said to be at once universal and local or sub-global. There can be no doubt that global integration has made many Muslims seek to appropriate universalist institutions by what might be called Islamic cloning. We thus hear more and more about "Islamic science", "Islamic Human Rights", an "Islamic international" (Arjomand, 2003).

The increasing integration of the Middle Eastern states into the international system has exposed them to the global wave of democratization and the promotion of the rule of law. This exposure has introduced a new element of legal pluralism and generated ambivalent reactions throughout the Middle East. The impact of the human rights revolution on the legal culture of Middle Eastern societies has been significant, and constitutional and supreme courts of a few Muslim countries, such as Egypt and Malaysia, have insinuated international rights provisions into their national legal systems (Islam, Globalisation, 2011).

An increasing number of Muslim intellectuals are defending the right to the freedom of expression by insisting that religious liberty and freedom of conscience are clearly deducible from the text of the Koran. A number of Quranic verses strongly imply a form of 'natural religion' among mankind, which entails religious liberty, and make explicit freedom of conscience and religion, most notably, 'there is no compulsion in religion' (Quran, 2.256). In Iran, Abdol-Karim Sorush, the erstwhile chairman of the Council for Islamic Cultural Revolution, has gone as far as putting the world religions on an equal footing in a title, *The Straight Paths* (saratha-ye mostaqim), a sacrilegious pluralisation of a fundamental Quranic concept (Arjomand, 1996: 331-347).

Islam is a whole culture. It is not synonym of fundamentalism as all religions have their extremist. It is not against multiculturalism but it is against consumerism that globalisation and deregulation bring with them. Islam writes Bobby S. Sayyid, (Sayyid, 1997) rejects the planetary culture of consumerism. The kind of message and global youth culture that "MTV generation" diffuse is not welcome in Muslim culture. It is known that fashion, music and sport are the targets of capitalist. Everything is for sale. Even women have become a commodity.

Here Islam opposes consumerism that leads kids, teenagers, and women to be corrupted by media and their messages. In Algeria, for example says Haynes (Haynes, 1998), the reforms claimed by Islamists wanted a stricter dress code for women, more religious broadcast on radio and television, and the banning of consumption of alcohol in public places...On the women question, there can be no compromise because "a community is what women want it to be" and Islam is about community. That is why, for Martin Riesebrodt, (Marty and Appleby, 1992: 134). Islamic fundamentalism is essentially a patriarchal protest movement against selected aspect of secularised modernity such as the western women's liberation movement.

According to Olivier Roy, a leading French scholar on Islam, neo-fundamentalist movements, in particular, Al-Qaeda, as a direct response to globalization pressures exerted by Western cultural and economic values. A significant number of neo-fundamentalists are found in countries that are not predominantly Muslim, Roy said. The movement tends to draw people who feel cut off from what they see as a traditionally Islamic lifestyle, including converts to Islam in European countries, such as Britain, France, and Germany. At the same time, neo-fundamentalists find themselves unable to fit in to the respective societies in which they are living. The neo-fundamentalists have "recast religion outside of cultural contexts", Roy said. As such, neo-fundamentalists tend to hold idealized notions about Islam.

He added that the lack of a firm grounding in traditional Islamic cultural values left neo-fundamentalists vulnerable to propaganda calling on them to express their faith in violent forms. Roy's theories on the nature of the neo-fundamentalist movement challenge some of the notions supporting the Western strategic response to radical Islamic-inspired terrorism. Many experts in the West consider the democratization of the Islamic world as the key to containing terrorism. Roy calls this notion only "half true". Democratization would help "isolate" Islamic neo-fundamentalists, he said, but it would not likely dispel the sense of economic and cultural alienation that drives the movement. (Wirsing, 2004: 165-178).

The internet and satellite communication have weakened the very tight control of the states over national radio and television networks that had once compartmentalized the Muslim world into differently oriented nation-states, and have stimulated the growth of a new, transnational Muslim public space within the global context. These effects of globalization on Islam are interpreted very differently by different observers. Some see the combined effect of globalisation as it affects upon the world's one billion Muslims.

They point to the growth of education and vigorous discussion of Islam in books and in public debates in the press, the audio-visual, and the electronic media as contributing to an Islamic reformation. In this view, the current Islamicization of social life has been both far-reaching and dispersed, lacking any focus or single thrust. Whether or not one concurs with the value-judgment that it constitutes reformation, it is undeniable that there is an unmistakable dispersion of the current trends in Islamization. The opposite view holds that globalization has put Islam on the front lines of a "Jihad versus McWorld" confrontation, creating a sharply focused and vehement anti-Western as well as anti-universalist struggle. This latter view tends to obliterate the distinction between Islam and Islamic fundamentalism.

The negative view on Islam and globalization, though widely shared by journalists and commentators, seems essentially mistaken. Not only is there a variety in Islamic fundamentalism, but Islamic fundamentalism is by no means identical with all the contemporary manifestations of Islam as a Universalist religion. Urbanization, development of roads and transportation, the printing revolution, and other contemporary processes of social change, including globalization, simply reinforce trends toward expansion and intensive penetration of society that are typical of Islam as a Universalist religion.

The increasing integration of the Middle Eastern states into the international system has exposed them to the global wave of democratization and the promotion of the rule of law. This exposure has introduced a new element of legal pluralism and generated ambivalent reactions throughout the Middle East. The impact of the human rights revolution on the legal culture of Middle Eastern societies has been significant, and constitutional and supreme courts of a few Muslim countries, such as Egypt and Malaysia, have insinuated international rights provisions into their national legal systems.

As anti-globalisation movement is advancing, Islamic fundamentalist movements find a strong presence to support their cause. The movement against the "inevitable" global advance of capitalist power has not been cowed by the imperialists' military and ideological offensive in the name of the "war against terrorism". Indeed their offensive has underlined and exacerbated the dangerous instability of global capitalism. And the growing sense of "global Islamic brotherhood" could, with little tact, revive all these people in an Islamic perspective! But for this to happen, Islam must be presented and reflected in a new way. Islam fundamentalism and the "gates of Interpretation" of the Shariah must be re-opened in a kind of revolution, not slammed shut forever, because if a genuine anti-Capitalist coalition is to appear in the world, it cannot happen without Islam.

References

Arjomand, S.A. (1986), 'Social Change and Movements of Revitalization in Contemporary Islam' in James Beckford (ed.), New Religious Movements and Rapid Social Change, London: Sage Publications.

Arjomand, S. A. (1992), "Constitutions and the Struggle for Political Order: A Study in the Modernization of Political Traditions",

Archives européennes de sociologie/European Journal of Sociology 33(4).

Arjomand, S.A. (1995), 'Unity and Diversity in Islamic Fundamentalism', in M. Marty and R.S. Appleby (eds.), *Fundamentalisms Comprehended*, Chicago, IL: University of Chicago Press.

Arjomand, S.A. (1996), "Religious Human Rights and the Principle of Legal Pluralism in the Middle East", in J. Van der Vyver and J. Witte (eds.), *Religious Human Rights in Global Perspective,* Vol. 2, Legal Perspectives, Dordrecht: M. Nijhoff.

Arjomand, S.A. (2002), "The Reform Movement and the Debate on Modernity and Tradition in Contemporary Iran", *International Journal of Middle East Studies* 34:7.

Arjomand, S.A. (2003), 'Thinking Sociologically About Islam', in M. Juergensmeyer (ed.), Global Religions: An Introduction, Oxford: Oxford University Press.

Brown, N. (1997), The Rule of Law in the Arab World: Courts in Egypt and the Gulf, Cambridge: Cambridge University Press.

Dalacoura, K. (1998), Islam, Liberalism and Human Rights, London: I. B. Tauris.

Eickelman, D.F. (1998), "Inside the Islamic Reformation", *Wilson Quarterly,* 22:1.

Gellner, E. (1981), Muslim Society, Cambridge: Cambridge University Press.

Gellner, E. (1994*),* Conditions of Liberty: Civil Society and Its Rivals, London: Hamish.

Gerber, H. (1994), State, Society, and Law in Islam. Ottoman Law in Comparative Perspective, Albany, NY: State University of New York Press.

Gray, John (2003), Al-Qaeda and What It Means to Be Modern, New York: The New Press.

Haque, Faatin (2007), 'Islam and the West: Bridging the Misconceptions', cited at, http://www.ihmsaw.org/resourcefiles/1260034335.pdf, accessed on 24-01-2012.

Hassan, Riaz (2003), Globalization's Challenge to Islam, cited in http://yaleglobal.yale.edu/content/globalizations-challenge-islam, accessed on 12-02-2012.

Haynes, Jeff (1998), *Religion in Global Politics*, London, Longman.

'Islam and Globalization' (2011), *Islam Encyclopaedia*, cited in http://islamweb.us/islam-globalization.html, accessed on 05-02-2012.

Jabbour, Nabeel T. (1994), "Islamic Fundamentalism: Implications for Missions", *International Journal of Frontier Missions*, Vol. 11:2 April 1994.

Khan, Lal (2000), 'The Menace of Islamic Fundamentalism and the Hypocrisy of Imperialism', *In Defence of Marxism*, cited at, http://www.marxist.com/islamic-fundamentalism-hypocrisy-imperialism.htm accessed on 11-01-2012.

Marty, Martin E. and R. Scott Appleby (1992), The Fundamentalist Challenge to Modern World, Boston: Beacon Press.

Milton-Edwards, Beverley (2005), Islamic Fundamentalism since 1945, New York: Routledge.

S. Sayyid, Bobby (1997), A Fundamental Fear, Euro Centrism and the Emergence of Islamism, London: Zed Books.

Wirsing, Robert G. (2004), 'Political Islam, Pakistan, and the Geo-Politics of Religious Identity', in Yoichiro Sato (ed.), Growth and Governance in Asia, Honolulu, Asia-Pacific Centre for Security Studies.

10

Human Trafficking and Human Security

M.J. Vinod

Introduction

Human trafficking is complex, multifaceted and a modern day form of slavery. An estimated 8,00,000 to 9,00,000 people are trafficked across international borders each year, besides the phenomenal number trafficked within borders. Of the 9,00,000 trafficked across borders, approximately 80 percent of the transnational victims are women and girls, and up to 50 percent are minors. Nationalities of people trafficked are as diverse as world cultures. Research into trafficking in human persons in any country is a very challenging exercise. At any given point of time, the International Labour Organisation estimates that 12.3 million people are in forced labour, bonded labour, forced child labour and sexual servitude.

About 2 million children are exploited in the global child sex tourism. UNICEF estimates that approximately 300,000 children under 18 years of age are currently exploited in more than thirty armed conflicts worldwide. Trafficking in persons is a brutal abuse of human rights that affects nearly every country in the world. The Congressional Research Service and the US State Department estimate that between one to two million people are trafficked each year worldwide with the majority originating in Asia—over 1,50,000 from South Asia and 2,25,000 from South East Asia.

The 10th Annual Trafficking in Persons Report outlines the continuing challenges across the globe, including in the United States. The Report, for the first time, includes a ranking of the United States based on the same standards to which it holds other countries. The report notes that the United States takes its first-ever ranking not as a reprieve but as a responsibility to strengthen global efforts against modern slavery, including those within America (Trafficking in Human Persons Report, June 2010).

Trafficking in persons is simultaneously a development and a criminal justice problem. Victims may be deceived by false promises of legitimate work, defrauded, tricked, threatened with force, coerced, abducted or even sold by their parents. Women are often more vulnerable to traffickers because of lack of education or access to work near their homes, or because of the prevalence of gender-based abuse and violence. Victims are exploited for sexual purposes, such as prostitution or pornography, or for labour without compensation in homes, farms, factories or other businesses. Those who are sexually exploited may become infected with HIV or other sexually transmitted infections (Trafficking in Persons: USAID's Response: 2004).

Human trafficking is a form of modern day slavery. On may define trafficking as "the recruitment, transportation, harbouring or receipt of persons, by means of the threat or use of force or other forms of coercion, of abduction, of fraud, of deception, of the abuse of power or of a position of vulnerability, or of the giving, receiving or payments of benefits to achieve the consent of a person having control over another person, for the purpose of exploitation (Article 3 of the United Nations Protocol). Exploitation shall include, at a minimum, the exploitation of the prostitution of others or other forms of sexual exploitation, forced labour or services, slaver or practices similar to slavery, servitude o the removal of organs". By definition 'trafficking' involves 'force, fraud and coercion which typically involvers 'confinement' and physical' and 'psychological' abuse.

The paper will revolve around the following hypotheses:

1. Human trafficking undermines the health, safety and security of the South Asian states.
2. Human trafficking has serious public health implications

as it involves physical and psychological traumas.

3. Trafficking in human persons is a major threat to the human rights of individuals, as well as a major national security threat.
4. Globalization of markets and labour force and relaxation of trade barriers have spawned new trafficking routes and scenarios.
5. Internal trafficking take place within each country, typically bringing rural women and children to cities in order to work as prostitutes, domestic servants and forced labourers.

The State Department categorises trafficking into three "tiers," based on individual countries efforts to combat the scourge. These include:

1. Tier 1 groups of countries that are in compliance with the minimum standards of the Trafficking Victims Protection Act of 2000 (TVPA). The TVPA is the most comprehensive anti-trafficking legislation passed in the US. It focuses on US involvement in prevention measures by increasing assistance to victims, and by enhancing penalties for perpetrators. The PVTA focuses on the 'three P's approach' viz., 'prevention', 'protection' and 'prosecution'.
2. Tier 2 includes countries that do not fully comply with the TVPA minimum standards, though they are making efforts to comply.
3. Tier 3 groups countries that are not making significant efforts to combat the problem.

The State Department prepares the annual *Trafficking in Persons Report* in response to a congressional mandate.

Strategies Used by Traffickers

Traffickers take advantage of the following strategies to lure potential victims:

One, traffickers take advantage of the poverty levels of many women and children in recruiting and luring victims into the traffic industry. For instance, women may enter voluntarily but be deceived as to the conditions under which they would be forced to work. Some are forced to work twenty four hours a day receiving little pay, not being able to leave, and being forced to endure physical abuse. The ILO Convention Number 182 of 1999, Article 3 (Worst Forms of Child Labour) declares that "all forms of slavery or practices similar to slavery, such as the sale and trafficking of children, debt bondage, serfdom and forced or compulsory labour, including forced or compulsory recruitment of children for use in armed conflict" represent a set of practices prohibited by the ILO Convention of 1999 (Stopping Forced Labour: A Global Report, 2001).

Two, women may be recruited through debt bondage. Parents, friends, or other close acquaintances may sell a child or woman for employment in return for cash.

Third, women and children are lured, deceived, kidnapped, or tricked in other ways into prostitution. Women and children are deceived by recruiters who gain their trust and promise a higher paying job somewhere else. The fact is they are lured and deceived.

Major Push and Pull Factors

The following are some of the major 'push' and 'pull' factors that sustain and complicate the problem of trafficking of persons in South Asia:

1. Poverty.
2. Lack of employment opportunities.
3. The commercial sex industry.
4. Violence against women and children.
5. Demand for prostituted women, boys and girls.
6. Discrimination against women.
7. Corruption.
8. Various forms of armed conflict.

Very often traffickers pose themselves as 'employment agents'. Parents are induced to part with their children into prostitution and domestic servitude ad a commercial enterprise. Victims are exploited for sexual purposes, such as prostitution or pornography, or for labour without compensation in homes, farms, factories or other businesses. Markets for sex and cheap labour in destination countries and the growing sex tourism industry fuel the demand. Weak rule of law, porous borders and widespread official corruption provide the context that allows human traffickers to operate with impunity.

UNICEF reports that, in the last 30 years, trafficking in women and children for sexual exploitation alone has victimized more that 30 million people in Asia. The International Organization for Migration (IOM) estimates that 2,00,000 to 2,50,000 women and children are trafficked every year in Asia. The US Department of State suggests that 1,50,000 South Asians are trafficked every year. The IOM estimates that nearly one-third of the global trafficking trade in women and children are trafficked from South-East Asia. About 50,000 women and children were trafficked annually to the United States from other countries. Of this, approximately 60 percent originate from South Asia.

In South Asia, Bangladesh and Nepal are the main countries of origin for human trafficking. There is an estimate by the Global Alliance against Trafficking in Women (GAATW) that 3,00,000 Bangladeshi women have been trafficked to India and 2,00,000 to Pakistan, and over 2,00,000 Nepalese sex workers are reported to work in India, one fifth of who are supposedly under the age of sixteen years (Sanghera, 1999).

South Asian Scenario: An Overall Perspective

India: India is a 'source', 'destination' and 'transit' country. In India, trafficking largely takes place for two reasons:

1. One, for 'forced labour'.
2. Two, for 'commercial sex exploitation'.

The Ministry of Home affair in India estimates that 90 percent of India's sex industry is for purposes of 'commercial sex exploitation' and 'forced marriage'. Children are often subject of various forms of 'involuntary servitude'. The

Parliament of India however had passed a law in 2006 banning the employment of children in domestic work.

The USAID Mission in India is working with the United Nations Development Fund for Women (UNIFEM) and a number of Indian NGOs active in anti-trafficking throughout the country. Activities include information centres and shelters, psychological counselling, and educational and vocational opportunities, including for children of prostitutes in order to prevent them form falling victim to traffickers. Training helps communities advocate against trafficking and reach at-risk groups with prevention efforts. USAID also supports information-sharing networks among NGOs and local law enforcement, and training for judiciary and law enforcement officials on the causes, nature and magnitude of trafficking. Awareness campaigns are under way at state and national levels using a variety of media (Trafficking in Persons: USAID's Response, 2004).

Trafficking in women also takes place across the India-Bangladesh and the India-Nepal borders. India has not been able to effectively guard its long and porous borders with both these countries. The Government of India prohibits various forms of trafficking. The immoral trafficking Prevention Act penalties range from seven years to life imprisonment. Various acts like the 'Bonded Labour Abolition Act', the 'Child Labour Act' and the 'Juvenile Justice Act' are other important Acts passed by the Parliament of India.

Pakistan: Pakistan is a 'source', 'destination' and 'transit' country. At one level, trafficking takes place from countries like Afghanistan, Sri Lanka, Myanmar, India, Nepal, Central Asian States for purposes of 'commercial sexual exploitation' and for various forms of 'involuntary servitude'. At another level women are trafficked through Pakistan from countries like Sri Lanka, Nepal and Myanmar. Many Pakistani boys trafficked to the Middle East serve as camel jockeys, sex workers and dancers. Internal trafficking also takes place within Pakistan where by rural women and children are brought to cities in order to work as prostitutes, domestic servants and forced labourers.

Pakistan has increased trafficking-related prosecutions and convictions, strengthened implementation of its 2002 Prevention and Control of Human Trafficking Ordinance, established an Anti- Trafficking Unit within the Federal Investigation Agency, and co-sponsored several public awareness campaigns.

Sri Lanka: Sri Lanka is a 'source' and 'destination' country for the following reasons:

1. Different forms of 'involuntary servitude'—when an individual is faced with restrictions on movement, threats, physical or sexual abuse and debt bondage.
2. Commercial sex exploitation.
3. Child soldiers used to be recruited by the erstwhile Liberation Tigers of Tamil Eelam (LTTE).

The US State Department has placed Sri Lanka in tier 2 Watch List in its June 2007 'Trafficking in Persons Report'. The report contends that this is due to Sri Lanka's "failure to provide evidence of increasing efforts to address trafficking... especially in its efforts to punish trafficking for involuntary servitude". The report says that Sri Lanka needs to improve its record of prosecution and conviction of sex and labour trafficking crimes, and need to institute a formal procedure to identify victims of trafficking among vulnerable groups, such as women arrested for prostitution, to ensure that they are not punished'. Though in April 2006, Sri Lanka amended the 'Penal Code' prohibiting all forms of trafficking, yet many loopholes remain in the implementation of the code. However, over the years there has been a marked improvement in Sri Lanka's trafficking prevention efforts.

Bangladesh: Bangladesh is basically a 'source' and 'transit' country for 'commercial sexual exploitation' and various forms of 'forced labour'. In Bangladesh, women and children are falling victim to trafficking mainly for the purpose of prostitution, sexual abuse, forced labour, camel jockeying, cheap labour, bonded labour, domestic servitude, selling of organs and marriage. In case of women and girls, the destination is usually the sex-market both within the country and outside. In the case of boys, the destination is usually Middle Eastern countries where they are engaged as camel jockeys. In most cases, the girls, who are trafficked abroad, are trafficked to India. In case of the boys, India is usually treated as a country of transit to the Middle East. On the other hand, within the country, an alarming number of boys and girls are forcefully engaged in prostitution. The girls are engaged both in brothels and the street sex-market, while the boys are almost exclusively engaged in the street sex market (Ali, 2004).

The Bangladesh National Women Lawyers' Association (BNWLA) has established 13 watchdog sites to monitor trafficking cases and provide legal assistance to victims. It repatriates victims from other countries, facilities the release of those trafficked within Bangladesh and reintegrates them into community life. In 2003 for example, BNWLA repatriated 29 women, children and men from various countries, affected the release of 32 women and children form internal trafficking and provided information that led police to arrest 76 traffickers. In the same period, 16 traffickers received convictions (Trafficking in Persons: USAID's Report, 2004).

Bangladesh established an inter-ministerial anti-trafficking committee to oversee its national efforts to combat trafficking, created a national anti-trafficking police monitoring unit with presence in all 64 districts. However, Bangladesh continues to have difficulty confronting the trafficking problem due to generalized corruption of public officials who in many cases are complicit in the human trade. The 'Repression of Women and Children Act, 2000' was amended in 2003. Besides many safeguards, the Act also prohibits the buying and selling of minors for prostitution.

Afghanistan: Based on specific cases and trends and employing the legal framework of the 2000 Protocol to Prevent, Suppress and Punish Trafficking in Persons, Especially Women and Children, which supplements the UN Convention against

Transnational Organized Crime, the International Organization for Migration (IOM) believes that the following forms of trafficking are taking place in Afghanistan.

1. Exploitation for prostitution (forced prostitution and prostitution of minors).
2. Forced labour.
3. Slavery and practices similar to slavery—abductions for forced marriage, marriage for debt relief, and exchange of women for dispute settlement.
4. Servitude—sexual servitude and domestics servitude.
5. For removal of organs.

Afghan trafficking victims are drawn from the most vulnerable communities. Displaced, destitute, and indebted persons and families, young people seeking economic opportunity abroad, and rural women are all targets for targets for trafficking crimes. Afghanistan's chronic insecurity, massive displacement, and poverty born of conflict and drought contribute to making many people vulnerable to this kind of exploitation. The role of women and girls as objects for dispute resolution, the power of local assemblies which often apply customary rather than constitutional (or Islamic) law, and the limited autonomy of women in marriage decisions, are additional factors that contribute to trafficking and make it difficult to combat. The problem of trafficking in Afghanistan is deeply intertwined with the country's other problems as it emerges form decades of lawlessness.

The IOM recommends action in the following areas:

1. To create a legal framework ranging from a constitutional prohibition on slavery to laws enforcing the various international agreements to which Afghanistan is a signatory to laws protecting women from the most extreme versions of customary justice.
2. To manage education and outreach regarding trafficking in persons to target Government officials, traditional leaders and members of the community, paying special attention to decreasing the stigmatization of victims.

3. To ensure that programmes to reduce economic insecurity, including training and education, micro-credit, and food security take into account trafficking risk factors in selecting beneficiaries.
4. To include trafficking issues in security sector reform programmes such as the Afghan New Beginnings Programme.
5. To strengthen and sensitise the police and courts to address all forms of trafficking and sexual violence.
6. To re-examine cases in which persons now held in jail may in fact be the victims of trafficking.
7. To work with traditional leaders to provide culturally appropriate support mechanisms for victims.
8. To provide a mechanism to file complaints about past violations (Tristan Burnett: 2004).

Nepal: Nepal is primarily a 'source' country for commercial sexual exploitation and involuntary servitude mainly to India and the Middle East. Nepal has a National Plan of Action to combat trafficking and a National Rapporteur on trafficking. Women police cells have been established in many districts. In spite of safeguards like the 'Human Trafficking Control Act, 1986', there have been cases of corrupt government officials facilitating trafficking along the India-Nepal border.

The Nepalese government's law enforcement effort works side-by-side with non-governmental organizations (NGOs) to provide protection and assistance for the victims. The government has established anti-trafficking "vigilance committees" in high-priority districts, conducts mandatory "safe migration" orientation sessions for workers travelling abroad, and carries out national public awareness campaigns.

Observations

Today, in a globalized world, trafficking is facilitated by the following factors:

1. Sex tourism.
2. Child pornography.

3. The global demand for cheap, vulnerable and illegal labour.

Of these, sex tourism and child pornography have become world wide industries and totally commercialized. Child sex tourism is the dark side of globalization, and this is fuelled in South Asia by weak law enforcement, poverty, corruption, besides the role of technology in the form of internet and digital cameras. The link between child sex tourism and child pornography is also very strong.

Jyothi Sanghera aptly summaries the scenario in South Asia as follows: "In the contemporary reality of south Asia women and increasingly young girls are the new migrants, the new movers and shakers. Traditional as well as on-going male out-migrate for employment, together with an increasing insecurity of funds and sustainable livelihoods, act to push women and girls into assuming new roles for their families. Limited access to the public world and safe channels for mobility, as well as the lack of recourse to legal measures and social protection intensify for women and minors vulnerability during the process of migration" (Joyti Sanghera: 2000).

In South Asia the number of victims of severe forms of trafficking is increasing significantly. South Asian countries are trying to cope with the problem of trafficking internationally in the framework of the South Asian Association for Regional Cooperation (SAARC), which adopted the Convention against the Trafficking of Women at its 11th Summit in Kathmandu in 2002. Many countries in the Asian region have legislation that criminalizes trafficking, but in most cases the existing legal framework does not offer adequate controls. Implementation of current laws is limited, and law enforcement officials lack adequate training.

Though prosecution is increasing, much more needs to be done. Most Asian governments are stepping up public awareness and victim assistance programs on their own and in conjunction with NGOs and international organizations. These programs often are very modest due to resource constraints.

Several states are beginning to collaborate on investigations and have signed cross-border agreements to regularize the return of victims. However, the need for coordination and information sharing among the countries of the region remains great (Trafficking in Persons: USAID's Response, 2004).

Many NGOs in the South Asian region are working in the areas of prevention, rescue, care and support either as a principal activity or as an important aspect of a broader social development project. Activities to improve local conditions for women and children that also incorporate messages to reduce vulnerability to trafficking are being implemented by NGOs through South Asia, with varying levels of government support. A number of NGOs in Nepal, India and Bangladesh are conducting women's leadership training courses, family life education, livelihoods skill building programs for adolescent girls and the formation of women's cooperatives (for group savings and credit activities). These Programmes seek to improve conditions that have often been identified as being the underlying causes of trafficking. NGOs in the region are also implementing programs that directly address the vulnerability of persons to trafficking. Awareness-raising activities directed at the general public (through street theatres, rallies and community meetings) and community leaders are common elements in many of the prevention programmes. [1]

Human trafficking is a 'human rights' and 'national security' issue, and hence needs to be seriously addressed by the South Asian states both individually and collectively. Perhaps the time has come to strike a balance between he two. There is the need for greater coordination or the 'law enforcement' efforts to 'investigate' and 'arrest'. Repatriation measures also need to be improved and streamlined. This is necessary to prevent victims from being re-trafficked' and from being 'further victimized'.

The South Asian states need to enhance cooperation between the 'source' and 'destination' states. Moreover, efforts need to be made to 'investigate', 'prosecute', 'convict' and 'sentence' public officials who participate or facilitate various forms trafficking. (Many South Asian Countries have passed legislations that criminalize trafficking. Yet in many cases, the existing legal frame-work does not offer adequate controls. Implementation of current laws is limited, and law enforcement officials often lack adequate training).

The causes, magnitude and inter-linkages of trafficking are very complex. The time has come to bring together representatives from 'government', 'law enforcement', 'civil society', 'academia', 'media', 'film industry' and 'private industry'. Learning and sharing the 'best practices' could be one of the best ways to combat the menace of human trafficking. This human rights abuse is universal, and no country, developing or developed can claim immunity from its reach or from the responsibility to tackle it.

End Note

1. Anti-Trafficking Programs in South Asia: Appropriate Activities, Indicators and Evaluation Methodologies (2001), Summary Report of a Technical Consultative Meeting, September 11-13, Kathmandu.

References

Ali, A.K.M. Masud (2004), 'Trafficking in Persons: Towards an Inclusive Paradigm', paper presented at the *Seventh Sustainable Development Conference,* 8-10 December, Islamabad.

Brown, Louise (2001), Sex Slaves: The Trafficking of Women in Asia, Virago Press, New York.

Burnett, Tristan (2004), 'Trafficking in Persons: An Analysis of Afghanistan', presented at the *Seventh Sustainable Development Conference*, 8-10 December, 2004, Islamabad.

International Labour Office, Stopping Forced Labour: A Global Report, The International Labour Conference, 89 Session 2001 Report 1(B), Geneva.

Lim, Lin Lean (1998), The Sex Sector, International Labour Organization, Geneva, Office of Women in Development (2004), *Trafficking in Persons: USAID's Response*, Washington.

Sanghera, Jyothi (2001), 'Towards the Construction of an Empowered Subject: A Human Rights Analysis of Anti-Trafficking Legal Interventions and Trends in South Asia' *Seminar on Anti-trafficking*

Programs in South Asia, Kathmandu.

Sanghera, Jyoti (1999), 'Sexually Abused and Sexually Exploited Children and Youth in South Asia: A Qualitative Assessment of their Health Needs and Available Services', *GAATW Newsletter*, January 6-8.

11

Conflict and Resistance under Globalization

Mohanan B. Pillai and P.M. Joshy

Introduction

The demise of Soviet Communism and the advancement in science and technology has accelerated the process of neo-liberal globalization. Globalisation means the unfettered flow of finance capital across the world. However, predatory globalization has given birth to too many resistance movements. People are fighting everywhere to protect their natural resources like water, soil, and broadly the environment from profit-thirsty multinational corporations (MNCs). For the past twenty years, the neo-liberal world order has subordinated human life to the dictates of market forces. The outcome of this process is unprecedented structural violence, especially in the Third World countries. In fact, the State has failed to handle the problems that emanated from the extreme concentration of capital and the resulting marginalization.

In the neo-liberal era, the State functions as the facilitator for global finance capital and acts in accordance with the dictums of the global financial institutions. In the welfare capitalist phase the State functioned as a major provider in the society. However, in the neo-liberal period the changed nature of the State has very much adversely affected the most vulnerable sections in the society. On the one hand, the State has withdrawn from implementing social security measures for uplifting the historically marginalised sections in the society and on the other hand, it has become increasingly militaristic in the execution of laws and treaties in the market and society. The State has been reduced to a mere agent of the MNCs in its area of influence. In short, the progression from the age-old *leizess faire* economism of Adam Smith to the "market fundamentalism" (Somers and Block, 2005: 260-261) under the neo-liberal regimes the world over has led to the total alienation of the excluded.

The neo-liberal/New Right line of thinking is structured on the premise that 'individuals are responsible for their destiny'. It can be better understood by a 'simple' comment from Thatcher, one of the practitioners of the New Right ideology: "there is no such thing as society…there are individual men and women and there are families" (Thatcher, 1987; for a discussion on New Right see Green, 1987; Gunn, 1989; Harvey 2005). This line of thinking gives importance to the individual rather than the society in general. The neo-liberal position is that all natural resources including water should be transferred to private hands. The community has no ownership stakes and "goods" such as housing, food, education and health care are not human rights at all, but mere commodities allocated by the market.

In this theoretical context, the liberalisation, privatisation and globalisation (LPG) policies have helped the private monopolies—MNCs to establish commercial and economic relations all over the world. The acute debt crisis during the 1980s forced the Third World countries to follow the dictums of the global financial institutions and consequently those States changed their approach to the society regarding the security of the common people. The MNCs have begun to assert their hegemony over all natural resources like water that were once under the ownership of the communities. The neo-liberal State has been protecting the interests of the MNCs and in this context the communities have lost their rights to all basic resources. This has prompted them to struggle for their basic right—the 'Right to Life.' The neo-colonial attempt to take away natural resources from the people is also destroying the basis of their socio-cultural existence.

The loss of public authority over the natural resources and the resultant social problems has forced people to fight against the MNCs. There are many victorious movements across the world which dethroned the profit motivated MNCs. The successful struggle of the native people of Plachimada in Palghat district of Kerala against the Coca Cola Company is the finest example of the New Social Movements in contemporary India. At this point let us discuss some theoretical aspects of the New Social Movements with a view to through more light on the significance of Plachimada movement.

Social Movements: A Theoretical Overview

Generally speaking, social movements are large informal groupings of individuals and organisations focused on specific political or social issues. Herbert Blumer says: "Social movements can be viewed as collective enterprises to establish a new order of life. They have their inception in a condition of unrest, and derive their motive power on the one hand from dissatisfaction with the current form of life, and on the other hand, from wishes and hopes for a new scheme or system of living" (Blumer, 2008: 64). In the West, the social movements emerged in response to the developments in an industrialised society. What makes social movements modern is not their collective behaviour but their distinct political character.

Modernity is defined as a condition loosely identified with industrial revolution and Enlightenment. The western modernity claimed continuous progress, which was thought to be achievable by incorporating principles of rationality into aspects of public and artistic life (Elliott and Turner, 2001: 111). However, the movements which come under the category of the 'new' social movements are claiming something "new" from the "old" social movements.

The old social movements are identified with the industrial revolution in the western world. They represented the movements of the Working Class, Peasants, Whites, Aristocrats, Protestant men etc., These movements are usually cantered on some materialistic goals like improving the standard of living. To a greater extend the old social movements absorbed energy from the Marxist paradigm of development.

According to this stream of thought, social inequalities are the result of economic inequalities and it is only a radical transformation in the society that can eradicate the disparities (Marx, 1967). However, during the 1960s many movements emerged in the West under the banner of 'new social movements,' which fundamentally differed from the traditional social movements (Buechler, 1999: 46). But there are controversies about the question what is "new" about the new social movements? (Day, 2005: 68-70). By analysing various view points, Richard Day concluded that "the New Social Movements hope to achieve effects on a *limited number of* axes, rather than on all axes at once" (Day, 2005: 68-70).

However, thinkers like Alberto Melucci viewed the controversy as a 'futile exercise' (Melucci, 2008: 223). He explains: "Contemporary movements have passed from sequence to coexistence. Slices of experience, past history, and memory coexist within the same empirical phenomena" (Melucci, 2008: 223). Indeed, the new social movements are the result of development of a post-industrial capitalist society. The people are confronting diverse issues and the old paradigms of social thought are not sufficient enough to address these complicated issues. Habermas notes: "...the new conflicts are not sparked by *problems of distribution*, but concern the *grammar of forms of life*" (Habermas, 2008: 201).

These movements are unique, different and the new movements concentrate on 'less materialistic qualities of the life' which under the 'old social movements' were totally ignored. It should be noted that the social conflicts have moved to previously untouched terrains and new practices have developed. The new movements are a response to the developments in the post-industrial capitalist society and it indicates 'autonomy from the conventional political arenas' and 'emphasis on the cultural aspects' (Escobar and Sonia, 2008: 240).

Those movements include feminist movements, gay rights movements, peace movements, civil right movements, environmental movements, the Free Software movement, anti-nuclear movements etc. The new social movement theory looks at various collective actions in the society, specifically the people's identity and their relations to culture, ideology and politics (Pichardo, 1997: 411). It tends to emphasize social changes in identity, lifestyle, and culture rather than pushing for specific changes in public policy or for economic change. Thus, socio-cultural and the civic aspects are seen by New Social Movements as more important than that of economic or political aspects (Buechler, 1995: 441).

The 'old social movements' can be seen as embedded in Western modernity, while the 'new' social movements are the reflection of a 'post-modern condition.' Lyotard explains the nature of post-modern knowledge: "It is not simply a tool of the authorities; it refines our sensitivity to differences and reinforces our ability to tolerate the incommensurable" (Lyotard, 1984: 25). The new social movements draw energy from postmodernism (Scott, 1990; Tarrow, 1989; Dalton, 1990; Off, 1990). The movements were described as a mix of groups who inhabit the periphery rather than core of industrial production and are linked together by a common critical attitude towards growth.

They express an implicit rejection of the conventional objectives pursued by the traditional labour movement. Postmodernism generally means the fragmentation of authority (Lyotard, 1984). It has been epistemologically supporting the empowering of the voices which were discarded by the socio-political models of Western modernity. Post-modernity is used to describe the economic or cultural condition of society which is said to exist after modernity. The term is closely linked with a rejection of bourgeois, elitist culture (Ahluwallia, 2001: 4). Postmodernism provides epistemic support to the local cultural celebrations and identity assertions, and it may act as a counter-hegemonic force against the dominant social values.

The statement quoted below is a testimony for the intermeshing of postmodernism with the New Social Movements.

An epic is unfolding at the grassroots. Pioneering social movements are groping for their liberation from the "Global Project" being imposed upon them. Seeking to go beyond the premises and promises of modernity, people at the grassroots are reinventing or creating afresh intellectual and institutional frameworks without necessarily getting locked into power disputes.

Ordinary men and women are learning from each other how to challenge the very nature and foundations of modern power, both its intellectual underpinnings and its apparatuses. Explicitly liberating themselves from the dominant ideologies, fully immersed in their local struggles, these movements and initiatives reveal the diverse content and scope of grassroots endeavours, resisting or escaping the clutches of the "Global Project" (Gustavo and Madhu, 1998: 9).

The New Social Movements are engaging themselves with the problems that are neglected by the old social movements. The problems like water, soil and environment degradation by the MNCs are examples. In the conventional Marxist analysis, these types of issues are reduced to the levels of class conflict and failed to address the specificity of the problem. However, garbed in post-modernist thinking the New Social Movements address the multi-dimensional nature of the problems.

For example, the water crisis is the crisis of a cultural system, a threat to the very human rights of the people, a threat to the existence of the entire humanity. Water is the basic property of a community. The privatization of water challenges the very existence of that particular community. However, these dimensions of the issues are not taken into account by the traditional social movements. The new social movements provide space for historically undermined problems and also address the new issues which have emerged out of the developments in the post-industrial capitalist system.

New Social Movements: Some Critical Questions

The New Social Movements positions have been criticized by the Left on various reasons. Also the new social movement perspective has been condemned by the Left. The question is to what extent these types of scattered struggles and movements can challenge the existing exploitative system. Capitalism is working in complex ways and the State has been transformed as a mere agent of global finance capital. The new social movement's slogan is that 'it is possible to change the world without changing the power equations in the State apparatus'. In fact, the state is the codified form of power relations in a society.

Without changing the existing power equations how can we change the existing perverted social system? For re-making the society in favour of the deprived sections, controlling the state power is essential. The new social movement perspective totally discarded this aspect from their discussion. Of course, the new social movements are addressing certain issues which are adding some new flavours to the possibilities for thwarting the system, but which are not sufficient to change the existing system. They have failed to address the issues in a larger context. The new social movements which heavily draw from post-modern critical tools lack a powerful agenda for social change. In fact, postmodernism imbibed the American liberal values and it also lacks a powerful agenda for social change (Amin, 2004: 20; Cole, 2003).

To some extent, they fall in the lap of neo-liberalism, at the same time as they claim to be fighting neo-liberalism. It should be noted that postmodernism generates a sort of fragmentary politics which enables neo-liberal appropriation. Neo-liberalism also advocates a new wave of the fragmentary and decentralized culture of development. By romanticizing development and culture the present capitalist system has been creating an 'apolitical' space which is aimed to scatter the working class, appropriating their anti-systemic feelings and ultimately 'silencing' them. In spite of these criticisms, the successful stories of certain movements like the Plachimada struggle in Kerala under the banner of new-social movements promote a different perspective.

Plachimada Struggle

In accordance with the neo-liberal dictums the national governments are forced to support the MNCs and their subsidiaries in their attempt to convert water to a commodity. Meanwhile, the State apparatus has become overly militaristic regarding the implementation of the neo-liberal policies in the society. However, protests against MNCs are emerging and gaining strength at unbelievable speed in Bolivia, Argentina, Brazil, Ghana, Indonesia, South Africa, Poland, Paraguay, France, Canada, Germany, Mauritius, America, Panama, Honduras, Hungary and Sweden. Both the civil and political societies have joined hands in their battle against the MNCs. Environmentalists, political parties, trade unions, political activists, human rights activists and NGOs are fighting to protect water bodies as public property. Such movements have emerged and gained momentum in most of the states in India.

These include caste movements, feminist movements, and anti-dam movements like the Narmada Bachao Andolan, movements by the excluded sections for land, and movements for protecting the forest. The ongoing struggle for land by the Dalits and Adivasis at Chengara and Muthanga, Silent Valley movement and Plachimada struggle are the noted movements in the Indian State of Kerala under the banner of New Social Movements. Strong protest movements are being organized in places like Plachimada in Palakkad District of Kerela against the Hindustan Coca-Cola Company. It seems to be a success story on the part of the civil society and the new social movements in general.

The Plachimada struggle is one of the best examples of resistance by the local people against the neo-colonial attempts of exploitation by the MNCs (Bijoy, 2006; Nair, 2008). Plachimada is situated in the Perumatty Gram Panchayat in

Palghat district. [1] Most of the villagers are landless *Adivasis* (indigenous people), classified as scheduled tribes and scheduled castes or *Dalits* (outcastes). The Hindustan Coca-Cola Beverages Private (HCCB), registered as a subsidiary of Coca-Cola of Atlanta, in 1993 got license to manufacture a range of products which includes, Coca-Cola, Fanta, Sprite, Limca, Kinley Soda, Maaza and Thumbs Up. In accordance with the policy provisions, Coke acquired 34.64 acres, mostly paddy fields for the plant in 1998. The Perumatty Panchayat granted a license to Coke on January 27, 2000. The plant was commissioned in March 2000 (Vijayalakshmi 2003; Raman 2005; Bijoy, 2006).

Six months after the company was commissioned, the people in the neighbourhood noticed slight changes in the quality and the quantity of the well water. The water in the ponds and wells turned milky white and was no longer fit for the household purposes. It was reported that nearly 100 people complained of stomach-aches in the nearest hospital because of consumption of water from their traditional water sources. The farmers became anxious about the drying up of the wells so fast. Within two years, the people around the plant experienced problems that they had never encountered before.

The receding of the water table and the drastic change in the quality of water within the 1-1.5 km radius of the plant naturally generated a sense of insecurity among the villagers (Bijoy, 2006; Nair, 2008). The Company made attempts to solve the problem by providing tank water to the villagers. But people understood the seriousness of the situation. They demanded a long-term solution to the problem. Protest against the company began with an initiative by the villagers Swaminathan and Mayilamma of Vijayanagar Colony in Plachimada. It soon gained global dimensions beyond expectations (Krishnayyar, 2004: 7-9).

The agitation, which initially was held through participation of Adivasis, gained the support of many tribal-dalit groups, environmental activists, progressive religious organisations, human right activists and political parties

(Falgunan, 2004: 19). Though the struggle began as that of Adivasi Samrakshana Samiti, later, to widen the popular public base, it was renamed as 'Coca-Cola People's Struggle Committee' (Ranjith, 2004: 63; Bijoy, 2006).

The Perumatty Gram Panchayat in association with several voluntary associations in the civil society had organized a three day Water Conference in Plachimada on January 2004. The debated topics were 'privatisation of water,' 'climatic changes and the environment,' 'corporate control of water' and 'dam implementation in India.' The dharna (Gandhian model of non-violent sit down protest with placards and slogans) outside the factory premises had continued for two long years and the participants in the water convention also joined hands with the agitators.

The leading speakers at the conference, including José Bové, leader of the Conféderation Paysanne, a farmers' organization in France, Maude Barlow, chair person of the Canada based council of Canadian Public Advocacy Organisations and activist Vandana Siva, inspired the people and the Plachimada problem got international attention. The active involvement of the local administration and the civil society had made the movement distinct from many other movements. The presence of a vibrant civil society and its active involvement had totally changed the destiny of the movement. In the popular imagination the struggle got an image of a massive campaign against US imperialism (Bijoy, 2006).

Environmentalist Medha Patker came to Plachimada for the inaugural ceremony of her national campaign against globalisation and communalism. At the meeting, Siddha Raj Dande disclaimed the Padmashri Award (an award by the Government of India to outstanding figures in the field of art and culture) conferred on him and proclaimed his empathy with the movement (Azhikkodu, 2004: 27). Vandana Shiva came to the venue to inaugurate the first anniversary of the struggle. On the 787th day of the struggle, activities like forming a human wall and blockades were organized in front of the factory by the Anti Coca Cola People's Struggle Committee (Shiva, 2003: 8). The agitators followed a kind of Gandhian model of struggle, which is characterized by its non-violent way of approaching the issue. The agitation in Plachimada has primarily adopted the method of sit down strikes. Apart from this, tactics such as demonstrations, hunger strikes, harthal (a peaceful way of mass protest by closing down an area, which may exclude hospitals, press etc.) and boycotts (avoid goods and services from an opponent party) have been adopted.

During the 2005 Mumbai World Social Forum (WSF) meeting in Mumbai, Plachimada became a central topic of discussion and green politicians, environmentalists, social activists and NGOs from all over the world, expressed their solidarity with the villagers who had been engaged in a battle for their 'right to life' for over 2 years. The Plachimada declaration adopted at the end of the conference began with an assertion that "water is not a private property or a commodity, but a common resource and fundamental right". It indicated that a country's water policy should be formulated on the basis of this outlook. The conference called all to resist the attempts to marketize, privatize and corporatize water. This conference redefined people's fight for water for survival in India and the world at large (Bijulal, 2004: 141-154).

The struggle against Coke was staged on two grounds: (i) the Adivasi's resistance against the Coke with the strong support from the civil society, and (ii) the legal battle by the Perumatty Gram Panchayat against the Coke (for details see Bijoy, 2006; 2008; Raman, 2005). The natives followed a non-violent form of struggle/resistance against the company. The Gandhian ways of struggles like 'Dharna' and 'Pradarshan' (demonstration) caught world attention. It was also a struggle between the Government and the community. In its initial stage, the Kerala government stood in favour of Coke, expecting more investment in the state. So it was viewed as a struggle against the State and finance capital combined. At the initial stage of the struggle, the Janata Dal, the then ruling party of the Panchayat gave little attention to the issue.

But later on they changed their position and different organisations in the civil society and the political society offered support to the strike. [2] In parallel with the strike, there was a series of legal battle between the Perumatty Panchayath and the Coke. However, after finding pesticides in soft drinks, the CPI (M)-led LDF (Left Democratic Front) government in Kerala banned manufacture and sale of Coca-Cola on August 11, 2006. Followed by this, recently, the Kerala State Legislative Assembly passed a bill to set up a tribunal for realizing compensation from Coke for the 'losses' its plant at Plachimada allegedly caused to the people in the area.

Conclusion

The New Social Movements are a response to the conflicts and contradictions in a post-industrial capitalist society. People are facing diverse issues and the old social thoughts are said to be not sufficient enough to address these complicated issues. The New Social Movements are taking up socio-cultural issues than that of 'economic' or 'political' problems that were taken up by the old social movements. At the epistemic level the New Social Movements are a reflection of a 'post-modern condition.' Post-modernism provides epistemic support to the local cultural celebrations and identity assertions, and in such a way it might be a 'counter-hegemonic force' against the dominant social values.

However, Leftist criticism on New Social Movements sticks on to a particular point that by absorbing energy from postmodernism it lacks a powerful agenda for social change. The Marxists are addressing the issues in a wider canvas. The question is to what extent these scattered struggles and movements can challenge the existing exploitative system. It falls in line with the dominant paradigm of neo-liberalism. By romanticizing development and culture, the present capitalist system has created 'apolitical' space aimed at disintegrating the working class, appropriating their anti-systemic feelings and ultimately 'silencing' them.

However, there is no doubt that the struggle of the people in Plachimada against Coca Cola Company was a great success. The Plachimada struggle shows that the movements in the civil society have the power to direct the political society towards certain ends. But the question remains: is it sufficient to check the 'violence of capital' beyond a space? These movements are fragmented in many ways. Different organizations pursue distinct objectives in diverse ways. The lack of a common agenda can hamper their ability to challenge established institutions and practices. In spite of these limitations, the extensive use of internet widens the horizon of new social movements. The movement against capitalism is part and parcel of struggle for democracy.

End Notes

1. The panchayati raj system is the core mechanism for decentralised governance in India. It is a three-tier system in which the Grama Sabah's are the cells which ensure people's participation in matters of common concern. The Gram Panchayat (the village representational body) is the basic representational body and above it there is block panchayat (taluka level) and zilla panchayat (at the district level).
2. Organisations from the civil society like the Shastra Sahitya Parishat (SSP), Adivasi Samrakshana Sangham, Adivasi Struggle Committee, All India Coordinating Forum of Adivasi, All India People Resistance Forum of Karnataka, All India Students Association, Dalit Liberation Party of Tamil Nadu, Tamil Nadu Green Movement, Jananeeya Cheruthunilpu Vedhi, Jananeethi, National Front of Tribal Self Rule, Planimalai Adivasikal Vidythalai Iyakkum of Tamil Nadu, Peoples Union for Civil Liberties of Kerala, PUCL of Tamil Nadu, Philip Morris Carbon Plant Activists, Telangana Jana Sabha of Andhra, Vyavasayikal Thozhilalar Munnetra Sangam of Tamil Nadu, Porattam, Vikas Adhyayan Kendra, Peoples World Water Forum, Green Peace, Pattika Jati Pattika Varga Munnani, Viplava Sthree Vedhi, Gandhi

Yuvadarshan, Ayyankalippada and the organisations from the political society like the Jnatha Dal, Samajvadi Jana Parishad, SUCI, All India Youth Federation (AIYF), Democratic Youth Federation of India (DYFI), Communist Party of India (Marxist), Communist Party of India (CPI) and Communist Party of India (Marxist Leninist) etc. has extended their warm support to the struggle. The leading newspapers in India like The Hindu, The New Indian Express, Times of India, Mathrubhumi, Malayala Manorama, Deshabhimani, Mangalam, Madhyamam etc. supported the struggle by publishing articles and editorials.

References

Ahluwallia, Pal (2001), Politics and Post-Colonial Theory, London, Routledge.

Amin, Samir (2004), The Liberal Virus: Permanent War and the Americanisation of the World, Delhi, Aakar Books.

Antony, Elliott and Bayan S. Turner (2001), Profiles in Contemporary Social Theory, New Delhi, Sage.

Bijoy, C.R. (2006), "Kerala's Plachimada Struggle: A Narrative on Water and Governance Rights", *Economic and Political Weekly*, October 14.

Bijoy, C.R. (2008), "The Plachimada Struggle", *Economic and Political Weekly*, November 15.

Bijulal, M.V. (2004), "Livelihoods Rights Question at Mumbai World Social Forum: Reminiscence of a Delegate", *Mumbai: Social Action Quarterly Review of Social Trends*, April-June.

Bulmer, Herber (2008), 'Social Movements' in Vincenzo Ruggiero and Nicolo Montagna (ed.); Social Movements: A Reader, London, Routledge.

Cole, Mike (2003), "Might It be in the Practice that it Fails to Succeed? A Marxist Critique of Claims for Post-modernism and Post-structuralism as Forces for Social Change and Social Justice", *British Journal of Sociology of Education*, Vol. 24, No. 4, September 2003.

Dalton, Russel J. and Manfred Kuecher (eds.) (1990), Challenging the Political Order: New Social and Political Movements in Western Societies, Oxford, Polity Press.

Day, Richard J.F. (2008), Gramsci is Dead: Anarchist Currents in the Newest Social Movements, Hyderabad, Orient Longman.

Escobar, Arturo and Sonia E. Alvarez (2008), 'Theory and Protest in

Latin America Today', in Vincenzo Ruggiero and Nicola Montagna (ed.), Social Movements: A Reader, London, Routledge.

Falgunan, P.K. (2004), "Varandunangunna Nellar", *Deshabhimani Weekly,* February 29, Kochi.

Green, D. (1987), The New Right: The Counter Revolution in Political, Economic and Social Thought, London: Wheatsheaf Books.

Gunn, S. (1989), The Revolution of the Right: Europe's New Conservatives, London: Transnational Institute/Pluto Press.

Gustavo, Estavo and Madhu Suri Prakash (1998), Grassroots Post Modernism: Remaking the Soil of Cultures, London, Zed Books.

Harvey, David (2005), A Brief History of Neo-liberalism, Oxford, Oxford University Press.

Jurgen, Habermas (2008), 'New Social Movements' in Vincenzo Ruggiero and Nicolo Montagna, Social Movements: A Reader, London: Routledge.

Krishnayyar, V.R. (2004), "Water Patriotism-Plachimada Terrorism", New Delhi, *Mainstream Weekly*, March 27.

Lyotard, Jean Francois (1984), The Post-modern Condition: A Report on Knowledge, Manchester, Manchester University Press.

Marx, Karl, 'On the Jewish Question', in L D Easton and K H Guddat (eds.) (1997), Writings of the Young Marx on Philosophy and Society, New York: Doubleday.

Melucci, Alberto (2008), 'A Strange Kind of Newness: What's New in New Social Movements', in Vincenzo Ruggiero and Nicola Montagna, Social Movements: A Reader, London: Routledge.

Nair, K.N., Antoyto Paul and Vineetha Menon (2008), Water Insecurity, Institutions and Livelihood Dynamics: A Study in Plachimada, Kerala, Delhi: Daanish Books.

Nelson, A. Pichardo (1997), "New Social Movement: A Critical Review", *Annual Review of Sociology*, 1997, Vol. 23.

Offe, Claus (1990), 'Reflections on the Institutional self-Transformation of Movement Politics: A Tentative Stage Model', in Dalton, Russel J. and Manfred Kuecher (eds.), Challenging the Political Order: New Social and Political Movements in Western Societies, Oxford: Polity Press.

Parkling, F. (1968), Middle Class Radicalism, London: Manchester University Press.

Raman, Ravi K. (2005), "Corporate Violence, Legal Nuances and Political Ecology: Cold War in Plachimada", *Economic and Political Weekly,* June 18.

Renjith, K.R. (2004), Holly Water from the West, Thrissur, Kerala: Alter Media Publication.

Saad-Filho, Alfredo (2007) (ed.), Anti-Capitalism: A Marxist Introduction, New Delhi: Viva Books.

Scott, Alan (1990), Ideology and the Social Movements, Boston: Unwin Hyman.

Seethi, K.M. (2001), "Post-modernism, Neo-liberalism and Civil Society: A Critique of the Development Strategies in the Era of Globalization", *The Indian Journal of Political Science*, Vol. 62, No. 3, September.

Sidney, Tarrow (1989), Struggle, Politics and Reform: Collective Action, Social Movements, and Cycles of Protest, New York: Centre for International Studies, Cornell University Press.

Somers, M. and Block, F. (2007), "From Poverty to Perversity: Ideas, Markets and Institutions over 200 years of Welfare Debate", *American Sociological Review,* 70.

Steven, M. Buechler (1995), "New Social Movement Theories", *Sociological Quarterly*, Vol. 36.

Steven, M. Buechler (1999), Social Movement in Advanced Capitalism, London: Oxford University Press.

Sukumar, Azhikkodu (2004), "Varandunangunna Palakkad", *Deshabhimani Daily,* Calicut, 24th February.

Sydney, Tarrow (1994), Power Movement Collective Action, Social Movement and Politics, London: Cambridge University Press.

Thatcher, M. (1987), 'Aids, Education and the Year 2000', Interview in Women's Own, October 31.

Vandana, Shiva (2003), "Yee Samaram Yadhaartha Swaathantryathinu", *Keraleeyam Monthly,* Thiruvananthapuram, April 27.

Vijayalakshmi, E. (2003), Calling the Shots- Cola Major Gets a Taste of Panchayat Power in Kerala, *Down to Earth*, December 15.

12

Bridging the Digital Divide and Right to Development

Josukutty C.A.

The revolution in information and communication technologies (ICTs) is propelling the world towards an advanced information society. In the information society, knowledge is the key economic resource and medium of change and development, and therefore, the most important source of political power. According to the UN, ICT as an area is a 'powerful enabler of development goals (UN Millennium Project, 2005: 49); they are expected to bring about, 'greater social freedoms, increased knowledge and productive livelihoods (UNDP, 2001: 1).

The tremendous economic development that India has registered in the last decade or so is attributed to ICT. It is the fastest growing sector in India and many consider it as a panacea for India's developmental problems. It is projected that the knowledge economy would make India an economic super power by 2020. Information and knowledge are crucial to development and empowerment in many ways. Obtaining better prices for agricultural products to participatory democracy to exploiting business opportunities and building social relationships depend on ICTs.

The general arguments and expectations of the information society have been that it would usher in a participatory, prosperous and equitable economic and political order. The enormous quantity of employment opportunities opened up by the ICTs along with globalisation was optimistically predicted to reduce inequalities and ensure prosperity for all. But what has been unfolding is the increasing consolidation of the existing inequalities and deepening development deficits in the form of digital divide at the national and global levels. Digital divide is a major reason for increasing social and economic developmental gaps. The paper attempts to address the issue of digital divide through the normative prism of 'right to development' and examines how its values and principles could be used to resolve the issues of inequality and exclusion caused by digital divide.

Digital Divide

The term digital divide became part of popular parlance in the 1990s when it was found that large sections of people, especially the marginalised, were not using or incapable of using the new ICTs. In fact, this is an extension of the concept of 'technological dualism' introduced by Hans Singer, by which he meant unequal. [1] Gradually, this began to be defined as a gap between those who possess new technology and those do not. Digital divide refers to the gap between people with effective access to digital and information technology and those without.

According to the Organisation of Economic Cooperation and Development (OECD), the term 'digital divide' refers to "the gap between individuals, households, businesses and geographic areas at the different socio-economic levels with regard to their opportunities to access information and communication technologies and their use of internet. It reflects differences among and within countries" (OECD, 2001: 6).

To Hanimann and Ruedin, the term 'digital divide' essentially describes three distinctive divides: a geographical digital divide (between regions and countries), a social digital divide (between social classes), and an upgraded digital divide (between technology and humans) (Hanimann and Ruedin, 2007: 16). Scholars like Norris, Mark, and Branko suggest that there are at least three major divides: a global divide between the developed and undeveloped worlds, a social divide between the information rich and the information poor, a democratic divide between those who do and those who do not use the new technologies to further political participation (Norris, 2001; Mark, 2003 and Branko, 2005).

Digital divide is not merely a question of accessibility to a technology. It includes the imbalances in physical access to technology as well as the imbalances in resources and skills needed to effectively participate as a digital citizen. It is also a question of capabilities- on the part of the individual and the society—to use ICTs and to convert the information that ICT provide into useful knowledge (Thomas and Parayil, 2008: 410). Accordingly, there are different levels and orders of digital divide such as gap in access to use ICT (first order), gap in the ability to use ICTs (second order), gap in actual use (third order) and gap in the impact of use (fourth order).

Thus, the concept of the digital divide, over the years, focuses on four areas of ICTs: infrastructure, capacity building, resource usage and empowerment. It means that digital divide has economic, social, political and developmental dimensions. Economically ones employability and the ability to generate income depend on ICTs skills and accessibility. Social connectivity and interactions, ranging from peer groups to community belongingness are increasingly shaped by ICTs. Knowledge of new technologies is essential for effective political participation and delivery and receipt of governmental services. Thus, social, economic and political empowerment or deprivation (depending on cases) has become a function of the ICTs.

Inequality and Exclusion

Contrary to expectations, ICT enabled economic growth is characterised by a growing inequality between the information rich and the information poor. There is an unequal distribution of the benefits of ICT generated development among different categories of people. The impressive economic growth has not shown a corresponding improvement in other fronts of development. It is the most recent and refreshed face of inequality and non-inclusive development that the world witness in contemporary times.

Inequality and the resultant underdevelopment is not a new phenomenon in India or elsewhere. Since long back, India has been subjected to acute forms of exclusionary development patterns and inequality. Caste system justified inequality and exclusion on philosophical and religious grounds. British rule had witnessed frequent episodes of famine deaths and disempowerment. It was the logic of colonialism and capitalist industrialisation that defined development.

A combination of these factors culminated in the creation of an order based on inequality, exploitation and underdevelopment. The gap between the rich and the poor and between the North and the South in terms of development indices at different phases of history is reflective of the whole story of the non-inclusive patterns of development. That is, even though, digital divide is characteristic of the information society, it is a complex, historically rooted, social, economic and political phenomenon. It is, into this, entrenched inequities that the growth brought about by ICTs is integrated into.

It is not surprising that inequalities have increased in the last two decades between countries and within countries, both developed and developing (Cornia et al., 2004: 25-26). Two-third of the world population is outside the information society. In the so called information society only one out of hundred get an opportunity for higher education, six of them have control over 50 percent of the wealth, 50 percent of the people lack proper education, health care, food, shelter and clothing. In the US, between 2000 and 2005, when real money earnings increased only for 3.5 percent of the labour force (the highly educated), it decreased for 96 percent of the labour force (Scheve and Slaughter, 2007: 34-37).

In India, which is tipped to become an IT super power, the situation is no better. As per statistics, the internet penetration in India is only 10.2 percent whereas it is 78.3 percent in USA (World Internet Statistics, 2011). Ninety percent of people have no meaningful access to internet. According to the noted economist C.P. Chandrasekhar, India is online but most Indians are not (Chandrasekhar, 2006). As per the Global Information Technology Report, India is placed 69th in the Networked Readiness Index Rankings (World Economic Forum, 2012). Tele density in India is only 23 percent. By the middle of the century half of the blind and the largest number of illiterates will in India.

Seventy percent of the people in India will have no access to drinking water, all the mega cities in India will be polluted well above the danger level and majority of the child labours will be in India. The Human Development Index, 2011 gives India a rank of 134 out of 187 countries. The Human Poverty Index which focuses on the proportion of people below a threshold level in the same dimensions of human development as the human poverty index places India at 87th among 135 developing countries.

According to the new International Multi-dimensional Poverty Index, 55 percent of India's population is poor (Human Development Report, 2010). In Gender-Related Development Index, out of the 157 countries, 137 countries have a better ratio than India's. The US-based International Food Policy Research Institute has ranked India 67th in the Global Hunger Index for the year 2011, way below its South Asian neighbours Pakistan, Sri Lanka and China (International Food Policy Research Institute, 2011).

According to the NSS data 2008, 77 percent of India's population lives on ₹ 20 a day. As per the Planning Commission (2004-2005) 27.5 percent of people in India live below the poverty line. A new study based on a survey of the height and weight of more than one lakh children across six States has found that as many as 42 percent of under-fives are severely or moderately underweight and that 59 percent of them suffer from moderate to severe stunting [2] (HUNGaMA Survey Report, 2011). The top ten percent of the population increased its share of national wealth to 52 percent while the share of the bottom 10 percent fell to just 0.21 percent (Asia-

Pacific Wealth Report, 2008).

The Report says that the number of India's high net worth individuals (those have a net financial assets of at least US$ 1 million), increased by 205 percent and they control about half of India's GDP. In short, a large majority of people in India do not satisfy the three essential capabilities for human development as identified by the UNDP such as the capacity to lead a long and happy life, to be knowledgeable and to have access to resources necessary for a decent standard of living. At the same time a small minority is accumulating lion's share of the benefits of ICT-generated economic growth.

These figures are to be analysed against the fact that India's GDP has been growing at an annual rate of over 6 percent since the early 1990s, and over 8 percent from 2005-06. [3] Apparently, the benefits of IT-enabled economic growth have not reached people at large. The fruits of economic growth and employment opportunities generated by the knowledge industry are pocketed by a few-urban upper middle class and caste- to the exclusion of a large majority. Apart from the figure and facts already presented, a study of the IT workforce in Bangalore shows that their social composition is homogeneous—it is largely urban, middle class and high middle caste (Upadhya, 2007: 1863).

The process of exclusion that operates in education, in recruitment, ideology of merit leads to the creation of homogeneity resulting in the exclusion of large section of people. Another study of the efforts to bridge the digital divide by the governments in Kerala and Andhra Pradesh gave interesting results. [4] The capabilities to use ICTs and the capabilities to convert information into useful knowledge were found to be higher in Kerala despite the fact that Andhra Pradesh has a better concentration of knowledge-based-industries (Thomas and Parayil, 2008: 409). The results showed clearly that existing socio-economic conditions (in this case better healthy social indices such as high literacy, land rights etc. in Kerala) have a clear bearing on the ICT induced growth patterns. Two generally known inferences are possible from the functioning of digital divide. One, digital divide is leading to a system of social and economic organisation that give rise to categories of individuals and groups that challenges the elementary principles of justice or fairness. Two, it is a combination of factors that causes inequality and non-inclusive development. The solution lies in addressing this issue from a strong normative framework.

Human Right to Development

Human rights discourse and development discourse though emerged simultaneously after the Second World War, there was little in common between the two. The missing link was provided by the concept of 'Right to Development'. It is the most innovative of human rights that established the essential unity of rights with the potential to bridge developmental gaps and facilitate inclusive development. Right to Development is right to a process of development that ensures the realisation of all human rights. It is in this spirit Article 1 of the Declaration on the Right to Development adopted by the UN in 1986, states, "The right to development is an inalienable human right by virtue of which every human person and all peoples are entitled to participate in, contribute to, and enjoy economic, social, cultural and political development, in which all human rights and fundamental human rights can be fully realised" (UN Declaration on the Right to Development, 1986).

The Vienna Declaration and Programme of Action adopted by the World Conference on Human Rights held at Vienna in 1993 further emphasised Right to Development as 'universal and inalienable right and an integral part of fundamental human rights' (Vienna Declaration and Programme of Action, 1993: 30). It is based on the premise that development itself is human right. It implies that right to development is comprehensive economic, social, cultural and political process. A mere increase in GDP or output or rapid industrialisation is not development.

States are precluded from determining whatever

development policy that suits them. The declaration establishes the duty of states to formulate appropriate national development policies that aim at the constant improvement of the well-being of the entire population and of all individuals, on the basis of their active, free and meaningful participation in development and the fair distribution of benefits resulting there from (UN Declaration on the Right to Development 1986). Right to Development (RTD) also focuses on the interdependence of rights. It links the realisation of each right with the performance of other rights.

According to Arjun Sen Gupta, Right to Development is the vector of rights aimed at achieving equity, justice and freedom in the society through the realisation of a number of human rights (Second Report of the Independent Expert to the Human Rights Commission, 2000). Each element of the vector is a human right just as the vector itself is a right. It is a composite of social, economic, political and cultural rights. All the elements are interdependent.

For example, realising right to health will depend on the level of realisation of other rights such as right to food, to housing, etc. RTD will be realised if all the elements improve or if at least one improves and no other element decreases (Second Report of the Independent Expert to the Human Rights Commission, 2000). Thus, the human right to development has the potential to ensure a whole lot of rights to the benefits of all in the society.

Rights-based Approach

A rights-based-approach is core to the human right to development. The UN Office of the High Commissioner for Human Rights defines the right-based approach to development as, "a conceptual framework for the process of human development that is normatively based on international human rights standards and operationally directed to promoting and protecting human rights. Essentially, a right based approach integrates the norms, standards and principles of the international human rights system into the plans, policies and process of development...A right based approach to development include the following elements: express linkage to rights; accountability; empowerment; participation; and non-discrimination and attention to vulnerable groups" (Office of the High Commissioner for Human Rights, 2012).

A human rights approach places human rights as the basis and guiding principle of development. Development should be pursued in a human rights way or that human rights must be integrated into sustainable human development. Andre Fran Frankovits of the Human Rights Council of Australia calls it 'the rights way to development' (Frankovits and Earle, 1998: 8).

In the words of Julia Hausermann, human rights to development is that one puts people first and promotes human-centred development, recognises the inherent dignity of every human being without distinction, recognises and promotes equality between men and women, promotes equal opportunity and choices for all...promotes national and international systems based on economic equity, equity in the access of public resources, and social justices and promotes mutual respect between people...(Hausermann, 1998: 32). Development is seen not as a privilege but as a human right that could be legally enforced, claimed or asserted. It is the conceptual framework for the process of human development. [5] The principles of equity, non-discrimination, transparency, accountability, participation, and non-discrimination are the parameters of the rights-based approach to development.

Capability Approach

The Human right to development also includes the capability approach as enunciated by Amartya Sen. In his book, 'Development as Freedom', Sen argues that development is not the acquisition of more goods and services but the enhanced freedom to choose to lead the kind of life one values (Amartya Sen, 1999a: 16). These enhanced choices are called capabilities. In the capabilities discourse, capability is the option available to an individual to partake some valued dimension of life; function is the exercise of that option (Amartya Sen, 1999b: 30).

As such, development approach links development concerns to freedom, and because freedom implies the widening of choices in the civil, political, social economic and cultural spheres and it becomes a starting point for a human rights understanding of the development process. This approach has become the official policy of the UNDP, as reflected in the assertion...human development shares a common vision with human rights (UNDP, 2001: 9). Human development and human rights are mutually reinforcing, helping to secure the well-being and dignity of all people, building self-respect and the respect of others. Therefore, human development is a process of enhancing human capabilities. In this sense right to development can be described as a human right to human development—the entitlement to a process of enhancing human capabilities and freedoms.

Right to Development and Bridging the Digital Divide

The RTD framework proposes a qualitatively different approach, where considerations of equity, justice and respect for human rights standards determine the strategy for economic growth. Our experience of growth has been marked by inequality, unemployment and multiple disparities. Digital divide is its latest manifestation. Contrary to past perceptions, development cannot be viewed entirely in terms increasing national income. It has to be sustainable, equitable and balanced. Only a right-based economic growth can ensure equity and justice in development.

Development is seen as a process of development and should adhere to the principles of equity, non-discrimination, participation, accountability and transparency as enunciated by various human rights instruments. These principles need to be incorporated and applied while framing and implementing ICT policies. ICT policies should aim at ensuring equitable distribution of benefits and there must be special provisions for the marginalised and vulnerable sections of society.

To make policies non-discriminatory, there shall be no

discrimination on the basis of race, colour, sex, language, political or other opinions, property, birth or other status not only between the beneficiaries but also between agents. The beneficiaries should be a part of the decision making process in ICT policies. This would ensure a sense of belongingness and ownership of the policy and make it truly participatory. Accountability means establishing responsibility for non-performance of a right and applying corrective measures. ICT policies and programmes must identify duty bears and their obligations.

This is an effective method to deal with bureaucratic indifference and apathy. For transparency, all the programmes and policies must be open in its interrelations and linkages between different actors and actions.

If these principles are applied to the information and communication technologies, its developmental potential would become a tool to improve the enjoyment of human rights. The RTD is a capability building right that empowers persons and peoples to convert ICT-enabled knowledge to improve conditions of life. Capability in relation to technology means that it is accessible, affordable and generating capability that could lead to empowerment. Right to development facilitate capacity-building which enable the individual to use the information provided by the ICTs to useful purposes. It empowers an individual to make use of the goods and resources at his command to lead a life of his choice.

Again as a composite right and as a vector of rights, RTD can address multiple issues of exclusion simultaneously. It can ameliorate the adverse social and economic contexts of the underprivileged into empowering situations. The human rights framework enhances various dimensions of development and surrounds it with certain guarantees such as freedom of association and expression, the right to information, a role in planning, decision making and management. It is, in this framework and understanding that the Human Rights to Development become relevant as tool to bridge the digital divide.

To make it possible define issues of digital divide in terms of rights, relate them to the main human rights treaties and focus on obligatory provisions to respect, protect, promote, provide, apply prescribed methods and principles of RTD (Stephen P. Marks, 2005: 50-51). The policies, programmes and institutions chosen for bridging the digital divide should be based explicitly on the norms and values of human rights. It can address the question of digital divide beyond and deeper the surface of a technology access question.

Digital divide and the consequent digital exclusion is a development issue. Digital exclusion is social exclusion and non-inclusive development which has become characteristic of the information society. Right to development and its normative prescriptions explain the ways in which human rights can be applied to human development. Possession, accession and application of ICT by all people are a pre-condition for equitable and inclusive development. Growth that increases GDP but does not reduce the digital gap and excludes large sections of the people from its benefits is not development. The strategy to bridge the digital divide need to be guided by considerations of equity, justice and respect for human right standards as envisaged by the Human Right to Development .

End Notes

1. According to Singer, technological dualism is a process of scientific and technological advance' that in all its stage-basic research, applied research and blueprinting—has been concentrated in the richer countries. Digital divide in the global economy is a reflection of the same basic forces that give rise to international technological dualism.
2. The findings—contained in the Hunger and Malnutrition (HUNGaMA) report by the Naandi Foundation—stunting means that the height of children is much lower than the median height-for-age of the reference population.
3. Data published by the Central Statistical Organisation (CSO) available from Economic and Political Weekly Research Foundation (EPWRF).
4. Government of Andhra Pradesh lunched the 'inclusive community'

(i-community) project in the Kuppam area in Chittoor District in April 2002 and the government of Kerala started the Akshya computer literacy programme in Malappuram district in November 2002. These centres provided computer training and information about agriculture, health, education etc. to the participants of the programme.

5. The preamble to the RTD Declaration, defines 'development as a comprehensive economic, social cultural and political process', for more details see' Centre for Development and Human Rights, (2004), *The Right to Development: A Primer*, Sage Publications, New Delhi.

References

Asia-Pacific Wealth Report, 2008.

Asia-Pacific Wealth Report, 2006.

Branko, Milanovic (2005), Worlds Apart: Measuring International and Global Inequality, Princeton University Press: Princeton.

Chandra Sekhar, C.P (2006), 'India is Online But Most Indians are Not', The Hindu, September 25, 2006,Thiruvananthapuram.

Cornia, G.A., T. Addision and Kiiski (2004), 'Income Distribution Changes and their Impact in the Post-Second World War Period' in G.A. Cornia (ed.), Inequality, Growth, Poverty in an Era of Globalisation and Liberalisation, New York, Oxford University Press.

Frankovits, Andre and Earle, Patrick (1998), The Rights Way to Development: Manual for a Human Rights Approach to Development Assistance, Marrickvill; Human Rights Council of Australia.

International Food Policy Research Institute (2011), 'Global Hunger Index'.

Mark, Warschauer (2003), Excellent Technology and Social Inclusion: Rethinking the Digital Divide, MIT Press: Cambridge.

Marks, P. Stephen (2005), 'The Human Rights Framework for Development: Seven Approaches' in Arjun Sengupta et al. (ed.), Reflections on the Right to Development, Centre for Development and Human Rights, New Delhi, Sage Publications.

Norris, P. (2001), The Digital Divide: Civic Engagement, Information, Poverty and Internet Worldwide, Cambridge University Press: Cambridge.

Organisation of Economic Cooperation and Development (2001), Understanding the Digital Divide, OECD Publications, Paris.

Scheve, K.J. and M.J. Slaughter (2007), "A New Deal for Globalisation", *Foreign Affairs*, 86(4).

Second Report of the Independent Expert (Arjun Sengupta) to the Human Rights Commission, A/55/306, 17th August 2000, paras 23-25.

Sen, Amartya (1999a), Development as Freedom, New Delhi, Oxford University Press.

Sen, Amartya (1999b), Commodities and Capabilities, Oxford, Oxford University Press.

Sen Gupta, Arjun, Second Report of the Independent Expert to the Human Rights Commission, A/55/306, 17th August, 2000.

Singer, Hans (1970), "Dualism Revisited: A New Approach to the Problem of the Dual Society in Developing Countries", *Journal of Development Studies.*

Thomas, Jayan Jose and Govindan Parayil (2008), "Bridging the Digital Divide in Andhra Pradesh and Kerala: A Capability Approach", *Development and Change*, Vol. 39, No. 3.

Upadhya, Carol, (2007), "Employment, Exclusion and Merit in the Indian IT Industry", *Economic and Political Weekly*, Vol. 42, No. 20.

United Nations (1986), UN Declaration on the Right to Development, General Assembly Resolution 41/128.

UNDP (1998), Integrating Human Rights with Sustainable Development, New York, also see *Human Development Reports*, New York: Oxford University Press, 1990, 2000, 2001, 2002.

UNDP (2001), Human Development Report, 2001, Making New Technologies Work for Human Development, New York: Oxford University.

U.N. Millennium Project (2005), Innovation: Applying Knowledge in Development, Task force on Science, Technology and Innovation, London, Sterling.

Vienna Declaration and Programme of Action (1993), World Conference on Human Rights, DPI/1394-39399.

World Economic Forum (2012), Global Information Technology Report.

13

Sri Lankan Ethnic Crisis

G.D.R.U.U. Abeyrathne and
S.Y. Surendra Kumar

Introduction

Sri Lankan ethnic crisis has undergone serious scholarly treatments. The causes and effects and impacts of the ethnic crisis on society, politics and economy have been brought out employing different theoretical approaches. There are plenty of explanations of the causes and they had suggested many solutions in their own capacities as experts. In other words, Sri Lankan ethnic crisis has become an archive of scholarly work on conflict studies and management experimentations. This raises the issue, whether there is anything new to warrant the present study.

The Sri Lankan forces have wiped out the Liberation Tigers of Tamil Eelam (LTTE) together with the military supremo, Velupillai Prabakaran and the top leadership. However, the military defeat of the movement alone would not lead to peace and harmony in the deeply ethnically fragmented society in Sri Lanka. The President, Mahinda Rajapakse himself has admitted the above reality in his address to the parliament in May 2009. He prefers a home grown solution to the ethnic problem. Further, the secure Tamil diaspora seems to be favouring a negotiated settlement. Military victory and suggested development package for North and East provinces of the country where majority of Tamil reside would not lead to automatic integration of different communities in a single united Sri Lankan Nation. Thus, military victory is not the end of the conflict.

There are explanations as to why some conflict last long

and difficult to resolve. James Fearon has broadly identified them (Fearon, 2004: 275-301).

1. "Sons of the Soil" based civil conflict. Such conflicts are difficult to resolve and last long. These conflicts originate out of effort on the part of state initiatives dominated by majority ethnic group to migrate their members to areas inhabited by peripheral minority ethnic groups.
2. Conflicts which derive funding from contraband such as opium, diamond or coca etc.
3. Domestic conflicts that are significantly internationalized and where peripheral ethnic groups have close or real or imagined blood relations to neighbouring country's ethnic groups, especially to that of big neighbours.

In the case of Sri Lanka, it has all the factors which contribute to protracted conflict. The theorization or conceptualization of the conflict as unending or long lasting has become virtually irrelevant to understand why, once a popular and armed with sophisticated military technology movement both globally and domestically becomes that much weak and is wiped out. The available literature is not sufficient to comprehend the situation. Further, this kind of conflicts signifies the failure of social science engineering of post-colonial societies. The parties to the Sri Lankan ethnic conflict are now facing the challenge of finding a political settlement to the ethnic crisis. They are facing the dilemma of breaking the cage of "foundational thinking associated with nation state" which has been created by the political elite of respective communities. Now the political elite find it difficult to escape the cage of their own creation.

The Sri Lankan case has to be identified as a conflict between "State-Nation Building" and "Nation-State Making" both that share the essence of nation state project. The political elites in Sri Lanka have been divided on ethnic line largely drawing on colonial policies in their struggle for power. They had shown their inability to move beyond the foundational thinking associated with nation state conception of community self rule. This entanglement had resulted in enormous bloodshed and humanitarian crisis in the society. This trapping would continue into the future even after military defeat of LTTE. This makes it difficult to find political solutions to the ethnic crisis.

The objective of this article is to bring out the basic syndrome of the State-Nation and Nation-State building projects and the inapplicability of them in the geo-political reality of the day and political demography of the society in Sri Lanka. This article looks at the nature of the state-crafting inherited from the colonial times. It also examines the social realities of post colonial state, efforts of proselytization and the ethnic rivalries among elites in the Sri Lankan society.

The first part of the article explores the foundational thinking associated with the nation state. Then it proceeds to study the impacts of colonial policies in developing competition and notion of ethnic nation. The third, part of the article examines the State-Nation building project carried out by the Sinhalese elite. The fourth part is devoted to examining the response of the major minority group, the Tamil and to bring out what went wrong.

Nation-State Building and Impacts of Colonialism

There is certain pattern of thinking associated with nation state project. It has been created through complex political discourses of nation and the political elite had strived to internalize the notion of nation among the inhabitant of the language territories in their struggle to gain wealth and prestige. Political discourse on nation-building and state-crafting assume that there is a fixed human nature [whether naturally social or naturally free] that forms the necessary true foundation for politics (Peri and Peter, 2005: 12). This is the base of modern state. The colonies have to become nations to qualify sovereign states in the international system. Nation to the people in Non-Western Societies had been an unfamiliar notion. The task of political elite was to build nations out of multiple identity groups in their struggle to gain control over the resource allocation process of native society.

Nation building involves moral, social and cultural ideas and customs that justify the particular political institution which we call nation state (Peri and Peter, 2005: 18). The moral, social and cultural ideas and custom of the nation state were the loyalty to single political entity which is identified as nation and its co-riders state, individualism, unitary citizenship and equality before law. Further, identification by individual member with a nation state was thought necessary and natural order of the things and characteristic of a well ordered society. The place where power resides was thought to be the nation. Accordingly, the power of the state is thought to be emanated or originated from a central, symbolic place or position of nation state. It is natural to have political identity organized around the nation.

The nation building process in the Western European context involves an eraser of cultural identities of minorities for centuries by force and *ideological warfare* of imagined communities. The societies in Asia and Africa which the Europeans colonized had not inherited the tradition of erasing the identities of others in order to build a state based on the notion of nation but allowed the other to co-exist as distinct group in a hierarchically ordered society (Ludden, 2006: 33). The nation state involves an essential centralization of power and constructing members of same quality to uphold the unitary conception of citizenship and undivided and in-alienable sovereignty of the nation. This involves a conflict with others who do not identify with nation aspiring to become the state.

The realities of the colonial societies has been totally different that of the master countries. Sudipta Kaviraj elaborates the society and its political arrangement in the Indian context as follows: "They were decentralized in a peculiar way (though this does not appear to have been less repressive)...It had a determinate way of arranging its social space which has important implications for the relation between state and society. It did not have a clear hierarchy of classes presided over by a strong and fairly 'thick' state... traditional society seemed to work on a practical arrangement of, rent-receiving, partly marginal state. The structure of society is less integrated in terms of its ordering discourse, and can be likened to a circle of circles of caste and regional communities with state sitting at the centre. The state impinges on these communities economically, but its right of economic extraction is more by squeezing a sector than by restructuring it" (Kaviraj, 1997: 141-169).

In this process of governing, the rulers in South Asia, prior to colonial discovery, did not intrude into everyday life processes of the communities who inhabited the traditional state and they were disinterested in restructuring of social relations so long as their appetite for a reasonable rent was satisfied (Kaviraj, 1997: 141-169). As long as these ground rules of rent receiving and non-interference in social life was fulfilled, neither party cared on what goes on. This reality has provided a space where the group's identity has cut across the linguistic and religious boundaries of the hierarchically ordered social milieu. [1] What was important in Sri Lanka in ordering social relations was caste or *jati,* not language or religion at the beginning of Representative phase of government introduced by the British colonizers.

British rule in colonial societies in South Asia had to face a dilemma. The political rule then prevailing in the region was not acceptable to them. The political world familiar to them was a public order where government is based on a conception of public law. Secondly, the firmness of their power had relied on the cooperation of traditional layers of personal loyalties (Ludden, 2006: 24). Compelled to abide by the public law and secure the firm grip over colonial society, the colonial rulers, had resorted to elite layers of society to work as intermediary between the general public and the ruling class of the master nation. This has given the elite layers that were literate in English and native languages as interpreters of traditions, reforming tradition and influencing government (Ludden, 2006: 41).

The British rule had abolished all barriers that prevented the penetration of its power in the society. Firstly, it abolished the land holding system of the native societies. The land entitlement was made an important aspect of economy. This was driven by the profit motive of the colonial capitalism. For the purpose, the habitat of the native societies was surveyed. The people were counted according to the rank and file in the native society. [2] Progress was measured according to relative numerical criterion. Land survey and colonial census exercises have contributed to stop community migration within the native habitat in the first time in history except for the bilingually literate elite in English and native languages of the society.

The bilingual elite strata were still in the habit of integrating with each other on the basis their elite position in the native society and they were the natural representatives and intermediary of the territorially and linguistically confined communities. The bilingual in native languages and ethnically mixed communities had to identify them with the majority language community of the area. This was required for classificatory purposes and was found administratively expedient. This was extended not only to languages but also to caste etc. [3]

The entire project of colonialism was driven by the profit motive of the ruling classes of the master nation. However, the project was justified on a civilization mission. It was based on the goodness of progress. Colonial rulers have offered different justification for subjugating native people. Spaniards justified their acquisition of America by force on the ground that the natives had fanatic practices of human sacrifices which transgressed the divine law (Parekh, 1997: 173-193). Lock justified land acquisition on the ground that land is given by the god for rational and industrious utilization. [4]

Removing the fanatic practices and inculcating rationality and industriousness were the said objectives. To adhere to the said goodness of the colonial rule, they had given representation to the native society trough the native elite. The native elite of multi-cultural society, though cooperated on mutually beneficial manner, had quarrelled each other with the introduction of territorial based representation in countries with a big majority and minorities. Sri Lanka is a classic example of this kind (Bandara, 2007: 124).

In this process, the intelligentsia of the elite has started producing discourses on the historicity of particular communities. Producing such histories was a precondition for political independence because autonomy was given only to nations with a history in the international power project. This policy had lead to producing competing histories of nations in the plural colonial territories in South Asia, as the success of competing elites came to realize that the stake of theirs depend on the success of creating histories for different people. This is a specific feature of writing modern history in Sri Lanka. [5] The impartial and objective history writing has been cornered in this process. The phenomenon has to understand in the context of competition between power elites in Sri Lanka.

State-Nation Building versus Nation-State and Nation-Territory Making

The power competition at the beginning between the elite has given birth to two types of ethno nationalism i.e. the Sinhalese and Tamil Nationalism (Bandara, 2007: 141). The violent clash among the two after 1970s, has contributed to an emergence of a third, namely that of Muslim nationalism. [6] At present, we could identify three types of political projects that share the fundamentals of nation state project in essence. It has projected the one who does not embrace the essence of nation, i.e. loyalty to single entity called nation which is essentially a cultural construct as others and had strived to project that compel the others to embrace the cultural lifestyle of the dominant within the unit aspired by them or the forced the other to see a unit where they could pursue their own cultural life style. Thus, three types of Nation projects can be identified as follows:

1. State-Nation Building.
2. Nation-State.
3. Nation-Territory Making.

The first and second are the political projects of political elite of the two major ethnic communities in Sri Lanka. The third is the response of other minority i.e. Muslims to the first and second projects. To understand and grasp the nature of the problem, contextualizing the political demography of Sri Lanka is necessary. Sri Lanka is a country which has had a long history of multi-ethnic and multi-cultural co-existence. The Sinhalese community is the biggest component of the Sri Lankan population. They composed more than 70 percent of the total population. The elite and non-elite have cooperated with each other depending upon the proximity of the habitat. However, it must be noted that elite of the both communities found proximity as no bar to the familial relations. [7]

Majority of Sinhalese elite found championing community causes and politically expedient with the gradual introduction of territorial base representative system. As pointed out above, the self rule or sovereignty was given only to the Nations with a history. The failure of the elite lies in its effort of creating and making a history for the peoples of Sri Lanka. The politics of independence in Sri Lanka was never a mass movement and most of the so-called independent movement had opposed the granting of suffrage to the ordinary people (Gosh, 2003: 51-61). Tamil elite were not in a habit of thinking as a minority due to historical reasons such as the spread of modern education in Jaffna Peninsular.

They were far ahead of the other native legislators in the colonial legislature in intellectual dynamism, independence of outlook and political maturity. [8] Historically, they had enjoyed privileged post in the court of the king and among the Mahasanga i.e. Buddhist clergy. The granting of unwished suffrage to ordinary people to elect and the denial of the right to be elected has resulted in a boom of writing of subjective histories of the people. The elite who identified with the majority Sinhalese have found championing the ancient glory and prosperity. The better off minority, due to objective historical events were seen by others as unduly over-privileged (Wijetunga, 1999: 65).

Ultimately, this had lead to the creation of nation building project around the state. In this process, the political elite who had to depend on 70 percent of Sinhalese, started a process of identifying the state with the symbols of the majority culture, such as lion flag, public holidays etc. Thus, the post-independence nation building in Sri Lanka was essentially a waxing of state with the cultural artifacts of the Sinhalese and following a process of social reward allocation based on justifying the historical injustices to the majority community. [9]

This has given added imperative to think of alternate geographical area for the Tamil community, diverting of a desire to contain Sinhalese dominancy to a manageable level. The desire was in existence as early as 1938 when Ponnambalam was championing 50:50 formula to control majoritarian politics. S.W. R.D. Bandaranayake has formed Sinhala Maha Saba as a political expedient in 1937 though he was for a devolutionary form of government in 1940s. However, it is impossible to determine whether Majority Ethnic politics or Minority Politics has lead to the kind of political conflict among the people in Sri Lanka (Gosh, 2003: 51-61).

State-Nation Building versus Nation-State Building

The twin principles of population and territory in carving out electorate adopted under the first-past-the post system of representative democracy has favoured the majority Sinhalese population in forming the government in Sri Lanka. The developmental state that was prescribed by the international actors involves development of the economy and nation building. The nation building has been presumed to be an important element of development and precondition in attaining the developmental objectives.

The challenge was to create a nation out of the complex ethnic groups by the time of the political independence. On the one hand, the political independence in Sri Lanka was not a result of a mass movement that involved masses of different communities of the society. Rather, independence was a shrewd calculation of the profitability of keeping the colony under the British Raj. On the other hand, the political elites were trained in the tradition of unitary citizenship, individualism and democracy to which they have become familiar.

The ruling elite did not recognize that democracy is possible with multiple loyalties of different group in a united country. They have started a process of assimilation and exclusion of other communities into the majority using the power of the state. The first piece of legislation came with the introduction of the citizenship laws that deprived the citizenship of the migrated Tamil labourers of Indian Origin. [10] This has given weight to the Hill Country Sinhalese Representation in the National Parliament. The exclusionary process was substantiated by writing of history. The backwardness of the Sinhalese community in the spheres of economy, education and culture was a historical injustice done to the Sinhalese not only by the Western colonizers but also by the privileged minority of Tamils of Sri Lanka for generation.

This involves a replacing the other from within the native community after colonial power left the country. The overall policy adopted in building the nation was the building of a nation after the state which has come to be in existence as a result of colonialism and hegemonic international law based on nation. The Sinhalese elites which were in competition for power and privileges with Tamil elites, has found inspiration for this project in the Pali Chronicle that were basically histories of dynasties. [11] This enterprise of historiography has created a history of Sinhalese, an imagined community in line with the modern jargon of nation. [12]

They have started a process of building nation through state sponsored development. Industries have been located basically in majority community areas and agricultural development penetrated the areas of traditional habitat of minority ethnic groups making changes to the demography assuring the domination of majority community.

The next step embraced by the political elite is the identification of the state with cultural artifacts of state with the ones of the majority community. First step was the identification of the state with the Sinhalese language. The government in 1956 has made Sinhala; the official language, while the First and Second Republican Constitutions constitutionally recognizing it as the official language. [13] The other symbols such as National Flag, State Emblem etc. have given predominant status to the cultural symbols of the majority community.

This process of cultural identification of the state culminated with the adoption of the First Republican Constitution. Besides those policies, the constitution has dropped the provisions safeguarding the rights of minorities which have been in-existence under the Dominion Constitution granted by the British. The Second Republican Constitution has carried the process of Sinhalization [14] of the state while erasing the element of democracy and embracing the liberal and capitalist mode of economy.

The nation state project is the one carried out by the major ethnic minority community of Sri Lanka. The basic feature of this project is that the production of history for the community, first articulated painstakingly by the competing political elite of the major minority of the Sri Lankan populace. This process involves creating ethnic nations which spoke dialect of Tamil. In this process, they had produced a history of equally old as that of the majority community (Sitrampalal, 2004: 239-282). They have adopted every possible measure to articulate an imagined community of shared history and culture. This includes the self-proclaimed inclusion of Muslims of the country among the Tamil folds (Ameer, 2001: 71).

Conscious effort of assimilation of multi-dialect communities into their fold using public resources available to them was also carried out. This was evidenced in the claims for the inclusion for by dividing the harmonious and multi-lingual communities into their fold such as the people of Panam Pattuva in the Eastern Province. This process has gained a new vigour in the context of ethnicity based war waged between government of Sri Lanka and LTTE. By the time of political independence of the country, the Tamil elite were able to inculcate a mind set of ethnic nation among the Tamil Hindus and Tamil Christians of the Country.

However, this movement had not aimed at achieving a state for a nation. The initial demand was for a homeland within a federal set-up in the framework of United Sri Lanka. The failed attempts of negotiated settlement in 1950s and 1960s and the gradual political and economic domination of the majority community in every sphere and the removal of minority guarantees under the home-made constitution making exercises has lead the Tamil moderate to demand for a separate state for the nation of Tamils. The peaceful means of agitation were suppressed brutally by the government.

The Tamil United Party which won most of the Tamil speaking electorate in 1977 general election however proved that such an objective is unattainable in the context of existing state in Sri Lanka through democratic means. This has given birth to a militant movement lead by youth organizations to achieve the objective by military engagement. However, the LTTE led by Prabakaran, has not tolerated different military groups and democratic wing of the traditional political elite. It has eliminated the competing group from within the community. The LTTE also had followed the same policy of exclusion of resisting others.

First, they have forced the Muslims of North and ordered to go out of the Tamil homeland within 24 hours. The Muslims and Sinhalese in the Eastern province were targeted brutishly to create a mono-ethnic homeland. This project could be compared and contrasted with the State Nation project such as denial of citizenship to the Indian Tamils, Sinhala only policy etc. This process has become the essence of foundational thinking associated with the nation state while incorporating the elements of fascism.

Whether, it is State Nation building or Nation State Building they are fundamentally same and similar. The demand made by the Nation State Making Project by the LTTE and by extension Tamils in Sri Lanka has been unable to count on geo-political realities and demographic realities in Sri Lanka. We approach the defeat of the LTTE and the humanitarian crisis in Sri Lanka as symptoms of the essential failures of foundational thinking associate with the nation state project.

What Went Wrong in Post-Independence Sri Lanka?

The Tamil insurgency and terrorism under the LTTE has to be understood as an implication of challenge posed by the dissenting ethnic communities to subsume the State Nation Building project carried out by government of Sri Lanka since Independence in 1948. The governing Sinhala elite was unable to understand that the "ethnicity is next to nature and second nature". When a community has become identified as a nation, it is extremely difficult to erase the identity and not voluntarily identify with the state nation which privileges a particular community specially, in the present context of globalized society. Globalization not only de-territorializes the nation but also re-territorializes.

The imagined relatives throughout the globe are vigilant over the relatives in every nook and corner of the globe. The spoiler role played by the Indian government at the initial stage of the ethnic conflict has to be identified in this light. The governing elite in Sri Lanka had not identified this fact of reality. This ignorance and the migrated people of the minority had contributed to the militarization of the movement of the Tamil in Sri Lanka. This fact is still a valid reality that the ruling elite in Sri Lanka has to seriously taken in to account in facing the post-ethnic war challenge.

The separatist project carried out by the LTTE, was not seriously calculated the internal as well as external realities. The first is the demography of Sri Lanka. The Tamils of Sri Lanka is also not homogeneous community. They are internally fragmented. The Sri Lankan Tamils are deeply divided as Northern and Eastern. The division was deepened after Karuna's break away with LTTE. In addition to that, there is a significant minority of Tamils of Indian Origin surrounded by the majority community Sinhalese. Further, one third of the Sri Lankan Tamils live outside of the Northern and Eastern Provinces, the traditional homeland projected by the Eelam, the nation state for the Tamils become virtually plausible objectives to be pursued without jeopardizing the rest of the Tamil community. Next, the Eastern Province is not a mono-ethnic province. It contains significant minorities of Muslims and Sinhalese.

If the Sri Lankan Government failed to recognize the importance of the imagined relatives of the neighbouring India, the militant project also has failed to recognize the importance of the geo-politics of the region. A separate state out of Sri Lanka is the next to impossible to be tolerated by India given its diversity of ethnic communities and separatist problems that has been facing her since the very inception of the country. Further, the International law that governs the state formation is biased towards the existing state. The United Nations Charter deprives the intervention of International community to the affairs of internal matters of the member states. Further, the Islamic fundamentalism and terrorism has so contributed to privileged the nation state over self-determination by the ethnic minorities in addition to the emerging multi-polarity of the world powers.

We approach the Sri Lankan ethnic conflict as the obverse and reverse of the same social phenomenon of Nation state. Going beyond the essence of nation state whether it is State Nation building or Nation State building is required. As Rajapakse has formulated, home-grown solution could not reject that going beyond the reality of presently existing nations in Sri Lanka is a hallucinatory exercise. Of course, he should not copy the blue-print of others. However, he could learn from the other experiences of the world. The basic requirement of finding a political solution is envisioning of cooperative polity of different nations in a unified nation. The historiographers of both sides could ease this burden if they deconstruct the political histories of both nations and reconstruct the true history of mutual coexistence of diverse groups in Sri Lanka. This would help to reject the foundationalism of Nation State project as a whole.

Plausible Explanation for the Failure of LTTE

The LTTE has been recognized as the most dangerous and deadly extremist group in the world (Federal Bureau of Investigation Report, 2008). Their methodology of attaining the Nation State is the indiscriminate terror over imagined and real enemies of the Nation State. The LTTE perfected the use of suicide bombers more successfully than any other outfit in the world. It has killed around 4,000 persons in the past two years alone and assassinated two world leaders (India and Sri Lanka).

As natural of the Nation state, it has built its own army, navy and air force with avowed strong cadres ready to die for the nation and its destined territory, i.e. the *Eelam* [Tamil Homeland]. This implies that this is the first kind of present day nationalist movement as no other terrorist outfit possessed such capabilities. Apart from this, the strong Tamil diaspora ensured political and financial support for the LTTE. Despite all these strength, the Eelam War-IV, which began in July 2006, has finally led to physical elimination of top leadership of LTTE including its chief Prabakaran, followed by defeat of LTTE. Thus, the question arises as to why LTTE failed to achieve its ultimate objective i.e. *Eelam or Nation State.*

As we understand the phenomenon, the major causal explanation lies that the mono-nation building project whether it is state nation building project identifying the state with the majority community or nation state building project for a particular community alone is highly impossible in of the present South Asian geo-political context and under the international law biased to existing nation state. Apparently, the failure of the nation state building carried out by the LTTE has to understand in the context of it tactics and strategies. They involve many blunders/miscalculations that gradually weakened its struggle.

First, the assassination of Rajiv Gandhi, former Prime Minister of India, in May 1991 was a major blunder committed by LTTE that eventually led to decline of India's sympathy towards LTTE's struggle. As a result, India banned the LTTE and consistently requested the Government of Sri Lanka (GOSL) for the extradition of Prabakaran who is presently dead. Subsequently, this led to silencing the sympathetic voices in Tamil Nadu where the imagined relatives of the Tamils in Sri Lanka reside.

Moreover, with the United Progressive Alliance (UPA), a Congress-led government coming to power in 2004, India shifted its stand from being a neutral bystander to an anti-LTTE stand, which was reflected in its strong statement issued by the government such as "it has no sympathy for the LTTE". [15] This was a strong statement ever made by the government on an insurgent group. In addition, the UPA government went a step ahead by increasing its cooperation with GOSL in non-lethal military matters that strengthen the Sri Lankan Army (SLA) in combating LTTE effectively. Subsequently, the UPA government expressed its willingness to accept the APRC report's main recommendations—13th amendment to the constitution as final solution, despite main parties such UNP, JVP, and JHU were not party to it.

Secondly, during the Presidential Poll in 2005, the LTTE instead of supporting Ranil Wickremesinghe's candidature enforced the boycott of polls in the areas under its control. As a result, majority of Tamils were unable to vote for

Wickremesinghe, who was one of the architects of 2002 peace process and had won the hearts of the minority for his political commitment to address the Tamil issue. Thus, LTTE's miscalculation paved the way for Mahindra Rajapakse to become President with a thin majority. Rajapakse was championing a mono-nation state that was most chauvinistic and composed of ethnically oriented parties such as JHU and JVP. The LTTE had underestimated Rajapakse, who in his election manifesto had promised to eliminate LTTE and did so after being elected as President (R. Hariharan, 2009). Thus, the military success for Rajapakse in a short period was possible due to his determination and commitment to end the conflict by eliminating the LTTE. At the same time, his core group constituted younger brother Gotabaya Rajapakse, as Defence Secretary and Sanath Foneska as Army Chief who took most of the decisions without any opposition within the government.

Moreover, President Rajapakse was in charge of defence portfolio and his brother as defence secretary ensured constant budgetary support. The defence allocation for 2009 budget was Sri Lankan Rupees 1.771 billion, despite a weak economy, high inflation and acute shortage of essential commodities (Lele, 2009). In addition, Rajapakse government established the Media Centre for National Security (MCNS) in June 2006, to counter the LTTE's propaganda. At the same time, despite the pressure from international community, civil society and Tamil diaspora over the civilian causalities during the course of the war, Rajapakse did not bow down to pressure tactics and took bold steps to finish the war. Thus, LTTE's miscalculation of allowing Rajapakse to become President was a major blunder that led to the end of LTTE.

Problems of Prabakaran Cult

Prabakaran was the main strength of the organization and under his charismatic leadership the LTTE's struggle sustained for decades. Prabhakaran was a tyrant that he never allowed anybody who questioned his leadership or attempted to counter the claim of LTTE as the sole representative of Tamils. He did not allow the democratization within the organization and as a result, with his demise, the LTTE collapsed. As he suppressed and even eliminated his opponents, Sri Lankan Tamils did not have any strong and independent political party/organisation to represent their grievances.

In the beginning the LTTE enjoyed overwhelming public support, however due to Prabakaran's ruthless tactics; the public support began to decline. His tactics include atrocities on the innocent lives through ethnic cleansing; forceful displacement; extortion; indiscriminate killing and kidnapping of innocent persons; forceful conscription of many women and children and assassination of prominent Tamil leaders and activists. Apart from this, during March and April 2009, the LTTE used many innocent civilians under its control as human shield and even killed arbitrarily those civilians attempting to flee its territory. Thus, all these actions of LTTE have led to a decline of people's support and also resulted in large scale migration of persons due to prolonged war and also in search of greener pastures.

The lack of democracy within the organization and systematic discrimination against the Tamils of Eastern Province has contributed to a split in the organization. The big blow to LTTE came in 2004, when for the first time LTTE's claim as the sole representative of Tamils was seriously challenged [politically and militarily] by V. Muralitharan (Col. Karuna). He was the most efficient military commander in eastern province and also for decades prevented the SLA from taking over eastern province. Karuna stated that the discrimination adopted by the LTTE leadership against the Tamils of eastern province was the main reason for the revolt against the LTTE hegemony (Sambandan, 2004: 52-54). After the split, in October 2004, he launched a new political party, *Tamileela Makkal Viduthalai Pulikal* (TMVP) and even made his maiden "Hero's Day Speech" on 27th November 2004. [16]

Alignment of Karuna faction was a strategic gain for the

Sri Lankan military. The closing of the Mavil-Aru dam by the LTTE was counterproductive to its interests in the region. This provided an opportunity for the government to launch a war in the guise of humanitarian intervention. This can be regarded as turning point in the conflict, as LTTE was weakened in the East and it was an impetus for the SLA to intensify its attack on LTTE in the Northern Province.

International Isolation

The terror tactics adopted by the LTTE and its international penetration has contributed to the isolation of the Tamil movement. The global phenomenon of terror, made it impossible for the countries to adopt dual standards towards terrorist that go against established nation states. The 9/11 attacks, have resulted in further isolation of LTTE and banning of the organisation by countries like the US, EU, Australia, India, Sri Lanka and so on. As of now LTTE is proscribed by 32 countries around the world. This development ultimately affected the flow of funds for LTTE from the Tamil diaspora. The intense lobbying and campaigning by the GOSL had also affected the international funding. Hence, the ban on LTTE severely curtailed its means of procuring weapons and funds for its struggle and eventually weakened its political and military capabilities. Interestingly, to overcome the international isolation, LTTE had signed the Cease Fire Agreement (CFA) in 2002.

Strong Sri Lankan Military

Although, the LTTE and Sri Lankan military have fought many wars in which both have experienced success and failure for short periods. However, the Eelam War-IV ensured victory for the Sri Lankan military, as it was fully backed by the government, which ensured maximum morale and also political and financial support. Subsequently, with a strong political leadership in the form of President Rajapakse gave the military the momentum to fight an all out-war with the LTTE. The Government also ensured the continuity in the leadership of the troops by granting service extensions for many officers, including the army chief, Lt. Gen. Sarath Fonseka (Narayanan, 2004).

Moreover, GOSL through rigorous campaign at the international level ensured the stoppage of logistical support to the LTTE. The Government on the other hand started procuring weapons for itself from Iran, China, Pakistan, Ukraine and also from private arms dealers. As a result they were successful in militarily containing the LTTE. The lethal weaponry were primarily supplied by Pakistan and China and bought commercially from around the world. Significantly Pakistan's military assistance to Sri Lanka has tripled in past three years.

Apart from weapons, Pakistan also provided training support to the army. The Sri Lankan Air Force was trained in precision bombing by Pakistan. There were several countries supplying non-lethal weaponry to Sri Lanka including the US and India. Thus, free flow of required weapons and support strengthened the SLA, which was also supported by Sri Lankan Air Force and Navy.

In addition, the Sri Lankan military adopted multiple strategies learnt from the past defeats and ensured an overall change in the approach in fighting LTTE that has resulted in the military victory. For instance, it transformed the Lankan military from a ceremonial army of 15,000 soldiers at the commencement of the ethnic war to a real fighting force of up to 2,00,000 battle-hardened soldiers. It also intensified its recruitment process, as in 2008 itself they recruited around "40,000 troops to raise 47 infantry battalions, 13 brigades, four task force contingents and two divisions. The army by the end of the war had 13 divisions, three task forces and one armoured brigade" (Hariharan, 2009: 13). As a result, the Sri Lanka's ratio of soldiers to population is one of the highest in the world. Nevertheless, these drastic steps transformed Sri Lankan military to strong force, which defeated LTTE in short span.

Negotiation: Maximalist Position

The LTTE always worked towards its ultimate goal—Eelam, as a result it never seriously negotiated with GOSL for an amicable solution to the Tamil issue. Instead, it negotiated half-heartedly and avoided any compromising formula. The best example was during the 2002 peace process facilitated by Norway. It was the best opportunity for the LTTE to negotiate an amicable solution for the Tamils. Only once it showed some compromising attitude was in December 2002 talks at Oslo. Both GOSL and the LTTE agreed to develop a federal political system and Tamil internal self-determination in Tamil dominated areas of the Northeast. [17] However, these words were not translated into action and thus proved to be just another gimmick to woo the people of the island and the international community.

Subsequently, through Norway's good office, the LTTE's also submitted its proposal to the GOSL in October 2003, popularly known as 'Interim Self-Governing Authority' (ISGA), which seeks a complete autonomy—political and economic life of the northeast people. It also called for separate institutions to be set up for the north-east in respect of police, judiciary, elections, taxation, local and foreign grants and loans and trade among others. If this policy were to be implemented the LTTE would have absolute majority in the northeast. As a result, of which the GOSL expressed reservation on the content of the proposal and even President Kumaratunga called it "blueprint for separation". Thus, LTTE always negotiated for Eelam and not for federal solution. The previous settlement efforts also had the same attitude. Thus, one could say that LTTE has chosen and put forward proposals to avoid negotiated settlement to the conflict of Two Nation projects.

Moreover, during the peace talks, LTTE was more concerned over military advantages than finding a lasting solution through talks. For instances, in August 2006, the GOSL shut down the A-9 highway, after the battle with the

LTTE along the Muhamalai forward defence lines, in which around 130 government troops were killed. As a result, the innocent people in Jaffna peninsula faced serious shortages of food, medicine and fuel (Reddy, 2006: 11). The Geneva-II talks on 28-29 October 2006 broke down on this issue.

During the ceasefire period, the LTTE had grossly violated the agreement. According to SLMM, from February 2002-July 2006 the number of violations committed by the GOSL and the LTTE is around 277 and 3,944 respectively. [18] Major share of violations carried out by the LTTE includes the child recruitment, constituting 47 percent of total violations, followed by abduction of adults (16 percent), harassment (6.54 percent), and so on. [19]

Apart from this, there has been alleged involvement of LTTE in assassination of prominent officials and personality such as of Foreign Minister Lakshman Kadirgamar, [20]; Gen. Parami Kulatunga, Deputy chief of Staff of the Army; Maj. Muthalif of Army intelligence, Lt. Col. T. Rizvi meedin, Senior Military intelligence Officials, K. Loganathan, a Tamilan working for a negotiated settlement as Deputy Chief of the Sri Lanka Peace Secretariat. On the other hand, the GOSL has also been successful in knocking out some of the key LTTE leaders like S.P. Tamilselvan [21] and others with the help of Karuna faction, and 'Deep Penetration Units'. Hence, both the LTTE and GOSL did not make any serious negotiations and were more often used opportunity for its military advantages.

In a nutshell, although LTTE had legitimate cause for its struggle, but it adopted ruthless means and committed many blunders which ultimately led to its defeat. Hence, LTTE has to blame itself for not fulfilling the aspirations of innocent Tamils.

Road Ahead

The Rajapakse government has successfully defeated LTTE. However this does not mean the end of conflict, rather it is the beginning of another phase of conflict in which government is confronted with many challenges such as: First, the 'war for peace' had caused large scale civilian casualties and larger scale displacement. For instances, most of them from Killinochchi and Mullaitivu has been displaced and around 2.8 lakh internally displaced persons (IDPs) in Sri Lanka, housed in 29 temporary camps in the districts of Vavuniya, Mannar and Jaffna. [22] Unfortunately, most of them were put up in temporary welfare centres or camps, erected hurriedly to house the fleeing civilians from the rebel controlled areas at the borders of the conflict zone. Moreover, those 1,00,000 people, who were displaced during 2008 were still lodged in welfare camps in Vavuniya and other places and are leading a miserable life without proper resettlement or relocation. However, since the end of war, large-scale efforts carried out by GOSL and the international community, ensured the return of IDPs and as of mid-2010 there are only 60,000 IDPs in camps.

Despite the efforts, the GOSL still has many tasks such as: (a) providing continued assistance to 60,000 IDPs remaining in camps and also working towards bringing them back to their homes in safety and dignity, (b) continue to address the basic needs and requirements of those returned communities, like ensuring physical security, freedom of movement, providing services - health, water and sanitation, shelter and non-food items, education, self reliance and public participation, (c) continue its efforts to demine the northern region, which still remains a major problem, as LTTE before fleeing the areas had heavily mined the region, (d) continue to mobilize funds, as it needs more international aid for creating infrastructure facilities and building a source of livelihood for the returnees, and (e) finally, find an amicable political solution to the ethnic crisis, failing which international aid could be stopped. Hence, ensuring the safety and providing the basic immunities to the displaced persons remains the biggest challenge.

Secondly, with the military victory President Rajapakse is

now confronted with the challenge of evolving an amicable solution to Tamil issue. Even India and the international community have been insisting Rajapakse to work towards a politically negotiated settlement acceptable to all sections of the Sri Lankan society, but within the framework of an undivided Sri Lanka. In this regard, Rajapakse government has assured India and the international community that he would go for a home-grown solution to the problem by way of implementation the 13th Amendment, one of the recommendations by APRC at the earliest.

However, implementation of 13th Amendment would be a difficult task, since the main political parties such as UNP, JVP, SLMC and TNA were not part of the APRC deliberations. Further, managing the hard core ethnically minded JVP and JVP and it break away groups are destined to be problematic. Other aspect of the 13th amendment is that it is result of Indo-Sri Lanka Peace accord of 1987 which paved the legitimation for Indian military Intervention to prevent a Tamil state at her door steps. This also a rejected policy measures every stakeholder to the conflict including Rajapakse himself. Hence, implementation of APRC recommendations would be difficult task. Finding an amicable political solution with the involvement of all the stakeholders would be challenging task for the Rajapakse government.

Moreover, with the electoral victory in the Eastern Province, President Rajapakse had promised to implement the 13th Amendment in both letter and spirit, ironically even after two year, the police power has not been devolved in the eastern province (V. Suryanarayana, 2009: p. 8). Thus, India, International community and Tamil diaspora would closely watch President Rajapakse steps towards finding a lasting solution.

Overall, the defeat of LTTE has not necessarily resolved conflict, rather has created an opportunity for Rajapakse government and to Tamil Community to genuinely address the legitimate grievances and aspirations of Tamils. If Rajapakse fails to capitalize the opportunity, then there are chances of LTTE's re-emergence either in the present form or in other form, which would intensify the conflict in the long run and Sri Lanka would be back to square one, were innocent civilians would be at the receiving end.

End Notes

1. In Sri Lanka, Govigama Caste (Jati) who speaks Sinhala and Buddhists in Religion and Vellala caste who speak Tamil and Hindus by Religion are treated equally. Their interaction ranges from marriages and electoral support to Tamil Candidate even under the British Constitutional Reform over their Sinhala speaking Buddhist Karava Candidate in 1919.
2. One of the basic premises of the justification of the colonialism was progress. To measure progress, census of communities was a precondition. Based on these statistics, the progress could be gauged.
3. The Tamil chauvinistic elite have strived to extend their discourse to incorporate descendents of Kerala origin, Malayalam Speaking communities in Western seashore among their fold as it is being still done by the Sinhala chauvinist in the multi-identity group village in Panama, Ampara District. These people have been absorbing either by Sinhalese or Tamils. This absorption is compelled by the modern political project of nation state.
4. See: Arneil, 1996.
5. Besides Academic teaching and learning of the subject, numerous people are writing history. The writing of history is a highly political enterprise. On the part of mainstream history writing, it has become an enterprise of arguing for and against the historical homelands for different communities within the Sri Lankan boarders. There is also a new trend of writing histories of caste group in recent Sri Lanka. The academic teaching and learning also do not escape from this bias. There are little studies of studying history of common and shared history of coexistence, Competing History writing for the historical habitat of Sinhalese in North and East. See: Prajapala, 2000.
6. One could add one more, at least, the Plantation Tamil Nationalism (Ali, 2001).
7. There is strong opposition to marry outside of the group among

middle class. However this is not applicable to higher class people. This is equally applicable to urban slum dwellers.

8. De Silva, 2010.
9. The citizenship rights of the migrated Indians was denied in 1948, which has given over-representation to the Kandyan Sinhalese, the Language of the Majority community was given official language status in 1956, the education opportunities to the Jaffna youth were limited in 1970s.
10. The motive of the laws has been disputed. The Tamils of Sri Lankan Tamil collaborated with the Sinhala elite to deprive the political rights of the internal other to keep the class interests over the ethnic interests. Because they are labourers and had voted for the left.
11. Truly, these texts are not the history of people but the history of dynasties. See: Prajapala, 2000.
12. In this process, the Sinhalese project is successful in absorbing some caste groups that had claimed relatives within the Tamil Speaking Community. What really happened was the absorption of caste groups within the close language group.
13. The Thirteenth Amendment to the present Constitution has identified Tamil as an Official Language. However, this remained largely un- implemented.
14. The 13th amendment to the present Constitution has strived to remedy the situation by making Tamil as the Official Language. Yet it remains largely non-implemented.
15. Report of Roundtable Discussion, 'Recent Developments in Sri Lanka: Implications for India'. 6th February, 2009. Available at, www.ipcs.org/article_details.php?articleNo=2827&cID=8.
16. In the Hero's day speech, Col. Karun attacked the leadership of Prabakaran as "unfit to lead the Tamils…and responsible for large scale killing of Tamils". Subsequently, he questioned the LTTE as sole representative of Tamils. Later, he welcomed India to resolve the conflict. See: Sambandan, 2004.
17. The hypocritical, Tamil Diaspora and the intellectuals portrayed this as a move to return to the more politically realistic phase of Tamil movement under the moderate democratic leadership.
18. The SLMM since April 2007 has suspended rulings on ceasefire violations.
    www.peaceinsrilanka.org/peace2005/insidepage/AtaGlance/Ceasfire_Feb-July 2006.asp.

19. The violation by GOSL included—harassment (30 percent), Hostile acts against the civilian population (6.27 percent), abduction of adults (5.54 percent) and so on. The CFA violations by the GOSL have been on a rise significantly after the victory of President Rajapakse. The main violations are the setting up of high security zones (HSZ), which denied citizens access to their land and delays in implementing some of the provisions of the CFA, such as handing over schools and buildings to their owners. See: Kumar Rupesinghe, 'Sri Lanka: Paradigm Shift in the Peace Process', *FCE FORUM* 26th October, http://www.kumarrupesinghe.org/Article.aspx?ArticleID=144.
20. Kadirgamar paid the price for his successful efforts to have the LTTE that proclaimed itself the sole representative of Tamils, designated a terrorist organization by the US and the UK. This squeezed the fund-raising and arms smuggling capacities of the LTTE in various parts of world.
21. On 22nd October, 2007, S.P. Tamilchelvan, chief of political wing was killed during the attack by the SLAF bombing a gathering of LTTE leaders in Kilinochchi, the administrative headquarters of the tigers.
22. See: Mayilvagana, 2009 and Reddy, 2009.

References

Abeyrathne, Upul, 'The Ethnic Problem and Sri Lankan Political Culture', in Georg Frerks and Bart Klem, op. cit., pp. 101-116.

Ali, Ameer (2001), Plural Identities and Political Choices of the Muslim Community, (Marga monograph series on ethnic reconciliation), Marga Institute, Colombo.

Arneil, Barbara (1996), "The Wild Indian's Venison: Locke's Theory of Property and English Colonialism in North America", *Political Studies*, Vol. XLIV, p. 73.

Bandara, Navarathna (2007), 'Britanya yatat vijita yugaye sri lankave Jatika Vaparaya', Nationalist Movement during the British Era in Sri Lanka, Fast Publishing Private Limited, Colombo, p. 124.

De Silva, K.M. (1999), "Sri Lanka: The Bandaranayake in the Island Politics and Public Life", *The Round Table: The Commonwealth Journal of International Affairs*, 88:350, pp. 241-280.

Fearon, James (2004), "Why Do Some Civil Wars Last So Much Longer than Others?" *Journal of Peace Research*, Vol. 41, No.

3, pp. 275-301.

Gosh, Partha (2003), Ethnicity versus Nationalism: The Devolution Discourse in Sri Lanka, Sage, New Delhi, pp. 51-61.

Hariharan, R. (2009), "Why LTTE Failed?", *Frontline*, 22nd May, 2009, p. 13.

Kaviraj, Sudipto (1997), 'On the Construction of Colonial Power: Structure, Discourse and Hegemony', in S. Kaviraj (ed.) Politics in India, Oxford University Press, New Delhi, pp. 141-169.

Lele, Ajay (2009), "Time to Win the Peace", *The Pioneer* (New Delhi), 2nd May, 2009.

Ludden, David (2006), India and South Asia: A Short History, Gopsons Papers Ltd., New Delhi.

Naryanan, Sripathi, 'Lessons from Lankan Military Successes', 9th February 2009, available at, www.ipcs.org/article_details.php?articleNo=2802.

Newman, Saul (2004), "The Place of Power in Political Discourse", *International Political Science Review*, Vol. 25, No. 2, pp. 139-157.

Parekh, Bhikhu (1997), 'The West and its Others' in Keith Ansell-Pearson et al., Cultural Readings of Imperialism, London: Lawrence and Wshart, pp. 173-193.

Prajapala, Gunawardana (2000), 'Dravida Trustavadaya Ha Sinhala Visdum', Tamil Terrorism and Sinhalese' Solutions, Godage and Brothers, Colombo.

Reddy, Muralidhar B. (2009), "Devastated Lives", *Frontline*, 22nd May, p. 7.

Reddy, Muralidhar B. (2006), "An Unfolding tragedy in Sri Lanka", *The Hindu*, 4th November, p. 11.

Roberts, Peri, and Sutch Peter (2005), An Introduction to Political Thought: A Conceptual, Toolkit, Edinburgh University Press, Edinburgh, p. 12.

Sambandan, V.S (2004), "Another Heroes' Day Speech", *Frontline*, 31st December, p. 54.

Sambandan, V.S. (2004), "The Stalemate in Sri Lanka", *Frontline*, 31st December, pp. 52-54.

Sitrampala, S.K. (2004), 'Tamils of Sri Lanka, Historical Roots of Tamil Identity', in George Frerks and Klem, Bart, *Dealing with Diversity: Sri Lankan Discourse on Peace and Conflict,* The Netherlands Institute of International Relations, The Hague, pp. 239-282.

Suryanaraya, V. (2009), "Is it the End of the Struggle", *The New Indian Express*, 19th May, 2009, p. 8.

Wijetunga, Harischandra (1999), *Moolika Aiyteen Penva Uttareetara Aiythiya Paharagenima,* S. Godage and Brothers, Colombo, p. 65.

14

Technology and Public Governance

Ashalekshmi B.S.

Rapid growth in the field of information and communication technologies (ICTs) in the past two decades has induced changes in the ways governments function world over. This information age paradigm shift has redefined the fundamentals and changed the institutions and mechanisms of delivery forever. Knowledge-based society is expected to share vast amount of information on a global scale almost instantaneously, which consequently helps in selecting, absorbing and adapting relevant technology and services.

It was the changing development agenda that created a space for new technologies in Kerala. From the background of globalisation, information technologies could develop at a faster pace and they have got a stabilisation in the field of industries, administration, education and the like. The government sector recognised the importance of information and communication technologies and thereby paying attention for rendering speedy services through the introduction of ICTs. Many government services have been transformed into the e-mode by this time.

The application of technology in any society usually creates a technically subaltern group. This marginalisation emerges out of the separation between those people who have access to information and communication technologies and those who do not have. The Akshaya project has been hailed as a high profile project of Kerala IT mission to introduce computers even to the lowest stratum of the Kerala Society and thereby bridging the digital divide.

The Akshaya project initiated in November 2002 was officially started with the introduction of rural e-kiosks or technology centres in the district of Malappuram in May, 2003. The Akshaya project had a grassroots beginning. It was developed as a result of a proposal from the Malappuram District local government requesting state government support to give at least one person in every family basic training in computers. This was based on the belief that ICTs could promote the local economy and assist individuals to attain jobs. The government's goal was eventually to create the first 100 percent e-literate state in India.

Back Ground of the Akshaya Project

Akshaya is a community oriented ICT initiative introduced by the Kerala Information Technology Mission for bringing the benefits of IT to the Kerala society. The Kerala IT Mission has set out the objectives of Akshaya as follows:

1. To develop over 5,000 numbers of networked multi-purpose community based technologies centres that are Akshaya e-kendras to provide ICT access to the entire population of Kerala.
2. To make at least one person in each of 65 lakh+ families in the State, e-literate.
3. To enhance the quality of available IT infrastructure in the State and also by providing facilities for rural connectivity infrastructure.
4. To enable e-transaction and e-governance services through the centres.
5. Generate over 50,000 employment opportunities in 3 years.

With these objectives the Akshaya project was piloted in November 2002 in Malappuram District of Kerala, with a plan for spreading it to the other districts of the State later on. The project was designed by a group of IT professionals and senior bureaucrats with substantive involvement of the local panchayats. The Akshaya project in Malappuram District of Kerala is the first district-wide e-literacy project in India, and one of the largest known internet protocol (IP) based wireless networks

(Pardhasaradhi et al., 2009). In the first phase of this project the emphasis was on the objective of imparting computer literacy to the people. The second phase focused on the promotion of e-commerce through entrepreneurial development since it was felt that the e-literate local population would generate adequate demand for e-commerce activities which can be catered to by the Akshaya entrepreneurs (Mukhopadhyaya and Nandi, 2007).

The strategy adopted for implementing Akshaya project has four major components. Firstly, for ICT access, a network of Akshaya e-kendras is being set up in Kerala run by entrepreneurs. These centres will act as a self-sustaining unit with e-literacy programme and the centres were set up within 2 km apart. Development of these centres is expected to provide direct sustained employment to at least 25,000 people (5 per unit) in the IT sector. The strategy included equipping each centre with 5-10 computers, printers, scanners, web cam and other necessary softwares to carry out various ICT based service. According to the project report of the Kerala IT mission, each centre would entail an investment of ₹ 3.83 lakh for its 10 computers plus accessories and other working capital.

Secondly, the strategy encompasses providing e-literacy training with the help of a carefully designed content module in local language for fifteen hours for each of the 64 lakh families in Kerala. The third strategic vision was on the creation of micro ICT enterprises. The Akshaya e-Kendras were set up as pure entrepreneurial ventures of selected entrepreneurs with an investment of about ₹ 3.83 lakh per centre. The Government of Kerala had taken steps to popularize Akshaya project through extensive advertising in newspapers and at the local level through Panchayat offices. Out of 2,000 applications a total of 637 applicants were initially selected. For finding out the ideal locations for setting up of Akshaya centres, field surveys were conducted in all Panchayats in Malappuram. For setting up Akshaya Centres, MOUs were signed with selected entrepreneurs. Many entrepreneurs took loans from various nationalized and rural co-operative banks in order to start Akshaya venture.

Before the inception of the project, village panchayats took a leading role in carrying out house-to-house information dissemination about the e-literacy training, urging every house hold to send at least one member to the Akshaya centre. The project had appointed one Akshaya co-ordinator usually a local woman in every village panchayat of the district to carry out the information dissemination and advocacy work. An expert committee was set up to examine the curriculum for a course in basic e-literacy which was designed by Centre for Development of Imaging Technology (C-DIT). The course had a 15 hour training module to be administered in ten days. For imparting computer literacy, two to three computer trainees were hired from the local communities.

Another strategic approach in the establishment of Akshaya centres includes the Akshaya ICT access points, envisaged to provide G_2C, G_2G, and G_2B (Government to Citizen, Government to Government and Government to Business) information dissemination. Akshaya centres were considered to function as decentralized information access hubs that cater to a range of citizen needs that have an inbuilt integrated front-end collection for utility bills and taxes—being done through these ICT service delivery points.

Many studies have come up by the time indicating the social development after the introduction of Akshaya project. It is often hailed as the prestigious e-literacy programme of the Government of Kerala. But the economic dimension especially the plight of the entrepreneurs even though a crucial one is not often brought into light. This paper seeks to provide an overall look into this high profile project in a critical manner.

The survey on Akshaya project among beneficiaries of the project and Akshaya entrepreneurs in order to find out the impact on each category was conducted among 180 citizens and 30 entrepreneurs in six blocks. The blocks were Wandoor, Perinthalmanna, Mankada, Areacode, Thiroor and Malappuram.

The survey was conducted when the first phase of Akshaya e-literacy was over.

Compared to the younger generations, the older generations are having minimal representation in this kind of a newer initiative. The age group and the representation seem to be disproportionate after the representation of respondents belongs to the age group of 31-40. The Akshaya project was intended to impart e-literacy to at least one person in each family. The family members might have selected the younger ones since they are more interested in cutting edge technologies.

To the question regarding their financial affordability for computer education 71.2 percent were totally satisfied. For e-literacy course, the fee per student was ₹ 120 out of which ₹ 80 was the contribution from Local Self Government bodies. This amount was further being divided in to ₹ 60 by Grama Panchayat, ₹ 10 by Block Panchayat and the remaining ₹ 10 by District Panchayat. The amount that had to be paid by the beneficiary was only ₹ 40. If the student was from SC/ST community, the entire fee was paid by the LSG body itself.

In this connection, the beneficiaries were not facing a financial constraint for computer education. Akshaya was introduced at a time when computer education was somewhat expensive.

This financial aid on the part of government could definitely increase the number of Akshaya students. However 28.8 percent of the respondents could not afford even the remaining fee, ₹ 40. Among them 85.6 percent of the respondents informed their income as below ₹ 12,000 and the remaining respondents were from the category who did not inform their annual income.

In a situation where people from economically backward families could not afford even ₹ 40 as fee, the Government could have reconsidered its policy. Apart from giving financial assistance to a specific community, economic backwardness could have also been considered for financial aid.

In order to reach Akshaya centre every respondent had to travel within a reasonable distance. In the pilot project in Malappuram each Akshaya centre was set up at a distance of 2 km. apart. Majority of the respondents (91.9 percent) were satisfied with the transportation facility. But 8.1 percent was dissatisfied and they had the complaint on transportation particularly with regard to the delay in the construction and maintenance of roads. Regarding electricity/telephone facility, on the whole, 88.1 percent of the respondents had satisfaction. The fifteen percent who were dissatisfied, were lacking that facility due to regional constraints. In their opinion, government had to pay much attention to such matters rather than starting new initiatives like Akshaya.

The crucial problem which arises while introducing new technologies is the digital divide. One of the reasons behind the emergence of digital divide is the language constraint. The researcher could notice the same while conducting the survey. The beneficiaries of Akshaya project had an interest in advancing their computer knowledge. But their lack of knowledge in English language prevented them from advancing their e-literacy. In the survey a huge majority revealed that they were facing the language barrier while advancing their computer knowledge. It was under the circumstance of this digital divide, the Kerala IT Mission had initiated Malayalam Computing to overcome the language barrier and thereby promoting the impact of technologies in all spheres of life.

According to the majority, major progress after the implementation of Akshaya project is the attainment of computer literacy. They were totally enthusiastic of the low cost computer literacy programme. Another set of the respondents opined that e-pay facility is the major advantage of Akshaya programme. Before the project, in their opinion, the payment of bills had taken much time and effort and after Akshaya, they were receiving a convenient interaction. According to 11.1 percent of respondents the convenience of online checking of examination results is the major advantage after Akshaya.

Among the respondents 28.3 percent informed that, they lack adequate health care facility. They highlighted the plight of public health centres and Government hospitals. This response was mainly from the respondents who were having annual income below ₹ 12,000. According to 24 percent of the respondents, more schools had to be there in their locality. But 19.4 percent highlighted the problems in transportation including improper maintenance of roads. Lack of proper drainage system was the major infrastructural issue regarding 16.7 percent of the respondents. Another 4.4 percent informed about the lack of adequate water supply. But a similar portion of the respondents were in need of both better hospital facility and good transportation. The remaining 2.8 percent lacked proper housing. All these respondents had an opinion that in this modern world, new technology is necessary. But they added that implementation of new technologies should be there only after fulfilling the infrastructural necessities. If so, there will not be disparities in the distribution of benefits emerging out of technologies.

Entrepreneurial Versions in Akshaya

Entrepreneurship is the process of identifying opportunities in the market place, arranging the resources required to pursue these opportunities and investing the resources to exploit the opportunities for long term gains. It involves creating wealth by bringing together resources in new ways to start and operate an enterprise. According to Cole, "Entrepreneurship is the purposeful activity of an individual or a group of associated individuals undertaken to initiate, maintain and aggrandize profit by production or distribution of economic goods and services".

Kourilsky (1980) suggested that the following are most relevant for being an entrepreneur: need for achievement; creativity and initiative; risk-taking and setting objectives; self-confidence and internal locus of control; need for independence and autonomy; motivation, energy and commitment; and persistence. According to Gorman et al. (1997), propensity towards entrepreneurship is associated with several personal characteristics such as values and attitudes, personal goals, creativity, risk-taking propensity, and locus of control.

Of the personal characteristics, McClelland (1961) proposed achievement motivation, risk taking and locus of control as important characteristics. However, Robinson, Stimpson, Huefner, and Hunt's (1991) argued that self-esteem and innovation are more prominent in entrepreneurs than the need for achievement. Stewart et al. (1998) disagreed, finding that entrepreneurs had higher achievement motivation, risk-taking propensity, and preference for innovation than corporate managers and small business owners. Risk-taking may not apply to youth who have not undertaken significant economic risk and opportunity cost due to the loss of wages, or wealth risk associated with business failure.

From Table 14.1 it is clear that majority of the Akshaya entrepreneurs are young and of course they were in need of a job. The youth in Malappuram were very much enthusiastic with the inception of Akshaya project there. From the background of their unemployment, they opted for being Akshaya entrepreneurs. Among the respondents, 26 were men and there were only 4 women. This indicates the lesser degree of work participation of women compared to men. This is the clear evidence of disparity in the gender pattern of entrepreneurship in Malappuram District.

Table 14.1: Age Profile of the Akshaya Entrepreneurs

Age	No. of Respondents	Percent
20-30	20	66.7
31-40	9	30.0
41-50	1	3.3
Above 50	0	0.0
Total	30	100.0

Source: The Survey.

Among the entrepreneurs majority were degree holders and they were all in need of a job and this highlights the extent of unemployment (Table 14.2). The majority was followed by respondents having Pre-degree or equivalent qualification. There was only one respondent who held the qualification below S.S.L.C. The Government, for selecting the entrepreneurs, should set up Pre-degree or Plus two as the required educational qualification. But the researcher observed that after getting approval for starting the centres, in some cases, the actual entrepreneur's benamies were running the centres. Owing to this fake entrepreneurship, the Government decided to issue identity cards to all Akshaya entrepreneurs from November 2010 onwards.

Table 14.2: Educational Profile

Qualification	Below S.S.L.C	S.S.L.C.	Pre-degree/+2	Degree	PG	Total
No: of respondents	1	3	9	14	3	30
Percent	3.3	10.0	30.0	46.7	10	100

Source: The Survey.

On the question of the visit of beneficiaries per day, majority (53.3 percent) informed that it was in between 20 and 30. Only 7.7 percent had the visit of beneficiaries per day in between 50-100 and twenty percent of the entrepreneurs had it below 20 in number. The plight of the centres was quite bad which were having the number of beneficiaries per day below 20. However, 19 percent informed that it was in between 30 and 50.

It is very much noteworthy that an outstanding majority of the entrepreneurs were dissatisfied with the nature of co-operation received from government (Table 14.3). All of them highlighted the inadequate financial support on the part of government. The government was not providing fund in time. Only a small portion of respondents did not have any complaint and they were getting more beneficiaries of Akshaya e-literacy programme compared to others.

Table 14.3: Satisfaction with the Co-operation of Government

Response	No. of Respondents	Percent
Satisfied	3	10.0
Dissatisfied	23	76.7
Satisfied only to some extent	4	13.3
Dissatisfied to some extent	0	0.0
Total	30	100.0

Source: The Survey.

Besides, majority of the entrepreneurs (93.3 percent) were dissatisfied with the facilities of the centres. According to them the centres were most often suffering from connectivity faults. This complaint was predominant among entrepreneurs from rural centres.

But majority of the entrepreneurs (83.3 percent) informed that they had the feeling that beneficiaries were satisfied with the implementation of Akshaya project. Similar opinion was heard from beneficiaries also regarding the services from Akshaya Centres. Majority of the entrepreneurs (76.7 percent) revealed that they were not getting any complaint from the beneficiaries regarding Akshaya Centres.

Even though majority of the entrepreneurs was not satisfied with Akshaya project, they were of the opinion that Akshaya project was able to improve the governance since it could impart the popularization of computer literacy and e-pay facilities. They had the vision that people are now in a position to access the government services and information very fast. But 13.3 percent of the entrepreneurs had an opposite view. They highlighted that even though Government is implementing many programmes through Akshaya, the rural people are not in a position to access the services out of their socio-economic backwardness. The entrepreneurs further added that Akshaya could not bring all the citizens to the mainstream and the progress is not uniform at all. Regarding the question of popular participation in governance through Akshaya, majority of the entrepreneurs (43.3 percent) had the opinion that online interaction with government was not taking place and the citizens have not come up to that level. Hence, according to them, popular participation in governance through Akshaya is a distant dream. But 40 percent of the entrepreneurs held a different view. They were of the opinion that even though online participation is not impressive, compared to previous years citizens are now more in touch with government and this may lead to progress in governance.

Surprisingly, seventy percent of the respondents revealed their dissatisfaction as an entrepreneur of Akshaya project (Table 14.4).

Table 14.4: Satisfaction as an Entrepreneur

Response	Satisfied	Dissatisfied	Satisfied only to some extent	Total
No. of Respondents	3	21	6	30
Percent	10.0	70.0	20.0	100.0

Source: The Survey.

They opined that in the beginning, they were having a lot of expectations regarding the project. All of them considered Akshaya as an opportunity for employment. But reality seemed to be very distant from their expectations. The major cause of the dissatisfaction of entrepreneurs was lack of generating adequate income from their centres. Majority had an opinion that after commissioning the project, the government developed an indifferent attitude towards the entrepreneurs.

Interestingly, fifty percent of the respondents informed that better social contact is the major attainment they have received through Akshaya. They were satisfied in one aspect that they were in touch with people from all walks of life. Only 23.3 percent of the respondents considered the job as the major individual benefit through Akshaya while 13.3 percent could advance their computer knowledge. But 6.7 percent opined that they have not attained even a single benefit through the implementation of Akshaya project. Instead, they have become bankrupts (Table 14.5).

Table 14.5: Individual Benefits through Akshaya

Benefits	Employ-ment	Better social contact	Better computer knowledge	Better financial position	Nothing	Total
No. of Respondents	7	15	4	2	2	30
Percent	23.3	50.0	13.3	6.7	6.7	100

Source: The Survey.

Major Pitfalls

The researcher could find that Akshaya project had two types of impacts on the beneficiaries and the entrepreneurs. The common people in the district were enthusiastic on the introduction of such kind of a project there. They were getting computer education at a lower cost. The question emerged from the civil society was about the educationally backward position of the district and the limitations for the adaptation to such newer technologies. According to the officials, the earlier projects like Literacy Mission and People's Planning were successful. In this background they anticipated the success of the implementation of Akshaya project there.

The bureaucrats opined that digital divide was not operating since the content module was prepared in local language. But the survey reveals that about 71.1 percent of the people were facing the barrier of language for advancing their computer education and of the similar reason also they were not in a position to utilize their computer knowledge in future.

In consequence to this, majority of the respondents (68.1

percent) were not using their computer knowledge further. But all of them were satisfied in one aspect that they could at least familiarize a new technology at a lower cost. In general, they have overcome the fear of handling the computers.

However, the people were of the opinion that government should give weightage for providing basic amenities and infrastructural advancement rather than giving preference to the introduction of technologies. The researcher could find that the implementation of Akshaya project was a hasty decision on the part of government. The people even after receiving e-literacy through Akshaya were unaware of the programmes like e-krishi. The government in this connection should take initiative for effective and persistent awareness creation rather than concentrating on the peripheral implementation of the projects.

The focus on entrepreneurs could find out that majority of the entrepreneurs were dissatisfied with Akshaya project. Apart from making the people computer literate, the project had a mission to impart entrepreneurship development in the society also. But the intention of imparting entrepreneurship was not taken in an effective manner after the inception of the project.

There was a long gap between the two stages in the implementation of Akshaya project. The entrepreneurs had taken a loan of ₹ 2 lakh from banks for starting and running the centres. The contribution of the government to the entrepreneurs was minimal. The entrepreneurs received the fund from the government for the first stage only after 8 months from its completion. By this time the struggle for survival of the centres reached its zenith. The entrepreneurs had to remit the interest rate of 12.5 percent which was unaffordable. As a consequence, majority of the entrepreneurs became bankrupt.

Considering these circumstances, the Cabinet on February 17, 2010 decided to write off part of the loans taken by Akshaya Centres in Malappuram district. The centres would now have to repay only 75 percent of their loans from banks as part of the one-time settlement. The Government has decided to pay half of the dues reducing the amount payable by the entrepreneurs to 37.5 percent (The Hindu, February 18, 2010).

After a break a new initiative named 'Internet to Masses' was introduced through the Akshaya centres. But majority of the centres by the time had become too weak to run effectively. Only a few centres became active (just 150 out of 600 centres). But even these were suffering from connectivity failures. The government has not taken timely step for enhancing connectivity.

After selecting the entrepreneurs and starting the project, the government did not pay much attention to the centres for ensuring that the centres were run by the actual entrepreneurs.

Some entrepreneurs highlighted that e-pay facility was also facing many problems such as:

1. Connectivity fault.
2. Location of SBI at a distance above 20 km.
3. The irresponsibility of the concerned team.

Another major lacuna was the abundance of Akshaya centres in the district. In the pilot project the centres were set up at a distance of 2 km. apart. Owing to this reason, the government later allotted only 2-3 centres in a panchayat during the roll out of the project in other districts.

Akshaya project can be considered as both success and failure. In its social context, it is successful. But it could not achieve the commercial aspect. In this regard it is failure. Akshaya was a prestige project of the Kerala Government. The project has many advantages and disadvantages. But the researcher observed that majority of the entrepreneurs considered themselves as 'victims' of this initiative since the centres were running with huge financial loss and lack of timely assistance on the part of government.

On the whole, it can be found that Akshaya project had only a peripheral impact. The Government could have taken much more time for an in depth homework before introducing this project. Plight of the entrepreneurs is not only the creation of their limited entrepreneurial skill but also lack of proper co-operation from local self-government. Now it is high time on the part of the Government to be aware of anticipating the forthcoming lacunae in the implementation of newer projects like this.

Majority of the ICT projects are designed and framed by professionals and senior bureaucrats. They often do not have contact with common people or they are having anonymous responsibility. The responsible and accountable policy makers often may work with partisan objectives. Their commitment is political in nature. A more clear vision regarding changing trends in the preferences of people can be better provided by academicians, NGOs and media personnel. For the fruitfulness of e-governance projects, involvement and suggestions from academics, media and civil society organisations can be considered during the design process. Successful stories from private sector can be considered for reference while designing new programmes for avoiding the lack of technical expertise and experience. We are only adopting expertise not experience.

Even though, entrepreneurship development was one of the objectives of Akshaya, it could not sustain the commercial element and thereby in that respect the project has become a failure. In order to improve the commercial sustainability, job-oriented courses under government initiative in PPP model should be incorporated in the project.

Majority of the studies undertaken by the Government are in tune with interest of the establishment. The Government should conduct study to measure the impact of e-governance from a popular perspective.

References

Government of India, Governance Knowledge Centre, 'Akshaya: Innovative Operations and Service Delivery, Kerala', New Delhi, http://indiagovernance.gov.in.

http://www.angrau.net/StudyMaterial/AgExtension/AEXT391.pdf.

http://labsel.pesarosviluppo.it/Modules/ContentManagment/Uploaded/CMItemAttachments/Developingpercent20entrepreneurial percent20characteristics percent20in percent20youth.pdf.

Interview with A.D. Jayan, General Secretary, Association of IT Employees on 18th November, 2009.

Interview with Dr. Achuth Sankar S. Nair, Centre for Bioinformatics, University of Kerala, on 5th March, 2010.

Interview with Dr. K.V. Ravi, Akshaya Zonal Co-ordinator on 13th September, 2009.

Interview with P.K. Kunhalikutty, Former IT Minister, Government of Kerala on 29th August, 2006.

Interview with Shri Salim, District Secretary, Akshaya, Malappuram on 25th August, 2006.

Mukhopadhyaya, Swapna and Rajib Nandi (2007), "Unpacking the Assumption of Gender Neutrality: Akshaya Project of the Kerala IT Mission in India", *Gender, Technology and Development*, Vol. 11, No. 1, pp. 75-95.

Pardhasaradhi, Y., Rakesh Chetal and Namita Gupta (2009), E-Governance, and Indian Society: With Case Studies, Kanishka, New Delhi.

15

Governance and Social Empowerment

Devi Parvathy

The problem of governance is directly related with the quality of services provided by the government to its citizen and the ability of the administrative system to capitalise the benefits of quality services in favour of the government. Effective administration must be a dynamic process, involving blending and directing of available human and physical resources in order to achieve public objectives. Its basic purpose should be to provide focus and consistency to the action programme of government.

The role of government servants as service providers is an important variable in ensuring good governance. Various governments are increasingly following the neo-liberal policy by adopting various Structural Adjustment measurers. Modernizing Government Programme (MGP) which is introduced at the behest of Asian Development Bank (ADB) aims at revitalizing the administration of the Government of Kerala. The study mainly focuses on the question whether the implementation of the initiatives of MGP especially Service Delivery Project is a success in the social empowerment of the citizens in Kerala. In this context, the focal points of the paper are the citizen's charter initiative and the social auditing policy.

The objectives of the Third Administrative Reforms Committee (TARC), among others are the improvements in service delivery. The 3rd ARC came into being in May 1997, with the former chief minister E.K. Nayanar as its Chairman. Its plan was to suggest measures to eliminate delays, lethargy, corruption and nepotism in the administration and to make it result-oriented. It suggests measures to cut unnecessary and avoidable paper works and for using modern management techniques in administration. Some of the important recommendations include people-centred form of governance and decentralized governance. The committee emphasized the need for decentralized governance structure with clear functional domains, and the power, authority and resources to discharge the assigned functions autonomously. The Committee underscored the need for a simple and rational administrative system that caters to the needs of all citizens.

Modernizing Government Programme

MGP is conceived as a comprehensive reform package for overhauling government towards enhancing transparency, efficiency and effectiveness in delivery of services. [1] It affords planners and policy makers an opportunity to take a step back and look at the problems of Kerala more objectively. Above all, it creates a framework for developing a vision of what the state should be in future. The thrust of MGP is to facilitate public servants and elected officials to serve the citizens of Kerala more effectively, efficiently and equitably with greater accountability. [2] In implementing this scheme, Government has made a radical departure from the conventional, emphasis on results and outcome as against the usual emphasis on activity based management.

The important principles underlined MGP are performance and enforceability which can be attained through the implementation of outcome based governance. That is the extent to which the units delivering their output, measured against and what they are expected to do. Such output based plans shall be based on defined performance goals, established performance indicators, provide a basis for comparing actual programme results with the established performance goal. Accountability, another core area can be ensured by defining it as a right to the people; information presented in a simple format and brought under an internal audit system. Here, the decision makers are held responsible and answerable for their actions and use of public resources (Shastra Sahitya Parishad, 2005: 23).

MGP can be defined as a programme visualized for overhauling Government towards achieving greater efficiency and effectiveness. Lack of good governance is now widely accepted as the critical factor most responsible for governments' inability to put resource to the optimum use resulting in underdevelopment and poverty. The Tenth Five Year Plan of India recognized the importance of good governance in delivering development. A similar approach is being followed in Kerala also. The focus of good governance in Kerala is on increasing transparency, reducing administrative corruption and improving service delivery especially to the poor and weaker sections. The Government of Kerala has also given thrust to governance reforms. The governance reforms programme of Kerala, viz., MGP was started in 2002.

Service Delivery Project

The Service Delivery (SD) Project is one of the actions-research fast track projects of the MGP. The key focus areas are: setting of standards, resource allocation and social monitoring (Government of Kerala, 2006: 8). The Government of Kerala launched the Service Delivery Project in November 2003 by identifying the criteria of institutions and laying down basic tenets and outline of the project. The process of planning for improved service delivery in the selected institutions took definite shape in April 2004. Through a consultative process with IMG and Administrative Staff College of India, Hyderabad (ASCI), it was decided that planning would be facilitated in a workshop mode. A series of workshops were held to identify service delivery areas and item-wise requirement for each department. 'Master Trainers' were identified in each department who in turn trained those below them.

The basic principles of Service Delivery Project can be summarized as: people-centeredness, laying down clear standards, equity, transparency, accountability, integrity, fairness, good behaviour, rationality, efficiency, convergence, right to service delivery, grievance redressal, continuous improvement, changing attitudes and improving skills, sustainability and inclusion and holistic approach. [3] Every citizen has a basic right to expect high quality public service. The users of public service would have a voice in ensuring quality. This would be ensured by affording opportunities for participation at all stages. Clear standards of service would be laid down and every citizen can therefore expect a guaranteed minimum level. [4] The focus would be on the poor and disadvantaged groups who would be given the most favoured treatment not only through easy access but also through deliberate outreach.

The citizens will have the right to know the standards expected to be achieved, the cost of service, identity of service providers, out puts and outcomes achieved. Service providers would be accountable not only to the Government but also to the citizen. Delivery of public services would be built around high standards of integrity in public institutions. The principle of-first-come-first-served would be followed in all cases. Wherever exceptions are made, they would be in favour of the poor and disadvantaged through a well-published due process. Politeness and courtesy on the part of service providers would be ensured. All decision of service delivery would be taken on the basis of facts and data. The cost of service would be continuously monitored to optimize resource use and to avoid wastage.

Convergence of services would be attempted to enhance impact facilitating horizontal and vertical linkages. Quality service delivery should be recognized as right of a citizen. Towards this end a legislative framework for enforcement of this right would be developed. There would be a well defined system for redressing grievances of those who are dissatisfied with service delivery. Continuous improvement of methods, processes and standards will be achieved through a process of modernization based on adoption of e-governance tools, emphasis on simplification of rules, reducing redundant multiple levels in decision making and greater delegation of authority to levels that actually deliver public services.

The whole process would be backed by capacity building efforts to upgrade skills change attitudes and improve performance. The service Delivery improvements would be made sustainable by linking them with the planning and budgetary process. The policy would provide for conscious reaching out to include marginalized in the spirit of 'antyodaya' or- 'unto the last'. When improvements in service delivery are designed, the modes and procedures would be appraised in full to facilitate administrative process reengineering. SDP will help, develop and put service standards in place which would enable citizens, policymakers and service providers to track service performance and take corrective action where appropriate. Through SDP, ADB is assisting the Government of Kerala by issuing structural adjustment loans to overcome governance drawbacks like stake holder's consultation, improper co-ordination and low level monitoring. [5]

The Government of Kerala announced the Service Delivery Policy on September 2004 for improving and co-ordinating the service provided by the different government institutions and thereby giving due importance to the will of general citizens. Citizen's Charter and *Sevana Mudra* (Charter Mark) and Social Auditing are the main source of SDP in ensuring better service delivery. The Government of Kerala decided to institute an award system based on guidelines provided by the Government of India, on the lines of Charter Mark, UK, whereby they will recognize well performing institutions focusing on the tenants of the Service Delivery Policy. Such recognition will have twin objectives to provide much needed impetus for the performing institutions and to encourage others to emulate the well performing ones. [6]

Citizen's Charter

One of the difficulties that stand in the way of delivering

quality services is that the people in the organization in government department or agency do not possess a clear understanding of their organizations aim and what should be the standards of services it offers to customers (the general public). This prevents them from working with a heightened sense of purpose. Lack of co-ordination between policy development and service delivery is another reason. The service delivery policy is drawn up first by identifying the services and facilities that the organization is expected to render to the public.

It should be developed through proper involvement of the users of service who should contribute towards decision making being responsive to the needs and concerns of the community when planning and delivering services. It should also incorporate the contours of the training that have to be provided so that all staff is provided with training in respect of their delegation under the service policy. [7] MGP suggested several initiatives that directly impinge on the improvement of the standards of services offered by government. Citizen Charter and Social Audit are important among them.

The concept of Citizen's Charter espouses, "quintessentially, the idea of citizen's entitlements vis-à-vis the government : entitlement to easy, un-hassled access to public services, to services of stipulated quality and specifications, to efficient and courteous delivery of services, to a transparent conduct on the part of the service provider and so forth." (Sharma, 2004: 115). The Citizen's Charter addresses multiple concerns. Firstly, it should incorporate a statement of services which a bureau might offer. It indicates the service standards and the remedies available to users in the event that there might be a non-compliance with stipulated standards (Sharma, 2004: 115). The Citizen's Charter insists on the display of requisite procedures involved in obtaining the available services.

It provides a structure for obtaining user feed back. Institution of an easy-to-follow procedure for making complaints and provision for a grievance-redressal mechanism, indication of response-time for various public transactions, setting up of machinery for system-audit, performance monitoring and evaluation; and provision for independent scrutiny of the agency's performance are some other concerns of Citizen's Charter. Citizen's Charter is a document which represents a systematic effort to focus on the commitment of the organization towards its citizens in respect of standard of services, information, choice and consultation, non-discrimination and accessibility, grievance redress, courtesy and value of money. It enshrines the trust between the service provider and its users. The concept was first articulated and implemented in the United Kingdom by the Conservative Government of John Major in 1991. [8] The programme was re-launched in 1998 by the labour Government of Tony Blair which rechristened it "Services First".

In India, as part of action plan for effective and responsive government by Central and State Governments, formulation of citizen's charter started with those sectors having large public interface (e.g. Railways, Telecom, Posts, Public Distribution Systems etc.). The organizations with Citizen's Charter are advised to give publicity to their Charters through such means as print/electronic media and awareness campaign. Based on the principles of SDP a pro-poor and participatory approach, as also its commitment to keep its citizens well-informed of government policies, procedure and plans a series of workshops were held in the Institute for Management in Government (IMG), Thiruvananthapuram to introduce the Citizen's Charter concept to hundreds of public servants. These workshops were conducted by the IMG faculty who had been trained in the UK on the concepts and practice of Citizen's Charters (Sharma, 2004: 97).

The Citizen's Charter has the potential to provide:

1. Agreed and published standards for service delivery.
2. Openness and information about service delivery.
3. Choice and consultation with users.
4. Courtesy and helpfulness in service delivery.
5. Provision of redressal of grievance.

From the field experience, there found some interesting data about awareness of public about Citizen's Charter. Some of them are represented in Table 15.1.

Table 15.1: Presence of Citizen's Charter in Government Offices

Presence of Citizen's Charter	No. of Respondents	Percentage
Viewers	144	24
Non-viewers	456	76
Total	600	100

Source: Survey Data.

Citizen's Charter is a tool facilitating the delivery of services to citizens with specified standards, quality and time frame etc. with commitments from the organization and its clients (Sharma, 2004: 119). Citizen's charter should give citizens, the sense that these services are meant only for them, and that the government employees are their servants, not their masters. The table shows that majority of people (76 percent) are completely ignorant about Citizen's Charter and they have never seen it in any offices. Only 24 percent said that they had seen Citizen's Charter in the offices they approached. Citizen's Charter and its principles are of western origin and the people in our state are not much aware of it. The official arrangements for formulating and presenting Citizen's Charter are progressing.

Among the respondents about 75.5 percent viewed that Citizen's Charter will be helpful in getting access to the services offered to them at the right time (Table 15.2). They said that the absence of such a document is a major hindrance of our administration in meeting the real objective that is serving the public. Citizen's Charter will make aware the public, about their rights and their claims in case any right is denied. About 23.83 percent of the respondents said that these types of documents will cause confusion to the public. Only 0.67 percent viewed that Citizen's Charter has no impact on our administration because of our inertia-prone bureaucracy itself.

Table 15.2: Citizen's Charter and Prompt Service Delivery

Presence of Citizen's Charter helps in the awareness of services rendered	No. of Respondents	Percentage
Citizen's Charter will help in claiming prompt service delivery	453	75.50
Citizen's Charter will create confusion	143	23.83
No impact in administration	4	0.67
Total	600	100.00

Source: Survey Data.

But they have the opinion that if it is furnished properly with the initiative and interest of bureaucracy, this will be successful. Most of the public are doubtful in the success of Citizen's Charter because of the government servants' attitude towards changes. Declaration of the provider- obligations and acknowledgement of the user entitlements invests the initiative with the power to make things happen. But these are not backed by legal sanctions, the citizen's charter can at best and exert a moral pressure upon the bureau officials.

Social Audit

Social Audit gives an understanding of the administrative system from the perspective of the vast majority of people in the society for whom the very institutional/administrative system is being promoted and legitimised. Social Audit of administration means understanding the administrative system and its internal dynamics from the angle of what they mean for the vast majority of the people, who are not essentially a part of the State or its machinery or the ruling class of the day, for whom they are meant to work. Social Audit is an independent evaluation of the performance of an organisation as it relates to the attainment of its social goals. It is an instrument of social accountability of an organization

According to Government of Kerala's comprehensive

Document on MGP/SDP Activities, Annexure, "Social audit will promote accountability, equity, effectiveness and value for money, and has been used by national and international agencies". The social audit of the government would be conducted by accredited panels of eminent citizens of un-impeachable integrity and social commitment to be identified jointly by the Government and the opposition. The audit reports are published in a form readily accessible to the public. The Social Audit is a mean to exercise general supervision or oversight by local communities over the performance of public organisations. The corner stone of Kerala's strategy has been to foster transparency as a means of encouraging public scrutiny of local projects.

At the site of every public work, is mandatory to display information pertaining to the job done. In case of local bodies, information regarding the number of workers employed and wages paid, materials purchased, transport costs and contingency expenditure incurred etc are monitored by the monitoring committee of Grama Sabha. All Plan documents, including the beneficiary lists, the estimates of expenditure, and bills and vouchers related to the works have been accorded the status of public documents, whose copies can be obtained by the villagers, free of cost, on demand. Right to information campaign provided a robust support to the social audit movement. Social audit can only act as a powerful instrument in enforcing public accountability and good governance.

The potential of Social Audit to: (i) fight corruption, (ii) expose and make public the nexus between local elites, bureaucracy and the elected representatives, and (iii) as means for redistribution of power by the ensuring inclusion of the poor and marginalised in government benefits and giving them 'voice,' thus rendering them vulnerable to stiff resistance. Clearly, Social Audit has tremendous potential in working to strengthen social networks at the local level. It creates opportunities for mobilisation, spaces for deliberation and mechanisms to ensure accountability and transparency; thereby promoting social justice and strengthening democracy at the local level.

Another paradoxical fact found during the field study among the government shows that only a small percentage of employees (19.33 percent) are aware about social auditing which is a pioneering initiative of MGP (Table 15.3). If the case of government servants is like this then what will be the situation of the civil society? The percentage of people who are aware about 'social auditing' is very meagre and it also reveals the scantiness of awareness programme by the government.

Table 15.3: Awareness of Employees about Social Auditing

Awareness about Social Auditing	No. of Respondents	Percentage
Aware of Social Auditing	58	19.33
Ignorant about Social Auditing	242	80.67
Total	30	100.00

Source: Survey Data.

The Social Audit is aimed at evaluating outcomes of various initiatives and programmes, rather than inputs and outputs alone. [9] The Social Audit policy is now complete with the announcement of the policy by the Government of Kerala. The social audit of the government would be conducted by accredited panels of eminent citizens of unimpeachable integrity and social commitment to be identified jointly by the government and the opposition. They would be empowered to co-opt experts. In the case of local governments, in addition to panels of eminent citizens, the performance audit wing shall conduct a regular form of internal audit.

The social audit reports, which would be public documents, would be given to the organizations and departments concerned and the legislature. Legislature committees would go into these reports. [10]

Observations

1. In Kerala, like every other reforms SDP, as a part of MGP also faces several hindrances. Improper implementation of the policy within the stipulated time is a major draw back. Passiveness among the employees, irresponsibility among the government and political parties are other reasons. [11] Another irony is that the main principles like Citizen's Charter; Sevana Mudra, Social Auditing and the like are not implemented uniformly in the selected institutions. Moreover, the employees as well as the public are not much aware about these principles.
2. Lack of awareness from the part of public and the government servants is the first major drawback. The prime importance should be on making adequate awareness programme for the public. The media, local bodies and the political parties should be responsible for conducting this.
3. Since Citizen's Charters are likely to raise the aspirations of the users of the service, the departments should guard against the tendency to promise more than they can deliver. A realistic assessment of the capabilities of the service provider must be taken into account in drafting the Charter.
4. A critical review of the current systems and processes in the department should be undertaken to examine whether they are likely to have an adverse impact on the Charter.
5. Implementing the Charters without the staff owning them will defeat the purpose of the Charter. Motivating the staff and involving them in the preparation of the Charter are extremely important.
6. The Charters will remain merely a paper exercise of limited value if there is no consultation with the users. Departments should ensure user involvement at all stages of preparation and implementation of the Charter.
7. Complex systems for lodging complaints or poor access to officers for redressal of grievances defeat the purpose and

the spirit of the Charter. The critical success factor in the entire Charter initiative is developing close relationships with stakeholders throughout the cycle of the charter, from inception and development of standards to raising awareness, to monitoring and reviewing, and determining appropriate compensation for redressal of grievances.

8. Social Audit, by its nature is more inclusive, involving multiple agencies with plural, and sometimes, conflicting interests. Knowing this, many times, the facilitating agency screens participation of agencies and people, with conflicting interest, and attempts to manufacture a consensus. In such situations, Social Audit tends to be devoid of its real purpose.
9. While legislative and policy measures have been used to create such spaces, guaranteeing equal and easy access for the marginal and minority sections within the community, the capacity to secure such access remains marginal. In the case of Social Audit Forums, the community, and within it the marginal and minority sections face considerable difficulty in benefiting from such audits. The deprived groups are not able to marshal their collective strength because of social fragmentation; and their dependence on the dominant groups, which do not lead to a coherent social capital within the community to raise questions. In such a case, Social Audits afflicted by the politics of control and agency involvement result in reduced effectiveness in building future links within the community.

Conclusion

A comprehensive training programme for civil service is needed to develop a well trained and professional civil service, to adequately respond to the current and emerging development needs. [12] The State Training Policy approved by the State Training Council on November 5, 2002 recognizes that training is an obligation of the State Government to its employees. In this background, MGP aims at more training courses and better training infrastructure. MGP realized the fact that lack of regular training input has affected modernization and up gradation of skills. Ignorance leads to fear of new things and builds resistance to change. There is, however an urgent need for working to strengthen Citizen Charter Initiative and Social Audits. Legislative provisions and policy guidelines need to progress beyond symbolic measures. It is a process, whereby the citizens regain control over their lives and hold those that serve them accountable. Then only the implementation of charter initiative and social auditing measures will create 'voice' for the poor.

End Notes

1. 'Modernising Government Programme; General Information', http:// www.keralamgp.org, accessed on 19.08.2008.
2. Government of Kerala, 'Modernising Government Programme: Strategic Implementation Plan and Order Issues', G.O. (Rt.) 1/2002/MGP, dated 4.10.2002, Thiruvananthapuram.
3. Government of Kerala, 'A People-centred Service Delivery Policy for Kerala, Modernising Government Programme', Government Secretariat, Thiruvananthapuram.
4. An Interview with Dr. Vijayakumar, Service Delivery Assessment Specialist (MGP) on 07.08.2006.
5. Interview with S.M. Vijayanand, Principal Secretary to Government, Local Self-Government Rural, Administrative Reforms, MGP on 23.03.2006.
6. Government of Kerala, 'Approaches to Public Service Delivery, initiatives under the MGP', Thiruvananthapuram.
7. Government of Kerala, 'Modernizing Government Programme', http://www.kerala.gov.in, accessed on 08.10.2005.
8. Government of UK, 'A Guide to Quality Scheme for the Public Sector', http:// www.serviceifirst.gov.uk, accessed on 27.08.2009.
9. Government of Kerala, 'A Note on Approaches to Public Service Delivery Initiative under the Modernizing Government Programme', Government of Kerala, p. 3.
10. Government of Kerala (2004), G.O.(MS) No. 274/04/GAD, Government of Kerala.
11. Interview with. Sarada Muraleedharan, IAS, on 27.3.2006.
12. Government of Kerala, 'Core Government Functions',

http://www.kealamgporg.accessed on 09.10.2005.

References

Aravind K. Sharma (2004), Bureaucracy and Decentralisation, Mittal Publications, New Delhi.

Government of Kerala (2006), 'Approaches to Public Service Delivery Initiatives under the Modernizing Government Programme', Government Press, Thiruvaanthapuram.

Kerala State Sastra Sahitya Parishad (2005), *Bharana Naveekarana Padhati Oru Avalokanam,* Parishad Bhavan, Thiruvananthapuram.

16

Indo-Myanmar Relations: Assessing the China Factor

Veena R.

Mainland South-East Asia, also known as Indo-China is sandwiched between Asia's two largest and greatest powers- India and China. The changing relationship between these two Asian giants has an impact on the entire region. Over the decades, India's foreign policy was blank in its approach towards East Asia, since our policy framers were preoccupied with Nehruvian model and the moralistic discourse associated with it. Economics and trade occupy the central stage in the recent geo-political and globalizing world climate. An assertive and realistic approach towards East Asia is called for, as China and India compete for hegemony in the region. The *Look East Policy* is the logical outcome of this historical turn of events.

With India's obsession towards Pakistan and with its preoccupation with China, the South-East Asian region did not figure much in its foreign policy calculus till the early 1990s. South-East Asia was a growing market with rapidly developing countries like Malaysia, Singapore and Indonesia. China had already entrenched itself deep in most of these countries over a period of time. The post-Cold War globalizing world and the economic liberalization of 1991 gave India the opportunity to improve its relations with South East Asian nations with the enunciation of the '*Look East Policy*' in the early 1990s by then Prime Minister P.V. Narasimha Rao. Myanmar occupies a key position in India's Look East policy as it is considered as the "land bridge" [1] between India and ASEAN. India Myanmar rapprochement began in 1991 and gained momentum in the latter part of 1990s as evidenced in the growing political, economic and military relations since 1998.

Indo-Myanmar Relations

India and Burma [2] share both historical and cultural links. India always had a peculiar relationship with its Burmese neighbour. Buddhism is one of the cultural legacies which Burma has gained from Indian civilization. More than that Burma was deeply influenced by India during the colonial era, when Burma was one of the largest provinces under British India (1862-1948). The colonial history brought in large number of Indians to Burma and they dominated in every field like trade, property, financial lending system, educational system, civil administration, and military and police forces. This continued from the end of 19th century until Burma's separation from India in 1937 (Chakravarthy, 1971: 211).

After Independence, the biggest bone of contention between these two countries was the People of Indian Origin (PIOs). The predominance of Indians in the socio-economic configuration created strong resentment within Burma's indigenous majority "Burman" population. This has resulted in several anti-Indian riots in Burma in the 1920s and 1930s and ever since Burma has been suspicious of India. Indian academics often ignored or neglected the apprehension of the Burmese population and emphasized on the mutual friendship between Indians and Burmese (Rajshekhar, 2006: 34-38).

Indo-Myanmar relations were very cordial during the first few years after independence and both Nehru and U Nu were leaders in the creation of Non-Aligned Movement (NAM). Both countries signed the *Treaty of Friendship*, which was to remain in force "for ever thereafter" if neither side gave notice of its desire to terminate it six months before its expiry after five years (Lall, Marie 2006: 431). After the 1962 coup, relations came to a standstill despite its strategic importance. Nehruvian idealist tradition compelled India to ignore Myanmar due to the undemocratic regime that had taken over.

This has continued even during the regimes of both Indira and Rajiv though both of them visited Myanmar. India's Myanmar policy has to be viewed from a larger perspective of India's foreign policy formulations as a whole, which was largely based on moralistic principles at the global level and hegemonic designs at regional level.

The military coup by General Nu Win in 1962 started "Burmanizing" the economy and society which led to a self imposed political isolation of Myanmar (Holmes and Robert 1967: 188-197). India's security concerns about its north-eastern front always ignored its Burmese neighbour. However, Burma has a significant strategic magnitude as it shares borders with four North-Eastern States; Arunachal Pradesh, Nagaland, Manipur and Mizoram, a 1,643 km. long border and with a coastline of 1,930 km. wide open in the Andaman Sea and the Bay of Bengal facing Indian territories of the Andaman Islands (Renaud, Egreteau 2003: 2). Indian diplomacy sounds unusual and strange when they completely ignored Myanmar as it is the gateway to ASEAN also. Hence, the country should have a special position in India's foreign policy.

Although New Delhi strongly supported the democratic movements against the Military junta in 1988, a new era in Indo-Myanmar relations was ushered in by the visit of J.N. Dixit, the then foreign secretary of India to that country in the middle of 1993. India's "Look East" strategy had started under the P.V. Narasimha Rao-led Congress government but it was the Bharatiya Janata Party-led National Democratic Alliance government that took the first concrete step to implement it. Normalizing relations with Myanmar was seen as essential for India to leverage its geopolitical proximity to the South-East Asian region.

The then Foreign Minister Jaswant Singh made two significant visits to Myanmar in 2001 and 2002. These visits initiated a new Burmese policy based on realpolitik. The first visit was to inaugurate the India-Myanmar Friendship Road, and the second was to start talks on building the ambitious

Trans-Asia highway project. High-level military contacts started in 2000 when the Indian Army chief met with his Myanmarese counterpart. India has since started supplying Myanmar limited amounts of weaponry, and providing training to military personnel.

In early March 2006, President A.P.J Abdul Kalam visited Myanmar and it was the first ever visit by an Indian President which was actually preceded by that of the Senior General Than Shwe's visit to India in October 2004. Several MoUs were signed in areas such as trade and commerce, oil sector, promotion of Buddhist Studies and various other cross-border development projects such as roads, railways, telecommunications, IT, Science and Technology, power etc. The recent 2010 July visit of General Than Shwe was again an illustration of the forward progressing relationship between the two countries. The dramatic shift in India's approach towards the Myanmar junta is being coined as '*velvet policy*' by critiques. India's engagement with the military regime is being considered as its failure as a committed democracy in enhancing or promoting democracy in its neighbourhood.

The Indian policy towards Myanmar is marked by a dilemma (Chakraborti, 2008: 19) While she finds it difficult to renege on her earlier commitment to democracy and democratic ideals, she seems unable to 'give up the option of maintaining good relations with the established government of an important neighbour' at a time when India promises to 'Look East'. At one level, Indian interests in Myanmar are guided by the following considerations: One, containment of Chinese economic and strategic influences in South-East Asia in general and Myanmar in particular; two, helping Myanmar in exploring her virgin gas fields and thereby exploiting the energy resources; three, getting the military junta to come down heavily on the Northeast's insurgents and rebel groups that have been holed up and taken shelter there; and four, to obtain inter-modal transit facility for the goods and services being traded between India and other South-East Asian countries.

The paradigm shift which can be observed in India's policy

towards Myanmar can be explained with the help of a number of reasons and we can evaluate the strategic importance of Myanmar in our foreign policy framework due to the post-1991 developments in the world. The reasons behind the makeover broadly fall into three categories: the Indian North East, the increased role of economic factors in foreign policy decision-making, and most notably the China factor.

The North East

Improving Indo-Myanmar relations as an intrinsic part of its policy vis-à-vis the North Eastern states and their decades of anti-Indian insurgency fuelled by the centre's economic neglect of the region. As a result, economic regeneration of this region is one of the domestic priorities underpinning the new policy. Many of the tribes in the north eastern states have cultural and ethnic resemblance with the tribes in Myanmar. India since independence have been facing a tough time managing the ethnic insurgencies and separatist movements which is a burning domestic issue. Decades of instability in the north-eastern states which share borders with Myanmar are at the heart of the decision.

Violence has risen and economic liberalization policies have barely touched these backward states. Containing the insurgency in the region is at the base of India's new attitude towards Yangon (Egreteau, 2003: p. 2). The issues of common interest for both the countries take the North Eastern Region (NER) as an important aspect. The infrastructural and educational backwardness of the NER adds fuel to the discontent. However, joint military operation to tackle the insurgents by both the armies of India and Myanmar are not enough to address the issue. Cooperation between both these countries would lead to more trade by opening the boundaries which can bring prosperity and development to the NER. India is also aware of the fact that it needs the support of Myanmar to stem both drugs and arms trafficking for which the area is notorious. However, a comprehensive approach towards

Myanmar can unquestionably contribute en route for the socio-economic growth of the NER.

Economic Co-operation

As described above economic factors start playing a key role in foreign policy decision making in the post-Cold War era and this led to borders becoming gateways of development. Trade and commerce between India and Myanmar have been rapidly growing as a result of India's Look East Policy. Trade with and trade through Myanmar would bring prosperity not only to the NER but also to both the countries. India is today Myanmar's fourth largest trading partner after Thailand, China and Singapore (Yhome, K. 2008: p. 64). India starts engaging Myanmar both bilaterally and through other groupings like Bay of Bengal Initiative for Multi-sectoral Technical and Economic Cooperation (BIMSTEC), Mekong-Ganga Cooperation etc.

In addition, India launched Kunming Initiative (BCIM) (Bangladesh-China-India-Myanmar). These regional groupings helped India to interact closely with Myanmar after its self imposed political isolation. Closing the gap between New Delhi and Naypyitaw in the realm of economic relations could be seen with the signing of a MoU on trade and economic cooperation, particularly in terms of border trade in 1994.

Infrastructural projects like Trans Asia Highway passing through Myanmar, Indo-Myanmar Friendship Road, Trans Asian Railways, Optical Fibre Telecommunication projects etc, not only further bilateral cooperation and trade but will also open the South East Asian markets to Delhi and get India more involved in Asian trade. There are two Indo-Myanmar organizations based in Yangon: the India-Myanmar Association and the Myanmar-India Chamber of Commerce.

The India-Myanmar Association is a cultural organization and a platform for Indian expatriates. Its aims are social as well as helping businessmen. There are around 150 Indian companies across fields such as agriculture, pharmaceuticals, spare parts, steel, transmission lines, electrical goods and furniture registered with them. With regard to the pharmaceutical companies, there are Indian representatives and local distributors. However, marketing is done by Indian companies. All these efforts paved the way for India to have better diplomatic interaction with Myanmar and also enables India to check 'Rising China's' influence over the region.

Along with the China factor in Indo-Myanmar relations, the strategic significance of Myanmar and its status as a 'client state' of China should also be discussed.

Strategic Significance of Myanmar and the China Factor

Myanmar was one of the world's first oil producers, with some exports dates back to1853. After nationalization of oil and gas industry in 1962, Myanmar kept this sector under its direct control. In 1988, Myanmar liberalized the oil and gas industry and to lure foreign investment in the country, it allowed outside countries to operate their business corporations into Myanmar. South Korea and China were amongst the first to cash in on this opportunity. By 2004, Myanmar became an attractive place after it intensified the process of exploration by opening new areas to foreign investors. Natural gas tops Myanmar's export list.

In Pacific region, Myanmar occupied the leading position in gas trade movement with having transported 9.89 billion cubic meters. It was during the 2001 visit of Jaswant Singh to Myanmar that India started negotiations about buying gas from Myanmar. Oil and gas exploration and supplies were discussed as a part of other negotiations with General Than Shwe regarding infrastructure projects such as the joint construction of roads. The visit to India of U Win Aung in January 2003, mentioned earlier, also further boosted this cooperation in the hydrocarbon, power and energy sectors, particularly with regard to India's role in the exploration of Myanmar's onshore oil and gas reserves. [3]

According to the 'Ministry of Energy Report, "Myanmar's

27 contracts are active in 28 offshore blocks with 22 foreign countries in offshore areas". Today, Myanmar is projected to contain more than 18 trillion cubic feet of natural gas, and possibly also oil, under its offshore waters, which stretch from its adjacent border with Bangladesh in the Bay of Bengal down to Thailand coastline. There are at least 9 potential oil and gas bearing areas which are either least explored or not explored at all till this date. Myanmar occupies 22 offshore and onshore oil and gas fields which are open for new investors.

The country is also estimated to have 3.2 billion barrels of recoverable crude oil reserve. Oil and gas sector is the second fastest emerging field of foreign direct investment in the country. Currently, dozens of countries are engaged in this sector in Myanmar including Thailand, Malaysia, South Korea, Canada and Russia. Positioned between rival powers India and China, both nations view Myanmar as the ideal buffer zone to balance the power of the other (Panwar, Namrata 2009: p. 100).

Conventional wisdom has always been the primary driving force behind Chinese foreign policy. China and Myanmar share relations for over 50 years with a temporary period of lull during the time of Cultural Revolution in 1967 (Das, Paramita 2008: p. 10). Though initially the PRC extended all types of support and economic assistance to the Communist Party of Burma, the realistic approach of Deng Xiaoping altered their Myanmar policy and a good rapport was established with the military junta through his 'Open Door' policy. While Myanmar was away from the world due to its self imposed isolation, China has maintained good relations with them.

Bilateral relations have included the sale of Chinese armaments and machinery to the military junta, joint efforts to combat cross-border trafficking of narcotics, border trade of consumer goods, and Myanmar's exports of timber (largely through illicit smuggling) and precious stones to Yunnan, China's south-western province. China has shielded the Myanmar regime from Western and United Nations opprobrium and sanctions (Maung, Tin Maung, Than 2003: pp. 189-210).

China wants to increase trade and gain greater access to energy and resources. China's relation with Myanmar was crucial in accomplishing these objectives as a result of its location and natural resources.

Beijing is involved in over 62 hydro, oil, gas, and mining projects in Burma to feed China's growing energy needs. For example, Beijing is pushing for the construction of an oil pipeline through Burma to bypass the Strait of Malacca, the route used to transport approximately 80 percent of China's oil imports (Bronson, Percival 2007). Thus, China's interest over Myanmar is primarily economic in nature with an aim to use its natural resources for the economic development of China's western provinces, especially Yunnan and Sichuan. Myanmar can act as a doorway for China to the Indian Ocean and also to South Asia and this itself proves the strategic significance of Myanmar for both Asian giants.

China has other non-traditional security concerns also like flow of drugs, human trafficking, and growing HIV/AIDS epidemic etc. Scholar Bronson Percival points out that Burma is called a Chinese "client state", but that, if this is the case, "...it is a difficult, xenophobic client"(Bronson, Percival (2007). However, it is a practical relationship that benefits China by all means. Presence of Chinese troops in Myanmar could extend its range of power to the Bay of Bengal and the Andaman Sea. Countries in Asia and the West became worried about the Chinese ambition in the Indian Ocean. Myanmar gives China an opportunity to control over the Malacca Strait which is the main route for oil shipment.

As far as the energy market is concerned, Indian State owned Oil and Natural Gas Corporation has invested US$ 3.5 billion overseas since 2000, while Chinese owned China National Petroleum Corporation has made overseas investment of US$ 40 billion (Panwar, Namrata 2009: p. 100). Compared to China, the democracy in India has shown a slowdown in its political process which always kept India at a disadvantageous position abroad. As Stephen O'Sullivan, head of research at

United Financial Group said, "Whenever we have seen the Indians and Chinese tussle, the Chinese have been faster and more aggressive in attaining their objective". One report identifies 69 Chinese MNC's involved in 90 completed, current and planned projects in the hydropower and extractive sectors including oil, gas and mining in Burma.

The realisation of China's presence in the region subsequently increased India's level of comfort and trust with Myanmar's military regime. Since 1999, there has been a better understanding between Indian and Myanmar navies. Indo-Myanmar naval cooperation is developing at a faster pace. Moreover, India enjoys one of the most advanced and well equipped naval bases in the region with the Far Eastern Naval Command based at Port Blair in the Andaman Islands, a few nautical miles from Myanmar's Coco Islands. Myanmar has diversified its military dependence. It approaches India in addition to China for the arms supply and several bilateral agreements have made between Indian Air Force and its counterpart in Myanmar. However, India tactfully manages the China factor in Myanmar than its stated goals like counter insurgency in the north east and the commercial relation between the two countries.

Myanmar is dependent on the PRC economically, militarily and politically. In a way China's usage of its 'Soft Power' in South-East Asia brings Myanmar in its sphere of influence. And this soft diplomacy has been named the "Win Win" strategy by China which helps Myanmar indirectly get aid and support from China. The latest cooperation between these two countries reflected in the 2007 uprising against the military junta. The brutal suppression of non-violent protest was condemned by the entire international community except China which maintained silence throughout. China is never ready to lose its strategic partner and the result is the continuation of the military junta.

Apparently China has cultivated close ties with the countries which are not worried of Chinese naval presence in their respective region or those which seek to undermine or balance another dominant power influence by cooperating with China. At the other end, India has bitter relations with its neighbours who create big obstacles for India to have a strategic relation with Central and West Asia. However, China's "strings of pearls" theory worries India by which China extends its presence throughout the strategic ports in India's neighbourhood.

Though the assumption is that Myanmar is a client state of China, in fact Myanmar is smart enough to play the 'China card' so that it can effortlessly counter its ASEAN brotherly states like Thailand, India, and Japan. The military junta skilfully uses the moral and material support provided by China to develop a more "open" economy by inviting investments both from China and other foreign countries. Unlike its earlier stand, as a complete turnaround Myanmar's repressive junta tactically maintaining the regional balance through a realpolitik game. The regime's recent attempts to forge relations with other states, including India can be taken as an effort to counter even China's influence in the region. As a result Myanmar's oil sector has not come completely under the Chinese domination. [4] In Myanmar's effort to balance the pulls of outside influence, India plays a key role. Well aware of the competition and rivalry between China and India, the junta tends to play China against India in the negotiations over potential gas route (Zhang, 2008).

Sino-Indian rivalry and the complexities of their relation with Myanmar are intricate mainly due to two reasons; disparities of views and national interests. India's pragmatic engagement with Myanmar is balanced by its indirect and close ties with the democratic movements. India's trade and economic incentives has always been downplayed by China's upper hand over Myanmar and China has consistently outbid India in its influence over Myanmar. China doesn't favour a strong Indian presence or dominance in South-East Asia, especially over Myanmar. China is always aware of the historical and cultural ties between India and Myanmar and it is somewhat puzzled and intrigued by India's increasing presence in the region. Unlike China, being late comer in Myanmar, India does not carry much political and diplomatic weight in the region but has considerable say to exert its influence.

The significant developments in the recent years like increasing mutual sympathy and understanding between India and Myanmar resulted in the high level exchanges and new agreements between the two countries. India was urged by the international community to pressurize the military junta to restore democracy in Myanmar. Currently India's approach towards Myanmar is guided by the geo-political considerations than ideological values (Parthasarathy, G. 2008). From 1993 onward, India tried to deal directly with Myanmar's ruling military junta to prevent Burma from becoming a Chinese military "pawn" or a satellite against Indian interest's (Malik, Mohan J. 1994: pp. 137-156). Befriending Myanmar and India's constructive engagement with the present regime are the only available methods by which India can increase its presence in the region. This will possibly help India to have a considerable check on the 'Rising China's influence over India's eastern flank and other eastern neighbours. Hence, this 'velvet policy' can be considered as the result of a realistic stance by India.

Conclusion

The past decade has witnessed considerable progress in Indo-Myanmar relations. New Delhi and Naypytiaw have developed a positive approach towards each other. Though it is in New Delhi's interest to have a stable democracy in Myanmar, Its first priority should be to have a consolidated regional engagement, reduce Myanmar's dependence on China and use the gap provided by the western countries sanctions over Myanmar. The changes in Myanmar's strategic thinking also contribute to a fair relation between both the countries. India's constant effort to have a better image in front of the

Burmese in order to avoid "Indophobia" which is in fact a constraint to have strong relations between the countries should be addressed urgently.

The silent support from India for the political reforms of military junta and the depoliticized humanitarian assistance can be used as effective tools for winning the confidence of the people along with cultural interaction to befriend Myanmar. Moreover, being a Buddhist country it can be influenced by India through their common heritage and culture. Indian diplomacy should be innovative enough to win over the various ethnicities in Myanmar. As a responsible and successful democracy India can persuade Myanmar to have a democratic arrangement since political instability is not in the interest of both the countries. India's new 'velvet policy' towards the military junta has been criticized by the pro democracy Burmese activists and in reality India faces both overt xenophobia and more subtle perceptions of suspicion throughout multiple layers of Burmese society. This can be averted if India would be advised to do everything it can to help Myanmarsee political normalization.

Another important area in which India should break its silence is the pathetic condition of the Indian diaspora in Myanmar. India has been adopting a "hands off" policy towards them and the time has come to be open about it and India cannot avoid the fact that the diaspora has a significant role in establishing friendly relations between the countries and also stem it now before it develops into a bilateral issue.

Apart from that a stable and cooperative north-eastern region can really contribute towards healthy Indo-Myanmar relations. The local people should also be involved in the entire process so that they can share the benefits of improving ties. The region should not be seen just as a conduit for transit of goods but it should be included as a stakeholder in the effort of improving ties with Myanmar. India's ambitions in Burma have been annoyed by New Delhi's inability to coordinate effective counter-insurgency in the north east and its inability to increase bilateral trade, which lags far behind Sino-Burmese and Thai-Burmese economic cooperation. In contrast, India's primary satisfaction gained from its new Burma policy has been effectively "managing" the perceived military threat posed by a "rising China" in Burma. India has to frame a clear cut strategic policy towards Myanmar given the strategic importance of the north east and India needs to decide whether it is a gateway or border to South-East Asia and similarly to Myanmar.

In conclusion, India would be advised to have an inclusive and integrated proactive policy in its relation with Myanmar by which we can reduce the alarming Chinese presence in the region and at the same time a flourishing and developed North East. Thus, the new world order has prompted India to realize the fact that foreign policy should be driven not just by the moral perspective but should be preceded by economic and strategic significance of the area. It is in India's interest to engage the military junta in Myanmar on one side to have a better understanding and on the other side as a committed democracy India can silently persuade them to have political normalization through democracy.

End Notes

1. An assessment of the approach indicates that India's relation with ASEAN have strengthened and expanded in the recent past. India trade and military ties with the region have been consolidated. For instance, India's trade with ASEAN region has reached over US$ 12 billion and forms about 10 percent of India's total trade. India has also made its presence in regional and sub regional groupings such as ASEAN, ARF, Mekong-Ganga Cooperation and East Asia Summit.
2. The new junta that took over through a coup on 18 September in 1988 changed in May 1989 the names of the country and many geographical and historical names. From then on, ' Burma' has been known as 'Myanmar', 'Rangoon' as 'Yangon', the River 'Irrawaddy' as the River Ayeyarwarddy' etc.
3. At this meeting the other areas for cooperation discussed were key areas of cooperation between the two nations which include

agriculture, human resource development, education, biotechnology development of infrastructure to facilitate trade and tourism. available at, http://www.mizzima .com/archives/news-in-2003/news-in-jan/20-jan03-21.htm.

4. Foreign oil companies, from Australia, Britain, Canada, China, India, Russia, South Korea, in addition to three ASEAN member states, are operating in Myanmar. Xinhua News Agency, "Companies from China, Myanmar, S. Korea sign gas pact in Myanmar," Xinhuanet.com, December 24, 2008, available at, http://news.xinhuanet.com/english/2008-12/24/content_10555064.htm, (accessed on January 3, 2011).

References

Bronson, Percival (2007), The Dragon Looks South: China and Southeast Asia in the New Century, West Port: Praeger Security International, pp. 38-39.

Chakraborti, Tridib (2008), "BIMSTEC or the Big Leap Forward for India's Northeast?", *World Focus*, Vol. 29, No. 1, p. 19.

Das, Paramita (2008), "Sino- Myanmar Relations: Chain of Friendship', *World Focus,* Vol. 29, No. 3, p. 100.

Holmes, Robert A. (1967), "Burmese Domestic Policy: The Politics of Burmanization", *Asian Survey,* 7:3, pp. 188-197.

Lall, Marie (2006), "Indo-Myanmar Relations in the Era of Pipeline Diplomacy", *Contemporary South East Asia*, Vol. 28, No. 3, p. 431.

Malik, Mohan J. (1994), 'Sino-Indian Rivalry in Myanmar: Implications for Regional Security', *Contemporary Southeast Asia*, Vol. 16, No. 2, pp. 137-156.

Maung, Tin Maung, Than (2003), "Myanmar and China: A Special Relationship?", *Southeast Asian Affairs,* Institute of Southeast Asian Studies, Singapore, pp. 189-210.

Nalini Ranjan Chakravarthy (1971), The Indian Minority in Burma: The Rise and Decline of an Immigrant Community, Oxford University Press, London, p. 211.

Panwar, Namrata (2009), 'India and China competing over Myanmar Energy Resources', *Working Paper for BISA Conference,* University of Leicester, Leicester, p. 23.

Panwar, Namrata (2009), 'India and China Competing over Myanmar Energy Resources', *Working Paper for BISA Conference,* University of Leicester, Leicester, p. 10.

Parthasarathy, G. (2008), "Dal, Idli, Sambar and the Myanmar Sanctions", *The Hindu Business Line*, 1st January.

Rajshekhar, Myanmar's Nationalist Movement and India, 1906-1948, Delhi: South Asian Publishers, 2006, pp. 34-38.

Renaud, Egreteau (2003), 'India and Burma/Myanmar Relations: From Idealism to Realism' paper presented at a conference on *India and Burma/Myanmar Relations: From Idealism to Realism,* p. 2.

Yhome, K. (2008), 'India-Myanmar Relations (1998-2008), A Decade of Redefining Bilateral Ties', *ORF Occasional Paper*, No. 10, Observer Research Foundation, New Delhi, p. 64.

Zhang, 'China's energy corridors in Southeast Asia.'; 'China-Myanmar Oil Pipeline Project Approved,' *Alexander's Gas and Oil Connections-News and Trends: E and SE Asia,* 13, No. 7, April 15, 2008, http://www.gasandoil.com/goc/news/nts81610.htm (accessed December, 2010).

Index

Index